THE Sasha Kagan

SWEATER BOOK

THE *Sasha Kagan* SWEATER BOOK

BALLANTINE BOOKS · NEW YORK

CONTENTS

Editor Bridget Harris
Art Editor Michele Walker
Designer Polly Dawes
Managing Editor Amy Carroll

First published in Great Britain in 1984 by
Dorling Kindersley Limited
9 Henrietta Street
Covent Garden, London WC2E 8PS

Copyright for patterns © Sasha Kagan
Copyright © 1984 Dorling Kindersley

Library of Congress Catalog Card Number
85-90560

ISBN 0-345-31871-4

Manufactured in the United States of America

First Edition: August 1985

10 9 8 7 6 5 4 3 2 1

GEOMETRICS

FLOWERS

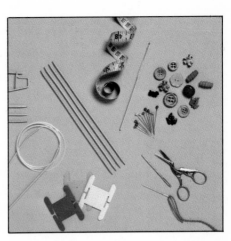

ETHNIC

NURSERY

INTRODUCTION

Through **The Sasha Kagan Sweater Book** I would like to share with every enthusiastic knitter the pleasure of making beautiful and carefully designed sweaters which are not only highly fashionable but also works of art.

Handknits are fast becoming a fashion staple and nearly all of us are prepared to spend time and money to find a sweater that is both well-designed and of high quality. Mass-produced machine knits no longer satisfy the majority of fashion conscious individuals and instead we tend to want sweaters that are original and carefully made, reflecting an element of handiwork as well as fashion. Over the past few years knitwear has undergone a complete revolution, but amidst today's trends for vibrant colors, foreign textures and evermore innovative shapes, I have intentionally tried to stand apart, designing sweaters that are not only fashionable, but that will also stand the test of time and warrant the care and attention that goes into producing each of these sweaters. My knowledge as a fashion designer, together with my avid love of knitting, have led me to attempt to produce work that encompasses beauty, style and craftsmanship, and I hope very much that in following the patterns in the book you too will share in the enjoyment of making such garments. A successful design, in my eyes, is one that can be worn year after year and will co-ordinate with whatever is in fashion at the time. More often than not, knitwear is one of the longest-wearing items in our wardrobes. Therefore it should be skillfully designed, well-made and based on shapes and patterns that are attractive, enduring and versatile. In **The Sasha Kagan Sweater Book,** I have put together a selection of what has proved to be the best and most successful of my summer and winter collections over the past few years. I sincerely hope that you will derive as much pleasure from making and wearing them as I have from designing them.

Sasha Kagan

Though trained as a painter, I have worked in knitwear for a long while and draw the inspiration for my patterns from a variety of sources. Many of my geometric and more linear designs come out of my head, and all I have to do to capture the feel and look of such a design in yarn is to draw it out on paper. In my studio I keep a store of hundreds of yarns from which I select the shades for these designs. Once I have an idea of the colors I will use, the design is then transferred to graph paper so that I have a basic block of pattern from which my knitters can work. In order to decide on the final color schemes I have many swatches knitted up, so that I can see just how the colors affect one another within the design. Once the colors and pattern are set, the graphs are sent to each knitter along with details of the garment to be made and accompanying instructions and samples of the yarns to be used, and this is essentially what I have provided for you to work from in the book. For my more complex and figurative designs, however, I look farther afield. Although I find the rural atmosphere of my surroundings in Wales an ideal environment for perfecting my designs, many of them derive from outside research. Textiles and embroideries from the past have greatly influenced me, and particularly in my early days, visits to the Victoria and Albert Museum and the Museum of Mankind in London triggered a multitude of ideas. Nostalgia, too, is a predominant influence on my work. Many of my more figurative patterns are of 1930s and 1940s origin. I try to adapt stitchcraft

Top and above, my studio and pinboard where I gather together ideas. *Left,* a selection of the old patterns which inspire many of my designs. *Right,* pattern charts in the making.

8

FIRESIDE YARNS

ORDER FORM

P.O. BOX 357
WHITEHOUSE
NEW JERSEY   08888

Please send me the following SASHA KAGAN yarn kits

Kit No.	Title	Yarn	Qty.	Price each	Total
20	Harriet Jacket	wool		$ 40.00	
22	Paintbox vest	cotton		20.00	
24	Desert Ribbons Cardigan	wool		35.00	
26	Optical Copper Waistcoat and Hat	wool/lurex		32.00	
28	Rib Sweater	wool		27.00	
29	Bramble sweater	wool		27.00	
32	Ribbons crew	wool		35.00	
33	Ribbons matching hat	wool		13.00	
34	Chequerboard crew	wool		35.00	
36	Squares on black Peplum	wool		40.00	
38	Copper Diamonds crew	wool		35.00	
39	Copper Diamonds crew	wool		38.00	
40	Maurice shawl collar waistcoat	wool with lurex		27.00	
44	Wallflowers envelope Crew	cotton		28.00	
46	Iris cardigan	wool/mohair		52.00	
48	Marigold waistcoat	wool/mohair		29.00	
50	Purple Pansy Long Crew	wool/mohair		56.00	
52	Roses Cardigan	cotton		30.00	
54	Daisy Waistcoat and Hat	wool/mohair		39.00	
56	Sweet Peas Camisole	cotton		20.00	
58	Pretty Pansies cardigan	wool/mohair		52.00	
62	Cactus Vest	wool		25.00	
64	Double Dutch Crew	wool		35.00	
66	Navajo Waistcoat	wool		25.00	
68	Pierrot Cardigan	cotton		35.00	
70	Sterling Zig-Zag Peplum and Camisole	wool		45.00	
74	Chittimacha Shawl Collar Waistcoat	wool/lurex		28.00	
76	Willow Pattern Waistcoat	wool		25.00	
78	Islamic Waistcoat	wool		27.00	
80	Leaves Autumn Cardigan	wool		40.00	
82	Mosaic Vest	wool		25.00	
86	Summer Scotty Cardigan	cotton		32.00	
88	Boys on Blue Cardigan	wool		40.00	
90	Teddy Bear Waistcoat	wool		25.00	
92	Seagulls Envelope Crew	wool		35.00	
94	Staring Cats Crew	wool		35.00	
96	Boys on black Crew	wool		35.00	
98	Butterflies Cable Waistcoat	wool		30.00	
100	Dachshund Waistcoat	wool		30.00	
102	Prowling Cats Crew	wool		25.00	
104	Alexander Beetle Banded Waistcoat	wool		38.00	
106	Raingirls Cardigan	wool		30.00	
108	Staring Cats Waistcoat	cotton		35.00	
110	Scotties V-neck	wool		23.00	
112	Scotties matching Hat	wool		35.00	
114	Scotties Cable Waistcoat	wool		13.00	
116	Scotties Matching Hat (Pale Grey)	wool		28.00	
120	Copies of SASHA KAGAN Sweater Book	wool		14.95	

Total
for $

Name ....

Address ....

Zip Code ....

Please allow 21 days for delivery.

I enclose my check made payable to FIRESIDE YARNS

US and Canadian delivery and packing included

designs such as embroidery motifs, petit point outlines and borders into knitting pattern formulae and use them to form the basis of many of my nursery and flower patterns. To do this, I translate the embroidery stitches into knitting stitches and then work them into a complete design which fits the proportions of a particular choice of sweater. I have a hoard of knitting patterns from the past which I inherited from my mother, and these provide a constant source of ideas for both the patterns and shapes that I use for my work.

While I tend not to design with a specific person or market in mind, I quite often derive ideas for my patterns from a particular climate, season or geographical area. My Cactus motif on pp. 62–63 is associated with a summer spent in south-western America. Normally a season's collection is constructed around a common theme – one year it might be geometrics, another it might be butterflies and birds, another it might be flowers or nursery images – and each collection is characterised by a particular range of colors.

Customers have said that my designs succeed to a great extent on their clever use of color, however, my criteria for choosing colors are little more than personal taste and trial and error. It is only through having the swatches made that I can see how the colors are affecting one another. Variety is of the essence in any perennial designer's work and so each season I tend to choose a few basic colors which are typical of that collection. In 1983 I used charcoals, grays and blacks, as in the Scotty dog patterns; in 1984 I have explored paintbox shades; other years I have used all pastels, as in the floral designs. By restricting myself to a few colors, my designs take on a more homogeneous look as a collection and by subtly varying the accent and background shades, I achieve variety but not confusion. What I like to do especially is to put two potentially clashing colors side by side within a design and it is this in particular that lends the versatility to my sweaters. A pale delicate pink may come next to a coarse rust mix; white mohair may blend into a strong oatmeal Shetland. I do not believe in monotones and by incorporating contrasting colors within one design I can appeal to several tastes.

Left, hard at work. *Right,* the same pattern worked in different colorways.

The shapes I prefer are classic, and meant to endure from season to season. In my collections I have chosen to limit myself to a select number of garments which all individually conform to basic proportions within which I can manipulate the patterns. Where a particularly complex design is involved, I make certain the shape into which it will be made is simple so as not to confuse the overall effect. Every collection includes a vest, a long-sleeved sweater and a cardigan. Vests, I feel, are versatile garments and something you could easily make for someone else. They are good garments to start off with as they are quick to make and allow plenty of potential to co-ordinate with other items in your wardrobe. More often than not, I work the backs of vests in striped rib, making them straightforward projects.

Long-sleeved sweaters are designed for warmth, and are therefore made in stronger outdoor colors as a rule. Sometimes the pattern is worked throughout on back, front and sleeves, but where a pattern is very dominant, such as the Double Dutch design, the sleeves are left plain to balance the overall effect. Cardigans are easy to wear and are useful for co-ordinating the rest of one's outfit. A plain dress or skirt worn with one of my cardigans makes a stunning and original outfit.

Whilst the basic outlines continue from year to year, I regularly introduce new details to keep pace with contemporary fashion trends and occasionally add a new shape. Shawl collars on vests, peplum skirts on jackets, and matching hats and berets all add new flavor to existing shapes and enhance particular designs.

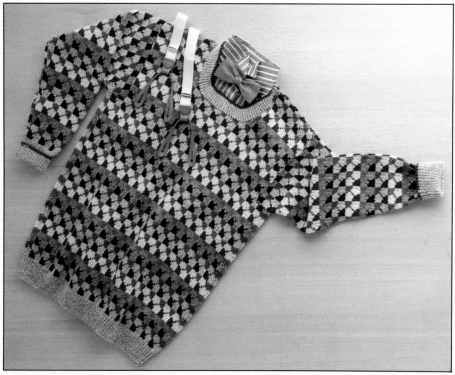

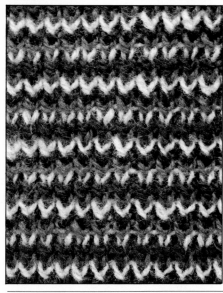

Basic shapes: *left,* crew neck sweater; *top,* short cardigan and peplum jacket; *top right,* crew neck sweater with plain sleeves; *right,* vest; *far right,* boat neck sweater. *Above,* a vest back worked in striped rib.

I also try to design my shapes with men in mind as well as women. Scattered throughout the book are several sweaters that are particularly suitable for men and these have been sized accordingly. Similarly, many of the nostalgic figurative sweaters should appeal to teenagers.

I usually prefer to work in Shetland yarn because it is found in a wide range of shades and because my knitters feel comfortable with it. It is particularly suitable for intricate patterns, and the fineness of the yarn is appropriate for the large amount of weaving in and carrying yarns across the back of the work that my patterns require. Since I am mainly concerned with pattern and color few of my styles use textured stitches. Occasionally, though, I incorporate mohair, silk, and lurex yarn, when I think this will add to my design. My spring and summer garments tend to be in cotton yarn. When working in cotton, I adjust my colors to be brighter and simpler; the straight outlines which the cotton yarn produces would kill a more intricate design, and therefore I stick to bolder figurative patterns. Most of the yarns used are fine-to-medium weight – Shetland yarn is generally the basis for my wool garments, with bands of mohair to separate certain patterns and flecks of lurex to accentuate others. A 4-ply yarn is used for the cotton garments.

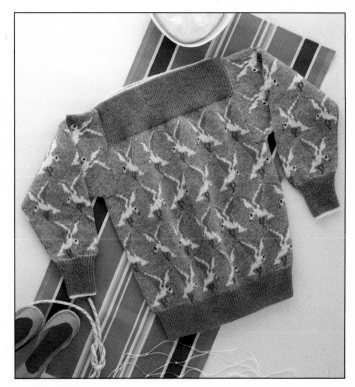

The possibilities for designing your own patterns
are endless. At the simplest level, you can follow
my designs but substitute colors of your own
choice. This can be done by merely changing the
shade of a background color, taking it up or down
so that the pattern becomes more or less predominant.
Alternatively you can replace one of my background
colors with a color you prefer better. For example,
when making the Seagull boat neck sweater on
pp. 92–93 you might use a navy blue background in
place of the pale background for a stronger effect.
When changing a background shade, remember to
consider the yarns that are going to be carried across
and woven in, taking care that they will not show
through the ground color.

At a slightly more complex level, you can borrow a
particular color scheme from another garment and
use it in one of the existing patterns. For example,
the colors of the Scotty dog sweaters might appeal
to you and you might like to translate these colors
into the Prowling Cats crew neck sweater on
pp. 102–103, making it more suitable for a man's
garment perhaps. When you do this try to make sure
that the number of yarns used in both patterns
correspond, or decide which ones you can afford
to forfeit.

You may find that one of my designs appeals to you
but none of my colors tie in with your wardrobe. In
this case you could change the color scheme
completely. To do this, first analyze the relationship
of one color to another; does it enhance the color
next to it, does it contrast with it, is it a neutral shade,
is it lighter than the next color or darker. Once you
have established this you can then select colors of
your choice which will have the same effect within
the pattern. You could translate the Dachshund
pattern into primary colors against a dark ground,
taking them away from their natural colors.

Similarly, you can change the colors of the Scotty
dog pattern so that you are using the same motif as
before but achieving a completely different style. By
using a gray ground and less vivid colors you can
convert the squares pattern into a much softer design
than the bold originals.

These are all examples of using my outlines and
patterns to suit your own tastes. But if you are feeling
adventurous you might like to try designing your own
patterns, translating a motif which appeals or has
particular sentimental value into a pattern formula.
When I put together a design I have certain maxims
I follow, which have evolved largely through trial and
error. Just as when building a wall, the bricks should
be staggered and not placed directly on top of each
other, so it is best to offset your pattern motif as it
moves up the work, so that only alternate rows of
pattern align. Similarly, if your design has a definite
horizontal direction, it is more effective to reverse the
direction on alternate rows to give 'movement'

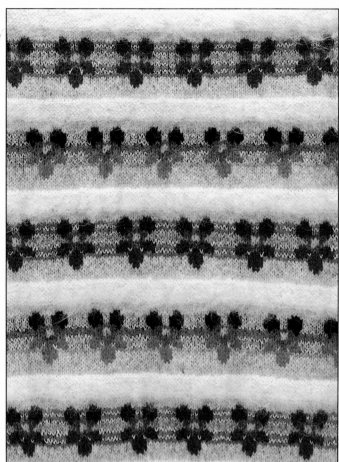

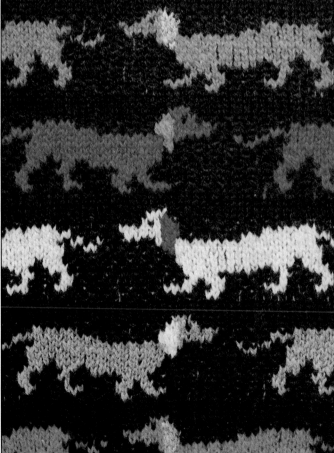

Above, bands of white mohair worked in reversed stockinette stitch are used to separate a repeating pattern. *Left,* examples of different backgrounds and colorways of patterns featured in the book.

within the garment. If your ground color is over-dominant you can introduce horizontal bands or stripes of different plain stitches, such as garter stitch, or different yarns in between the pattern rows, to break up the design quite simply. I have also found that border colors are of great importance and often work in the opposite direction to that which you would expect. They do not always have to be mute, back-up colors; it is sometimes possible to use a strong, perhaps contrasting shade; but experiment with yarns before making your final decision to ensure that you do not kill an otherwise subtle and interesting color combination within the pattern.

Once you have started thinking in terms of specific patterns and designs – whether they are of mine or your own inspiration – you will find that different designs will develop out of one another. The colors used in a bold figurative design might translate interestingly into a more miniature geometric design and vice versa. Do not be afraid to knit up smallish squares of your pattern incorporating any border design you might have envisaged, to see whether your ideas are effective.

I first trained as a painter at Exeter College of Art and then studied printmaking at the Royal College of Art. I concentrated on prints filled with patterns, and then went on to produce silkscreens based on various knitting stitches. My mother had been a great knitter and hoarder of scraps of yarn and was herself a professional needlewoman. I grew up to believe that knitting in many ways represents the ultimate in endeavour and application, and I feel lucky to have taken up the craft in our increasingly technological age at a time when it is becoming more appreciated and sought after.

I came to live in Wales in 1972 and found its compact ruralness a great advantage when I began to translate the repeat patterns and graphic qualities of prints into knitwear. In 1977 I was awarded a Welsh Arts Council bursary to set up a dye workshop and began organised production of my knitwear designs with four outworkers. Today my knitwear business is thriving; I have a core of around a hundred knitters who come from all over the country, and who produce the 800–1000 garments I now sell commercially in London, Milan, Berlin, New York and San Francisco. Buyers say that my unique designs have international appeal, and that customers appreciate the good finish and hand-made quality that distinguishes my work.

I am greatly indebted to the help and support I receive from the team of workers who contribute to the beautiful finish and commercial success of my sweaters. I would especially like to thank the following people for their industry: Marlene Richards for finishing the sweaters, Mrs M. Jones and Mrs E. Holmes for working pattern swatches and Maria Feltham for organising the production of the sweaters and co-ordinating sending the yarns and patterns to the knitters.

Individual patterns are given for each of the sweaters illustrated in the book, and these, along with the appropriate pattern charts, are found beside each photograph. However, I strongly advise those of you who are new to knitting patterns from charts to consult the Knitting Know-how section at the back of the book. There you will find a detailed breakdown of how these particular charts and patterns should be read when making the sweaters (see pp. 134–135). Also at the back of the book are a list of abbreviations, and illustrated step by step instructions for all the stitches you will require.

Above right, drawing charts for my knitters; *right,* choosing yarns to be sent off. *Top far right,* with my family; *below far right,* working out pattern swatches.

The majority of the patterns are given in several sizes where the design permits, and the sizes are quoted at the beginning of each pattern. A breakdown of the measurements corresponding to these sizes is given on pp. 116–123, along with sketches of each of the sweaters, to give a better idea of the proportions of each garment. These measurements and the measurements quoted within the pattern are calculated as though perfect tension had been maintained throughout. Instructions about working the yarns in the patterns given in the book, about maintaining and adjusting tension, and working the yarns to correspond with the pattern charts provided are given fully in the back of the book on pp. 136–137. I further advise you to consult these pages if this method of knitting is new to you. Obviously, if your tension is not exact and you decide to shape the piece you are working on a different row from that quoted, your pattern will not correspond with the photograph in the book. When several sizes are quoted, the measurements, yarn quantities and numbers of stitches for the larger sizes are quoted in brackets after the initial figure.

Many of the garments have been designed with a unisex element in mind. In those patterns I have given instructions for working right over left opening edges on cardigans and vests. However, if you wish to make the garments for a man, these can easily be reversed.

Finishing instructions are given at the end of each pattern, but fuller, illustrated instructions are given on pp. 140–141 in the Knitting Know-how section. Alongside the measurements charts on pp. 116–123 there are samples of the yarns which I have used, to help give you a better idea of the colors. Quantities of yarn quoted in the patterns are generally the minimum amounts required. In some cases, however, only very small quantities of a shade are required. For these you can use scraps of yarn if you have them, so study the pattern before you buy your own.

Yarn Information

I always use 2-ply jumper weight Shetland yarn manufactured by Jamieson & Smith. You can order yarn directly from them by writing to the address given on page 143. However, packs of the same type of yarn in sufficient quantities for knitting the sweaters in this book are available from Fireside Yarns Inc., whose address is also on page 143. If you would like to choose your own yarn, wool fingering yarn knits up in much the same way.

GEOMETRICS

HARRIET

A warm three-quarter length jacket for cold days,
with striped rib double borders and slit hip pockets.

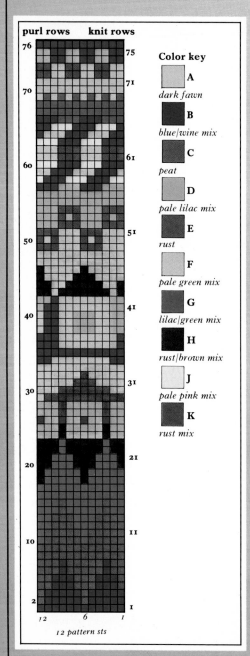

purl rows   knit rows

76   75
71
70
61
60
51
50
41
40
31
30
21
20
11
10
2   1

12   6   1

12 pattern sts

Color key

- **A** — *dark fawn*
- **B** — *blue/wine mix*
- **C** — *peat*
- **D** — *pale lilac mix*
- **E** — *rust*
- **F** — *pale green mix*
- **G** — *lilac/green mix*
- **H** — *rust/brown mix*
- **J** — *pale pink mix*
- **K** — *rust mix*

MATERIALS

Yarn
Use wool fingering yarn.
Yarn A 3½oz (100g) *(dark fawn)*
Yarn B 2¾oz (75g) *(blue/wine mix)*
Yarn C 2¾oz (75g) *(peat)*
Yarn D 1¾oz (50g) *(pale lilac mix)*
Yarn E 2¾oz (75g) *(rust)*
Yarn F 2¾oz (75g) *(pale green mix)*
Yarn G 1¾oz (50g) *(lilac/green mix)*
Yarn H 1oz (25g) *(rust/brown mix)*
Yarn J 1oz (25g) *(pale pink mix)*
Yarn K 1oz (25g) *(rust mix)*

Needles
1 pair no 3
1 pair no 2
1 pair no 1
Notions
8 buttons

MEASUREMENTS

To fit chest 36 (38)in (91, 97cm).
(See also chart on p. 116.)
Stitch gauge
32 sts and 32 rows measure 4in over Fair
Isle pattern on no 3 needles.

BACK

With no 1 needles and yarn A, cast on
142 (154) sts. **Work 7in in k1, p1
twisted rib in the following colors:
Row 1: Yarn C
Row 2: Yarn E
Row 3: Yarn A
Repeat rows 1–3 for 7in, ending with a
row in yarn A**. Increase across the next
(wrong-side) row as follows: (yarn C) rib 1
(7) sts, *rib 6 sts, rib twice into next st;
repeat from * 19 more times, rib 1 (7) sts –
162 (174) sts.
Change to no 3 needles and st st and
work Fair Isle pattern from chart, reading
odd (knit) rows from right to left and even
(purl) rows from left to right. Work the
pattern across knit rows as follows: *for the
smaller size (36in)*, repeat sts 1–12
thirteen times and then work sts 1–6 once
to complete row; *for the larger size (38in)*,
repeat sts 1–12 fourteen times and then
work sts 1–6 once. Work purl rows in
reverse. Continuing in pattern, work
straight until you have completed row 64
of the second working of chart and back
measures approximately 24½in.
Shape armholes: Continuing in pattern,
bind off 10 (12) sts at the beginning of the
next 2 rows – 142 (150) sts remain. Work
straight until end of row 62 (66) of third
working of chart and back measures
approximately 33 (33½)in.
Shape shoulders: Continuing in pattern,
bind off 11 (12) sts at the beginning of next
8 rows. Bind off remaining 54 (54) sts.

FRONTS

Left front
***With no 1 needles and yarn A, cast
on 64 (68) sts. Work as for back from ** to
**. Increase on next (wrong-side) row as
follows: (yarn C) rib 0 (4) sts, *rib 7 (5)
sts, rib twice into next st; repeat from * 7
(9) more times, rib 0 (4) sts – 72 (78) sts.
Change to no 3 needles and st st and
work pattern from chart. Work the pattern
across knit rows as follows: *for the smaller
size*, repeat sts 1–12 six times; *for the
larger size*, repeat sts 1–12 six times, then

work sts 1–6. Work purl rows in reverse.
Continue in pattern to end of row 22 (24)
of the chart.***
Pocket: Work pocket over the next 32
rows as follows: on the next row, work the
first 32 (38) sts in the row, turn, leaving
the remaining 40 sts on a spare needle.
Work the next 31 rows of the pattern on
these first 32 (38) sts – you should have
completed row 54 (56) of the chart. Then
leave these 32 (38) sts on a spare needle.
With right side facing, return to the 40 sts
on the other spare needle and work the
same 32 rows of pattern on these sts
ending at row 54 (56) of the chart. Now
slip both sets of stitches on to one needle
and continue to work straight in pattern
until end of row 64 of the second working
of chart and front measures approximately
24½in.
Shape armhole: Continuing in pattern,
bind off 10 (12) sts at the beginning of next
row – 62 (66) sts remain. Work straight
until end of row 39 (43) of the third working of chart.
Shape neck: Bind off 5 sts at the beginning of the next (wrong-side) row, then
work pattern to end. Continue in pattern,
decreasing one st at the neck edge on the
following 13 rows – 44 (48) sts remain.
Now work straight until end of row 62
(66) of the third working of chart and
front measures approximately 33 (33½)in.
Shape shoulder: Bind off 11 (12) sts at
the beginning of the next and following 3
alternate rows.

Right front
Work as for left front, reversing pocket,
armhole, neck and shoulder shapings.
When working the pocket, work the first
40 sts in the row (right-side facing) and
then work the remaining 32 sts.

SLEEVES

With no 1 needles and yarn A, cast
on 68 (70) sts. Work 7¾in in striped
rib as for back. Increase across last
row as follows: rib 2 (5) sts, *rib 3 (2)
sts, rib twice into next st; repeat from
* 15 (19) more times, rib 2 (5) sts –
84 (90) sts.
Change to no 3 needles and st st and
work Fair Isle pattern from chart.
Work pattern across knit rows as
follows: *for the smaller size*, repeat sts
1–12 seven times; *for the larger size*,
repeat sts 1–12 seven times and then
work sts 1–6 once to complete the row.
Work purl rows in reverse. Continue
in pattern, *at the same time* increasing
one st at each end of the 3rd and every
following 4th row until there are 144
(150) sts on needle. Work straight until
end of row 48 of second working of chart
and sleeve measures 22¾in. Bind off.

FRONT BORDERS

Measure 3½in up from edge of hem welt at front opening edges and mark points.

Right front

With right side facing, using no 1 needles and yarn A, pick up and knit 216 (220) sts up front opening edge from marker to start of neck shaping. Work 5 rows in twisted rib in the same three-color stripe sequence as for back welts.

Buttonholes: Make 8 buttonholes in the 6th row as follows: rib 6 (7) sts, *bind off 4 sts, rib 25 sts; rep from * 6 more times, cast off 4 sts, rib 3 (6) sts. Rib back along next row, casting on 4 sts over those bound off in previous row. Rib 8 more rows, then work the two buttonhole rows again. Work 5 more rows of rib; bind off.

Left front

With right side facing, no 1 needles and yarn A, beginning at start of neck shaping, pick up and knit 216 (220) sts down front edge to marker. Work 22 rows of rib to correspond with right front band, omit buttonholes. Bind off.

COLLAR

With no 1 needles and yarn A, cast on 116 (118) sts. Work one row in rib in yarn A. Using same color sequence as before, work collar in striped rib, increasing one st at each end of next and following 5 alternate rows. Then increase one st at each end of the next 6 rows – 140 (142) sts. Continuing in rib, work 4 rows straight then decrease one st at each end of the next 6 rows, then decrease one st at each end of next and following five alternate rows – 116 (118) sts. Work one row straight. Bind off.

POCKET

Pocket borders

Left front: With no 1 needles and yarn A, and with right side facing, pick up and knit 34 sts up the side of the pocket slit nearest the front opening edge. Work 12 rows of striped k1, p1 twisted rib, as before. Bind off.

Right front: Work in same way, beginning at opposite end of pocket slit.

Pocket linings

With right side facing, using 3mm needles and yarn A, pick up and knit 34 sts down the remaining edge of one pocket slit, behind ribbed border. Work 13cm in st st in yarn A; cast off. Repeat for other pocket.

FINISHING

Press all pieces from the wrong side avoiding ribbing. Join fronts to back at side and shoulder seams. Join sleeve seams, leaving 1¼ (1½)in unstitched at top of seam. Sew sleeves and collar in position in same way as Leaves cardigan (see p. 81). Fold cuff ribbings in half to inside and slip stitch inner edges in position inside sleeves. Fold front ribbed bands in half to inside, aligning double buttonholes in right front band. Slip stitch inner edge of bands in position down inside front edges and blanket stitch around double buttonholes. Fold up half of hem welt to inside and pin inner edge in position. Slip stitch to main body of garment, oversewing the double edges at front opening edges. Sew free sides of each pocket lining to back of cardigan fronts. Catch down sides of pocket borders. Sew 8 buttons to left front band to match buttonholes. Press seams from wrong side.

PAINTBOX

*Pretty paint-box colors, bordered with white,
make this an ideal garment for summer days. Bands of garter stitch
separate the pattern and the back is worked in plain white rib.*

MATERIALS

Yarn

Use No. 8 cotton yarn.

Yarn A 10½oz (300g) *(white)*
Yarn B 1¾oz (50g) *(yellow)*
Yarn C 1¾oz (50g) *(brown)*
Yarn D 1¾oz (50g) *(pale green)*
Yarn E 1¾oz (50g) *(pink)*
Yarn F 1¾oz (50g) *(rust)*
Yarn G 1¾oz (50g) *(mid-blue)*
Yarn H 1¾oz (50g) *(bottle green)*
Yarn K 1¾oz (50g) *(lilac)*

Needles

1 pair no 3
1 pair no 2
1 pair no 0

MEASUREMENTS

To fit chest 32 (36, 38)in (81, 91, 96cm)
(See also chart on p. 116.)

Stitch gauge

34 sts and 38 rows measure 4in over Fair
Isle pattern on no 3 needles.

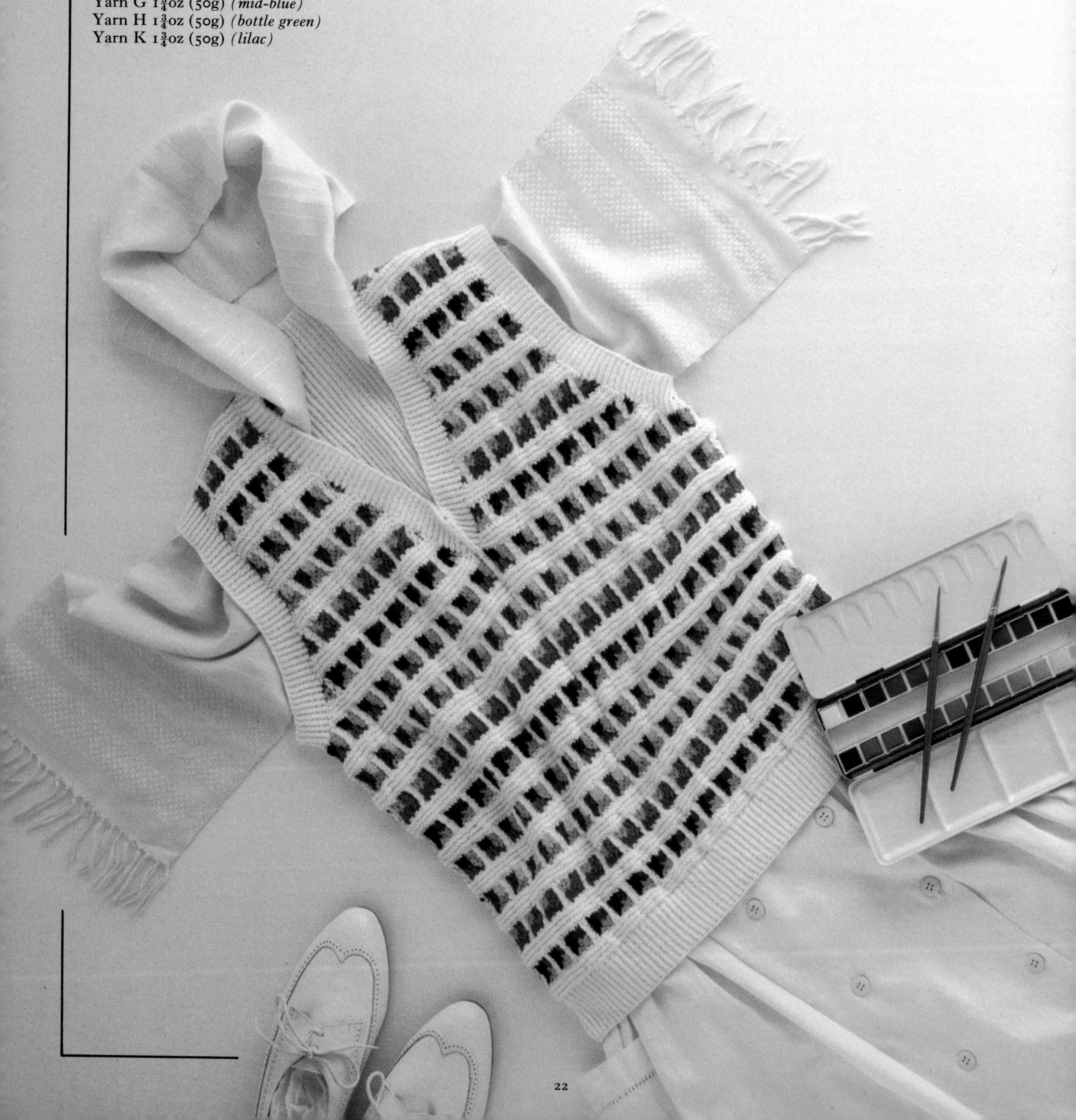

FRONT

With no 0 needles and yarn A, cast on 132 (142, 154) sts. Work 2 (2, 2¼)in in k1, p1 twisted rib in yarn A ending with a wrong-side row. Work one row in purl, increasing across the row as follows: p1 (7, 7) sts, *p6 (4, 3) sts, purl twice into the next st, p 6 (4, 3) sts; repeat from * 9 (15, 19) more times, p1 (7, 7) sts – 142 (158, 174) sts.

Change to no 3 needles and st st and work pattern from chart, reading odd (knit) rows from right to left and even (purl) rows from left to right. Work the pattern across knit rows as follows: *for the small size* (32in), repeat sts *1–8* seventeen times, then work sts *1–6* once; *for the medium size* (36in), repeat sts *1–8* nineteen times and then work sts *1–6* once; *for the large size* (38in), work sts *1–8* twenty-one times and then work sts *1–6* once. Work purl rows in reverse. Work the first six rows (1–6) in garter sts, knitting every row and then work rows 7–14 in st st. Continue thus in pattern alternating 6 rows of garter sts and 8 rows of st st until you have worked row 48 (54, 6) of the second (second, third) working of chart and the front measures approximately 12½ (13½, 14½)in from the cast-on edge.

Shape armholes and neck: Continuing in pattern, bind off 13 (14, 16) sts at the beginning of the next 2 rows – 116 (130, 142) sts. *At the same time,* divide here for neck: on the next row, k2 tog, then work pattern across the next 55 (62, 68) sts in the row, turn and leave the remaining 59 (66, 72) sts on a spare needle. Continuing in pattern on these 56 (63, 69) sts, work the next row straight. **K2 tog at the beginning of the next row, then pattern to end. Work next row straight in pattern. K2 tog the next row, then work pattern to the last 2 sts, k2 tog. Work the next row straight**. Repeat from ** to ** until 32 (35, 39) sts remain. Now work armhole edge straight but continue to decrease one st at the neck edge in the same way until

24 (27, 32) sts remain. Continuing in pattern, work straight until you have completed row 30 (38, 50) of the fourth working of the chart and front measures approximately 22 (23¼, 24¾)in from cast-on edge.

Shape shoulder: Continuing in pattern, bind off 8 (9, 12) sts at the beginning of the next row. Then bind off 8 (9, 10) sts at the beginning of the following 2 alternate rows. Now return to the remaining sts on spare needle. Slip the first 2 sts at the center on to a safety pin, then rejoin yarn to remaining 57 (62, 68) sts of right shoulder. Finish right neck, armhole and shoulder edges to correspond with left side, reversing all shapings.

BACK

With no 0 needles and yarn A, cast on 142 (158, 174) sts. Work 2 (2, 2¼)in in k1, p1 twisted rib in yarn A.

Change to no 2 needles and continue to work entire back in twisted rib in yarn A. Work straight until back measures the same as the front from cast-on edge to start of armhole shaping – approximately 12½ (13½, 14½)in.

Shape armholes: Bind off 8 (9, 11) sts at the beginning of the next 2 rows. Then k2 tog at each end of every alternate row until 94 (104, 118) sts remain. Work straight until the back measures the same

as the fronts from cast-on edge to start of shoulder shaping – approximately 22 (23¼, 24½)in.

Shape shoulders: Bind off 8 (9, 12) sts at the beginning of the next 2 rows. Then bind off 8 (9, 10) sts at the beginning of the next 4 rows. Leave the remaining 46 (50, 54) sts on a spare needle or stitch holder.

NECKBAND

Join front to back at right shoulder seam. With no 0 needles and yarn A, beginning at the left shoulder, pick up and knit 82 (90, 94) sts down left side of neck to center-front, mark with colored thread. Then knit the 2 sts on the safety pin at the center-front and mark again with colored thread. Then pick up and knit 82 (90, 94) sts up right side of neck, and knit the 46 (50, 54) sts on spare needle around back of neck. Work back along right side of neck to within 2 sts of marker on this side; slip 1, k1, psso, then purl the 2 sts at the center-front, then k2 tog, rib to end of left side. On the next row, rib back along the left side of neck to within 2 sts of the marking thread on this side, slip 1, k1, psso, knit the 2 sts at center-front, k2 tog, rib to end. Repeat these 2 rows four more times. Bind off in rib, still decreasing as before.

ARMBANDS

Join left shoulder seam and ribbing. With no 0 needles and yarn A, pick up and knit 174 (182, 190) sts round one armhole. Work 10 rows in k1, p1 twisted rib in yarn A. Bind off in rib. Repeat for other armhole.

FINISHING

Press front very lightly from wrong side avoiding ribbing. Join both side seams and press seams lightly.

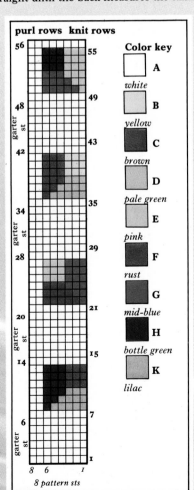

purl rows   knit rows

		Color key
		A
		white
		B
		yellow
		C
		brown
		D
		pale green
		E
		pink
		F
		rust
		G
		mid-blue
		H
		bottle green
		K
		lilac

8 6 ... 1

8 pattern sts

DESERT RIBBONS

*A short cardigan with three-quarter sleeves and front pockets,
worked in subtle desert shades of ribbon pattern.
It could easily be made in bolder shades for a livelier effect.*

MATERIALS

Yarn
Use wool fingering yarn.
Yarn A 5¼oz (150g) *(sand)*
Yarn B 3½oz (100g) *(ivory)*
Yarn C 1¾oz (50g) *(pale lilac mix)*
Yarn D 1¾oz (50g) *(mid-brown mix)*
Yarn E 1oz (25g) *(pearl)*
Yarn F 1oz (25g) *(sage green)*

Needles
1 pair no 3
1 pair no 2
1 pair no 1

Notions
5 buttons

MEASUREMENTS

One-size: to fit bust 34–36in (86–91cm).
(See also chart on p. 116.)

Stitch gauge
30 sts and 32 rows measure 4in over
Fair Isle pattern on no 3 needles.

BACK

With no 1 needles and yarn A, cast on
128 sts. Work 2in in k1, p1 twisted rib,
increasing across the last (wrong-side) row
as follows: *rib 7 sts, rib twice into the
next st; repeat from * 16 more times –
144 sts.
Change to no 3 needles and st st and
work Fair Isle pattern from chart, reading
odd (knit) rows from right to left and even
(purl) rows from left to right. Work the
pattern across knit rows as follows: work
sts *10–17* once at the beginning of the row
and then repeat the 17 pattern sts (*1–17*)
eight times across the row. Work purl
rows in reverse, working extra sts at the
end of rows. Continuing in pattern work
sides straight until you have worked row
18 of the third working of the pattern
chart and the back measures approximately 11in from the cast-on edge.
Shape armholes: Continuing in pattern,
bind off 8 sts at the beginning of the next
2 rows. Then decrease one st at each end
of every row until 108 sts remain. Work
straight in pattern on these 108 sts until
you have worked row 28 of the fifth working of the pattern chart and back measures
approximately 19¼in from cast-on edge.
Shape shoulders: Continuing in pattern,
bind off 6 sts at the beginning of the next
4 rows. Then bind off 7 sts at the beginning of the following 6 rows. Divide the
remaining 42 sts in half and leave each
half on a spare needle or stitch holder.

FRONTS

Pocket linings

Begin by making the pocket linings. With no 2 needles and yarn A, cast on 28 sts. Work 2¼in in st st in yarn A, ending with a purl row. Leave sts on spare needle. Make another lining in the same way.

Left front

With no 1 needles and yarn A, cast on 58 sts. Work 2in in k1, p1 twisted rib in yarn A, increasing across the last wrong-side row as follows: *rib 6 sts, rib twice into the next st; repeat from * 7 more times, rib 2 sts – 66 sts.
Change to no 3 needles and st st and work Fair Isle pattern from chart, working the pattern across knit rows as follows: repeat sts 1–17, three times and then work sts 1–15 once to complete the row. Work purl rows in reverse, working sts 15–1 at the beginning of the row. Continuing in pattern, work straight until you have completed row 14 of the chart.
Pocket: Introduce pocket in row 15 as follows: work the pattern across the first 19 sts in the row, then slip the next 28 sts on to a spare needle or stitch holder and in their place work the pattern across the 28 sts of one pocket lining on spare needle, then work the pattern to the end of the row. Continuing in pattern, work straight until you have worked row 18 of the third working of the pattern chart and the front measures approximately 11in from the cast-on edge.
Shape armhole and neck edge: Continuing in pattern, bind off 8 sts at the beginning of the next row and then work the pattern to the last 2 sts in row; k2 tog. K2 tog at the armhole edge on the next 10 rows and then work armhole edge straight. *At the same time,* continue to decrease one st at the neck edge on every following 4th

row after the first decrease on row 19 until 33 sts remain. Then work straight until you have worked row 28 of the fifth working of the pattern chart and front measures approximately 19¼in from the cast-on edge.
Shape shoulder: Continuing in pattern, bind off 6 sts at the beginning of the next and following alternate row. Then bind off 7 sts at the beginning of the next and following 2 alternate rows.

Right front

Work as for left front, but reverse pocket, armhole, neck and shoulder shapings.

SLEEVES

With no 1 needles and yarn D, cast on 62 sts. Work one row in k1, p1 twisted rib in yarn D. Join in yarn A and work a further 3¼in in k1, p1 twisted rib in yarn A, increasing across the last (wrong-side) row as follows: rib 11 sts, *rib twice into the next st; repeat from * 39 more times, rib 11 sts – 102 sts.
Change to no 3 needles and st st and work Fair Isle pattern from chart, repeating sts 1–17, six times across knit rows, and working purl rows in reverse. Continuing in pattern, work sleeve straight until you have completed row 18 of the third working of the pattern chart and the sleeve measures approximately 12¼in from the cast-on edge.
Shape top of sleeve: Continuing in pattern, bind off 8 sts at the beginning of the next 2 rows. K2 tog at each end of the

next and following alternate row, nine times in all. You should now have completed row 11 of the fourth working of pattern chart. Then work 24 rows straight, ending on row 7 of the fifth working of the pattern chart. K2 tog at each end of the next and every following alternate row, six times, then k2 tog at each end of every row, ten times. Bind off the remaining sts. This wide sleeve top will then be pleated into the armhole.
Make another sleeve in the same way.

Join fronts to back at shoulder seams.

FRONT BANDS

Right front

With right side of work facing, using no 1 needles and yarn A, beginning at the lower edge, pick up and knit 93 sts up the front opening edge to the start of the neck shaping; then pick up 92 sts around side of neck to center-back, including the 21 sts on the first spare needle – 185 sts. Work 3 rows in twisted rib in yarn A.
Buttonholes: Make 5 buttonholes in the 4th row of ribbing as follows: rib 4 sts, *bind off 3 sts, rib 18 sts; repeat from * 3 more times, bind off 3 sts, rib to end of row. On the next row (row 5 of ribbing) work back in rib, casting on 3 sts directly over those bound off in previous row. Work 4 more rows in rib in yarn A. Join in yarn D and work one row of rib in yarn D. Bind off in rib in yarn D.

Left front

With no 1 needles and yarn A, and with right side of work facing, knit the 21 sts from the remaining spare needle, then continue to pick up and knit 71 sts around neck to start of neck shaping, then pick up and knit a further 93 sts down front opening to lower edge – 185 sts in all. Work to correspond with right front band, omitting buttonholes.

POCKET TOPS

With no 1 needles and yarn A, rib across the 28 sts of one pocket on spare needle. Work 7 more rows in k1, p1 twisted rib in yarn A. Join in yarn D and work a further row in twisted rib in yarn D. Bind off in rib in yarn D. Repeat for other pocket top.

FINISHING

Press all Fair Isle parts lightly from the wrong side, avoiding ribbing. Join fronts to back at side seams. Join underarm sleeve seams. Pin sleeves into each armhole, pleating the fullness around the top of the sleeve as you pin in position. Sew sleeves into armholes. Join front bands at center-back of neck. Sew down sides of each pocket top and sew around the sides of each pocket lining on wrong side. Sew on 5 buttons to correspond with buttonholes. Press seams lightly from wrong side.

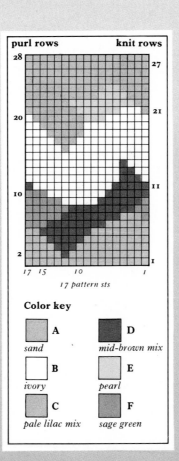

purl rows   knit rows

28
27

20
21

10
11

2
1

17 15   10   1

17 pattern sts

Color key

A — sand
D — mid-brown mix
B — ivory
E — pearl
C — pale lilac mix
F — sage green

MATERIALS Hat

Yarn
Use wool fingering yarn unless otherwise indicated.
Yarn A 1¾oz (50g) *(black)*
Yarn B 1oz (25g) lurex *(copper)*
Yarn C 1oz (25g) *(rust)*
Yarn D 1oz (25g) *(peat)*
Yarn E 1¾oz (50g) *(wine)*

Needles
1 pair no 3 (long or circular)
1 pair no 1 (long or circular)

MEASUREMENTS
One-size: to fit an average head.
(See also chart on p. 116.)

Stitch gauge
32 sts and 32 rows measure 4in over Fair Isle pattern on no 3 needles.

OPTICAL COPPER

*Matching vest and hat in dark shades with glints of copper
scattered throughout. The copper yarn could, however, be substituted
for a Shetland yarn to give a more subtle effect.*

Headband

With no 1 needles and yarn A, cast on
160 sts. Work in k1, p1 twisted rib in the
following three-color sequence:

Row 1: Yarn E
Row 2: Yarn B
Row 3: Yarn A

Repeat rows 1–3 until the band measures
approximately 4¼in, ending with a row in
yarn A. Increase for crown on the next
wrong-side row as follows: (yarn E), *p1,
purl into front and back of next st; repeat
from * to end – 240 sts.

Change to no 3 needles and st st and
work Fair Isle pattern from chart reading
odd (knit) rows from right to left and even
(purl) rows from left to right. Repeat the
16 pattern sts, fifteen times across the
rows. Work rows 1 to 54 on chart.

Shape crown: With right side facing and
continuing in st st, work in stripes,
decreasing as follows:

Row 1 (Yarn E) *k8, slip 1, k1, pass
slipped stitch over (psso); repeat from *
to end – 216 sts.
Purl one row (yarn B), knit one row
(yarn A).
Row 4 (Yarn E) *p7, slip 1, p1, psso;
repeat from * to end – 192 sts.
Knit one row (yarn B), purl one row
(yarn A).
Row 7 (Yarn E) *k6, slip 1, k1, psso;
repeat from * to end – 168 sts.
Purl one row (yarn B), knit one row
(yarn A).
Row 10 (Yarn E) *p5, slip 1, p1, psso;
repeat from * to end – 144 sts.
Then knit one row (yarn B), purl one row
(yarn A). Continue thus, working a
decrease row on every 3rd row (i.e.
decreasing 24 sts on every decrease row)
until you have worked the row *p1, slip 1,
p1, psso; repeat from * to end – 48 sts.
**Knit one row, purl one row. Next row,
k2 tog to end of row. Repeat from ** once
more. Work 2 rows straight – 6 sts. Break
yarn leaving 6in end. Thread end of
yarn through remaining 6 sts, draw up
and secure.

FINISHING

Press Fair Isle parts lightly from wrong
side. Join seam from crown to edge of
headband, with 6in length of yarn. Fold
headband in half, turning it in to wrong
side. Pin and slip stitch in place all around.

MATERIALS Vest

Yarn

Yarn A 3½oz (100g) *(black)*
Yarn B 1¾oz (50g) lurex *(copper)*
Yarn C 1oz (25g) *(rust)*
Yarn D 1oz (25g) *(peat)*
Yarn E 1¾oz (50g) *(wine)*

Needles

1 pair no 3
1 pair no 2
1 pair no 1

Notions

5 buttons

MEASUREMENTS

To fit bust 32 (34, 38)in (81, 86, 96cm).

Stitch gauge
32 sts and 32 rows measure 4in over Fair
Isle pattern on no 3 needles.

FRONT

Pocket linings

Begin by making pocket linings as
follows: with no 2 needles and yarn A,
cast on 28 (32, 36) sts. Work 2¾in in st st
in yarn A, ending with a purl row. Transfer the sts to a spare needle or stitch
holder. Make another pocket lining in the
same way.

Left front

**With no 1 needles and yarn A, cast on
66 (72, 78) sts. Work in k1, p1 twisted rib
in following three-color stripe sequence:

Row 1: Yarn E
Row 2: Yarn B
Row 3: Yarn A

Repeat rows 1–3 until the work measures
2in, ending on a wrong-side row**.
Change to no 3 needles and st st and
work Fair Isle pattern from chart, reading
odd (knit) rows from right to left and even
(purl) rows from left to right. Work the
pattern across knit rows as follows: repeat
sts (1–16) four times *for all sizes* and then
work sts 1–2 *for the small size;* sts 1–8 *for
the medium size* and sts 1–14 *for the large
size,* to complete the row. Work purl rows
in reverse. Continue in pattern until end
of row 20.

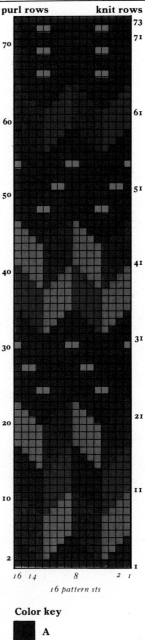

purl rows	knit rows

16 14 | 8 | 2 1
16 pattern sts

Color key

 A
black

 B
copper

 C
rust

 D
peat

 E
wine

continued on p. 31

RIB & BRAMBLE

*Two plain garments based on 1930s shapes. The Rib sweater is close-fitting with diagonal ribs moving outwards from a central panel.
The Bramble sweater has puff and darted sleeves.*

RIB & BRAMBLE

MATERIALS Rib

Yarn
Use wool fingering yarn.
12¼oz (350g) *(deep pink mix)*
Needles
1 pair no 2
1 pair no 1
1 crochet hook, size B
Notions
2 small buttons

MEASUREMENTS

To fit bust 36in (91cm).
(See also chart on p. 116.)
Stitch gauge
48 sts and 44 rows measure 4in over rib.
Note: To work the instruction 'up 1 pk' (see row 5 of back), work as follows: insert the right hand needle from back to front into the top of the stitch below the next stitch to be knitted, *purl* this loop in the usual way, then *knit* the next stitch on the left hand needle, so making one stitch. To work the instruction 'up 1 k' (see row 5 of back), insert the right hand needle from front to back into the top of the stitch below the next one to be knitted, *knit* this loop, then *knit* the next stitch on the left hand needle to make one stitch. To work the instruction 'up 1 p' (see row 11), insert the right hand needle from back to front into the top of the stitch below the next one to be knitted, *purl* this loop in the usual way; *purl* next stitch on left hand needle to make one stitch.

BACK

**With no 2 needles, cast on 136 sts.
Work the following rib pattern:
Row 1: (Right side facing) k1, *k2, p2; repeat from * to last 3 sts, k3.
Row 2: K1, *p2, k2; repeat from * to last 3 sts, p2, k1. Repeat rows 1 and 2 once more. Then start shaping for the side panels as follows:
Row 5: K1, k2 tog, (p2, k2) 11 times; p1, up 1 pk, (k2, p2) 9 times, k1, up 1 k, (p2, k2) 11 times, p2, k2 tog, k1.
Row 6: K1, p1, (k2, p2) 11 times, k2, p1, (p2, k2) 9 times, p3 (k2, p2) 11 times, k2, p1, k1.
Row 7: K1, p2 tog, p1, (k2, p2) 11 times, up 1 k, (k2, p2) 9 times, k1, up 1 k, k1, (p2, k2) 11 times, p1, p2 tog, k1.
Row 8: K1, (k2, p2) 12 times, (p2, k2) 9 times, p2, (p2, k2) 12 times, k1.
Row 9: K1, p2 tog, (k2, p2) 11 times, k2, up 1 pk, k1, (p2, k2) 9 times, up 1 pk, k1, (p2, k2) 11 times, p2 tog, k1.
Row 10: (K2, p2) 12 times, k1, (p2, k2) 9 times, p2, k1, (p2, k2) 12 times.
Row 11: K1, k2 tog, k1, (p2, k2) 11 times, up 1 p, (p2, k2) 9 times, k2, up 1 p, (k2, p2) 11 times, k1, k2 tog, k1.
Row 12: K1, *p2, k2; repeat from * to last 3 sts, p2, k1. Rows 5–12 inclusive form the pattern. Repeat them seven more times. Now work first increase row:
Row 69: (i.e. row 5) K1, (k2, p2) 11 times, k2, p1, up 1 pk, (k2, p2) 9 times, k1, up 1 k, (p2, k2) 12 times, k1.

Continue thus in pattern, decreasing one st at each end of the needle and increasing one st at each side of the center panel as before on every alternate row. *At the same time,* increase one st at each end of the needle on every following 6th row after the first increase row – i.e. after row 69, until there are 156 sts – (10 increasings in all). (*Note:* the side increasings are worked by continuing to increase one st each side of the center panel on every alternate row as before, but *omitting* the decreasing at each end of the needle on every 6th row as indicated on the first increase row. When you have completed the 10 increasings, continue without further increasing (i.e. you will now increase one st at each side of the center panel and decrease one st at each end of the needle on alternate rows as before, keeping the same number of sts on the needle) until the back measures 13¾in, measuring down the center of the work.
Shape armholes: With right side facing, still increasing at each side of the center panel on every alternate row, bind off 7 sts at the beginning of the next 2 rows. Then k3 tog at each end of the needle on every row until 124 sts remain**. Now continue in pattern, (i.e. increasing at each side of the center panel and decreasing one st at each end of the needle) until back measures 21¼in from cast-on edge. Bind off.

FRONT

Work as for back from ** to ** – 124 sts remain after armhole shapings. Continue in pattern as for back (increasing each side of the center panel and decreasing one st at each end of the needle) until front measures 18½in from cast-on edge, ending with a wrong-side row.
Shape neck: On the next row, k1, k2 tog, rib the next 39 sts, increase in next st, k3, bind off 32 sts, k2, increase in next st, work in rib to last 3 sts, k2 tog, k1.
Now continue in pattern on the last 46 sts, increasing at neck edge and decreasing at side edge on alternate rows as before for 3¼in. Bind off, with wrong side facing. With wrong side facing, rejoin wool to remaining 38 (42, 46, 50) sts at neck edge and work to correspond with first side.

SLEEVES

With no 1 needles, cast on 88 sts.
Row 1: (Right side facing) k1, *k2, p2; repeat from * to last 3 sts; k3.
Row 2: K1, *ps, k2; repeat from * to last 3 sts, p2, k1.
Repeat rows 1 and 2 once more. Change to no 2 needles and work as follows:
Row 5: K1, k2 tog, (p2, k2) 4 times, p1, up 1 pk, (k2, p2) 11 times, k1, up 1 k, (p2, k2) 4 times, p2, k2 tog, k1.
Row 6: K1, p1, (k2, p2) 4 times, k2, p1, (p2, k2) 11 times, p3, (k2, p2) 4 times, k2, p1, k1.
Row 7: K1, p2 tog, p1, (k2, p2) 4 times, up 1 k, (k2, p2) 11 times, k1, up 1 k, k1, (p2, k2) 4 times, p1, p2 tog, k1.
Row 8: K1, (k2, p2) 5 times, (p2, k2) 11 times, p2, (p2, k2) 5 times, k1.
Row 9: K1, p2 tog, (k2, p2) 4 times, k2, up 1 pk, k1, (p2, k2) 11 times, up 1 pk, k1, (p2, k2) 4 times, p2 tog, k1.
Row 10: (K2, p2) 5 times, k1, (p2, k2) 11 times, p2, k1, (p2, k2) 5 times.
Row 11: K1, k2 tog, k1, (p2, k2) 4 times, up 1 p, (k2, p2) 11 times, k2, up 1 p, (k2, p2) 4 times, k1, k2 tog, k1.
Row 12: K1, *p2, k2; repeat from * to last 3 sts, p2, k1.
Rows 5–12 inclusive form the rib pattern.
Row 13: (increase row) K1, (k2, p2) 4 times, k2, p1, up 1 pk, (k2, p2) 11 times, k1, up 1 k, (p2, k2) 5 times, k1.
Continue in pattern, decreasing one st at each end of the row and increasing one st at each side of center panel as before on every alternate row. *At the same time,* shape sides by increasing one st at each end of the needle on every following 6th row after the first increase row (row 13 above) until there are 142 sts on the needle – (27 increasings in all). (*Note:* the side increasings are worked in same way as on back by *omitting* decreasings at each end of needle on every 6th row.)
When you have completed the 27 increasings continue without further shaping, i.e. work increasings and decreasings on every alternate row as before, until the sleeve measures 19¾in from cast-on edge (measuring down center of work).
Shape top of sleeve: Continuing to increase at each side of the center panel, bind off 2 sts at the beginning and k2 tog at each end of every row until 73 sts remain. Then bind off 3 sts at the beginning and k3 tog at the end of every row until 43 sts remain. Cast off in purl.

FINISHING

The diagonal ribbing tends to distort the shapes so block each piece before finishing (see p. 139). Join the side seams, then join the shoulder seams from shoulder edge to within 1½in of neck edge. Join sleeve seams and pin sleeves into armholes gathering any fullness at top of sleeve. Sew in position. Crochet a button loop at each inner front shoulder edge. Sew button to back shoulder edge to match.

MATERIALS Bramble

Yarn
Use 4-ply sport yarn.
10½oz (300g) *(petrol blue)*
Needles
1 pair no 4
1 pair no 2

MEASUREMENTS

To fit bust 35–36in (89–91cm).
(See also chart on p. 117.)
Stitch gauge
32 sts and 32 rows measure 4in over pattern on no 4 needles.

BACK

**With no 2 needles, cast on 126 sts and work in rib as follows:

Row 1: (Right side facing) *k2, p2; rep from * to last 2 sts, k2.

Row 2: *P2, k2; rep from * to last 2 sts, p2. Repeat rows 1–2 for 8cm ending with row 2. Next row, rib 42 sts, p40, p2 tog, rib 42 sts – 125 sts.

Change to no 4 needles and work rib and Bramble pattern as follows:

Row 1: (Wrong side facing) rib 42 sts, *(k1, p1, k1) into next st, p3 tog; rep from * 9 more times, (k1, p1, k1) into next st, rib 42 sts.

Row 2: Rib 42 sts; p43, rib 42 sts.

Row 3: Rib 42 sts, *p3 tog, (k1, p1, k1) into next st; rep from * 9 more times, p3 tog, rib 42 sts.

Row 4: Rib 42 sts, p41, rib 42 sts.

Repeat rows 1–4 once more. Continuing repeating rows 1–4, shape sides by increasing one st at each end of 2nd and every following 6th row until there are 52 sts in rib at each side of center panel. Take extra sts into k2, p2 rib as they are made. Then work straight until back measures 12½in ending with row 3.

Shape armholes: Bind off 4 sts at beginning of next 6 rows**. Now work the Bramble pattern throughout, without the ribbed sides. Work straight until back measures 20½in, ending with row 3.

Shape shoulders: Bind off 9 (10) sts at beginning of next 6 rows. Leave remaining 61 sts on a spare needle.

FRONT

Work as for back from ** to **.
Change to Bramble pattern throughout and work straight until front measures 17¼in, ending with row 3.

Shape neck: Continuing in pattern, purl 44 sts, bind off 33 sts, purl to end of row. Continue in pattern on these last 44 sts, decreasing one st at neck edge on every row until 30 sts remain. Then work straight until front measures 20½in.

Shape shoulder: Bind off 10 sts at beginning of next and following 2 alternate rows. With wrong side facing, rejoin yarn to first 44 sts at neck edge. Work to match left side.

SLEEVES

With no 2 needles, cast on 66 sts. Work 2in in k2, p2 rib as for back. Decrease on next right-side row as follows: rib 18 sts, purl next 28 sts, ps tog, rib 18 sts – 65 sts. Change to no 4 needles and work sleeve pattern as follows:

Row 1: (Wrong side facing) rib 18 sts, *(k1, p1, k1) into next st, p3 tog; rep from * 6 times, (k1, p1, k1) into next st, rib 18 sts.

Row 2: Rib 18 sts, purl 31 sts, rib 18 sts.

Row 3: Rib 18 sts, *p3 tog, (k1, p1, k1) into next st; rep from * 6 more times, p3 tog, rib 18 sts.

Row 4: Rib 18 sts, purl 29 sts, rib 18 sts.

Continue repeating rows 1–4, increasing one st at each end of every following 6th row until there are 32 sts in each side rib panel. Now work straight until sleeve measures 18in, ending with row 3.

Shape top of sleeve: Bind off 4 sts at beginning of next 6 rows. Then work Bramble pattern throughout for 5½in. Bind off 20 sts at beginning of next 2 rows. Work 2in straight in pattern. Bind off.

NECKBAND

Join right shoulder seam. With right side facing, using no 2 needles, beginning at left shoulder, pick up and knit 84 sts around front of neck, then knit the 61 sts on spare needle at back of neck, decreasing one st at the end of this first row – 140 sts. Work 1¼in in k2, p2 rib. Bind off.

FINISHING

Do not press pieces. Join left shoulder seam and neckband, side and sleeve seams. Sew each side of center strip at top of sleeve to bound-off edge at each side to give fullness required at top of sleeve. Pin sleeve into armhole, gathering fullness and sew in position. Repeat for other sleeve.

Optical Copper continued

Pocket: Introduce pocket in row 21 as follows: work the first 19 (20, 21) sts in pattern, transfer the next 28 (32, 36) sts to a spare needle. In their place work pattern across 28 (32, 36) sts of one pocket lining on spare needle; then work the pattern across the remaining 19 (20, 21) sts in the row. Continuing in pattern, work straight until you have worked row 70 (1, 5) of the first (second, second) working of chart and front measures approx. 10¼ (11, 11½)in.

Shape armhole and neck edge: Bind off 8 (10, 12) sts at the beginning of the next (right-side) row then work pattern to the last 2 sts; k2 tog. Continuing in pattern, decrease one st at armhole edge on the next 14 (16, 18) rows. Work armhole edge straight. *At the same time,* decrease one st at neck edge on every following 4th row after first decrease, 8 (9, 13) times; then decrease one st on every following 3rd row until 24 (26, 28) sts remain. Then work straight until the end of row 1 (7, 13) of third working of chart and front measures 9 (9½, 9¾)in from start of armhole shaping.

Shape shoulder: Bind off 8 (10, 10) sts at beginning of next row, bind off 8 (8, 9) sts at beginning of next 2 alternate rows.

Right front

Work welt as for left front from ** to **. Change to no 3 needles and st st and work Fair Isle pattern from chart as before, reversing pocket, armhole, neck and shoulder shapings.

BACK

With no 1 needles and yarn A, cast on 132 (144, 156) sts and work 2in in k1, p1 twisted rib, working the same three-color stripe sequence as before.
Change to no 2 needles and continue in twisted rib. Work straight until back measures 10¾ (11, 11½)in from cast-on edge.

Shape armholes: With right side facing, bind off 3 (4, 6) sts at beginning of next 2 rows. K2 tog at each end of every row until 100 (104, 108) sts remain. Work straight until back measures 9 (9½, 9¾)in from start of armhole shaping.

Shape shoulders: Bind off 10 (11, 10) sts at beginning of next 2 rows. Bind off 9 (9, 10) sts at beginning of next 4 rows; divide remaining 44 (46, 48) sts evenly. Transfer each half to a spare needle.

Join fronts to back at shoulders.

FRONT BANDS

Right front

With no 1 needles and yarn A, and with right side facing, beginning at hem edge of right front, pick up and knit 93 (97, 101) sts up front opening edge as far as neck shaping. Pick up and knit a further 81 (87, 93) sts around neck as far as center-back, including 22 (23, 24) sts on spare needle – 174 (184, 194) sts. Work 3 rows of k1, p1 twisted rib in same stripe sequence in yarns E, B and A as before.

Buttonholes: Make 5 buttonholes in 4th row of ribbing as follows: rib 4 sts, *cast off 3 sts, rib 18 (19, 20) sts; repeat from * 3 times, bind off 3 sts and rib to end. Rib back across 5th row, casting on 3 sts over those bound off in previous row. Work 5 more rows in striped rib. Bind off in rib.

Left front

With no 1 needles and yarn A, beginning at center-back of neck, rib 22 (23, 24) sts from remaining spare needle. Continue to pick up and knit 59 (64, 69) sts around neck to neck shaping. Pick up 93 (97, 101) sts down front opening edge to lower edge – 174 (184, 194) sts. Work 10 rows in twisted rib as for right front band, omitting buttonholes. Bind off in rib.

POCKETS

Pocket tops

With right side facing, no 1 needles and yarn A, knit 28 (32, 36) sts of pocket top on spare needle. Work 10 rows of twisted rib as for front band. Bind off.

ARMHOLE BANDS

With no 1 needles and yarn A, pick up and knit 155 (161, 167) sts around armholes. Work 10 rows twisted rib. Bind off.

FINISHING

Join front bands at center-back of neck. Join side seams. Sew down the sides of the pocket tops. Sew the three sides of each pocket lining to back of vest fronts. Sew 5 buttons to left front band.

RIBBONS

*A loose-fitting long-sleeved winter sweater with a wide
boat neck and dropped shoulders. The matching pixie hat uses bands
of the same pattern, worked between a black background.*

MATERIALS Hat

Yarn
Use 4-ply sport yarn.
Yarn A 2¾oz (75g) *(black)*
Yarn B 1oz (25g) *(mustard)*
Yarn C 1oz (25g) *(green)*
Yarn D 1oz (25g) *(bright blue)*
Yarn E 1oz (25g) *(red)*
Yarn F 1oz (25g) *(peat)*
Needles
1 set of four *or* circular, no 3
1 set of four *or* circular, no 2
1 set of four *or* circular, no 1

MEASUREMENTS

One-size: to fit an average head.
(See also chart on p. 117.)
Stitch gauge
32 sts and 30 rows measure 4in over Fair
Isle pattern on no 3 needles.

Headband

With the set of no 1 needles or circular
no 1 needle, and yarn A, cast on 154 sts
(i.e. 51 sts on each of 2 needles and 52 sts
on the third needle). Work 6in in k1, p1
twisted rib in rounds, decreasing one st at
the end of the last round – 153 sts.
Shape crown: Change to no 3 needles
and work pattern from chart. Because you
are working in rounds, read all rows from
right to left and knit every row. Repeat the
17 pattern sts on chart nine times around.
Work rows 1–28 of pattern chart twice.
On the next round, knit entire round in
yarn A, increasing 3 sts evenly – 156 sts.
Change to no 2 needles and continue in
yarn A only, decreasing to a point as
follows:
1st decrease round: (K10, k2 tog) 13
times. Knit 19 rounds straight.
2nd decrease round: (K9, k2 tog) 13
times. Knit 19 rounds straight.
3rd decrease round: (K8, k2 tog) 13
times. Knit 19 rounds straight.
4th decrease round: (K7, k2 tog) 13
times. Knit 19 rounds straight.
Continue decreasing in this way, working
one decrease round and then 19 rounds
straight until you have worked the round
(k1, k2 tog) 13 times – 26 sts remain.
Knit a further 19 rounds straight.
Then (k2 tog) 13 times. Knit 6 rounds
straight. Break yarn leaving a 5in end.

FINISHING

Thread the yarn end through the remaining sts on the needle and draw up tightly.
Secure end and darn in. Make a pom-pom
from the remaining yarns and sew on to
end of hat. Press lightly from wrong side,
avoiding ribbing.

MATERIALS Sweater

Yarn
Use wool fingering yarn.
Yarn A 5¼oz (150g) *(peat)*
Yarn B 3½oz (100g) *(black)*
Yarn C 1¾oz (50g) *(red)*
Yarn D 1¾oz (50g) *(green)*
Yarn E 1oz (25g) *(bright blue)*
Yarn F 1oz (25g) *(mustard)*
Needles
1 pair no 3
1 pair no 0

MEASUREMENTS

To fit chest 36 (38)in (91, 97cm).
(See also chart on p. 117.)
Stitch gauge
31 sts and 30 rows measure 4in over Fair
Isle pattern on no 3 needles.

BACK and FRONT

With no 0 needles and yarn A, cast on
128 (136) sts. Work 2in in k1, p1 twisted
rib, increasing across the last wrong-side
row as follows: *rib 3 sts, rib twice into
the next st, rib 4 sts; repeat from * 15 (16)
more times – 144 (153) sts.
Change to no 3 needles and st st and
work pattern from chart, reading odd
(knit) rows from right to left and even
(purl) rows from left to right. Work the
pattern across knit rows as follows: *for the
smaller size,* repeat sts 1–17 eight times,
then work sts 1–8 once to complete row;
for the larger size, work sts 1–17 nine
times across the rows. Work purl rows in
reverse. Continue thus in pattern until
you have worked row 12 (16) of the fourth
working of the pattern chart and the work
measures approximately 14½ (15)in from
the cast-on edge.
Shape armholes: Continuing in pattern,
bind off 10 (12) sts at the beginning of the
next 2 rows – 124 (129) sts. Then work
straight in pattern until you have completed row 24 (28) of the fifth working of
the pattern chart and the work measures
approximately 19¾ (20)in from the cast-
on edge.
Change to no 0 needles and with yarn A
only work 4 (4¼)in in k1, p1 twisted rib
to form boat neck, increasing one st at
each end of the first row, *for the larger
size only.* When you have worked 4
(4¼)in, join in yarn B and work a further
row of rib in yarn B. Bind off in rib in
yarn B.
Make another in the same way for front.

SLEEVES

With no 0 needles and yarn B, cast on
60 sts. Work one row in k1, p1 twisted rib
in yarn B. Change to yarn A and work 3¼

(3½)in in twisted rib, increasing across the
last wrong-side row as follows: rib 5 sts,
*rib 2 sts, rib twice into the next st;
repeat from * 15 more times, rib 7 sts
– 76 sts.
Change to no 3 needles and st st and
work Fair Isle pattern from chart, repeating
sts 1–17 four times and then working sts
1–8 once across knit rows. Work purl rows
in reverse. Continuing in pattern, shape
the sides by increasing one st at each end
of the 7th and every following 4th row
until there are 132 (136) sts on the needle.
Take the extra sts into the pattern as they
are made. Then work straight in pattern
until you have worked row 24 (28) of the
fifth working of the chart and the sleeve
measures approximately 20¾ (21¾)in from
the cast-on edge. Bind off right across.

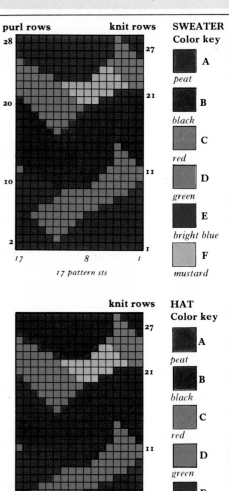

purl rows		knit rows	SWEATER Color key

17 pattern sts

SWEATER Color key

A *peat*
B *black*
C *red*
D *green*
E *bright blue*
F *mustard*

knit rows

17 pattern sts

HAT Color key

A *peat*
B *black*
C *red*
D *green*
E *bright blue*
F *mustard*

FINISHING

Press all pieces lightly from the wrong side, avoiding ribbing. Join front to back at side seams. Overlap the front half of the boat neck and the back half by ¾in and hold with a pin. Sew front of boat neck to back of boat neck from shoulder edge to point 2in in, lifting the front welt and catching down the underneath to the back welt so stitches are invisible. Join sleeve seams, leaving the last 1½in at top of seam unstitched. Pin straight bound-off edge at top of sleeve into top of armhole and pin either side of the unstitched sleeve seam across straight bound-off edge at bottom of armhole. Sew in place. Repeat for other sleeve. Then press seams lightly.

CHEQUER·BOARD

Chequered squares of pattern in a mixture of shades
make this warm wool sweater suitable for both men and women.
It has a crew neck and slightly dropped shoulders.

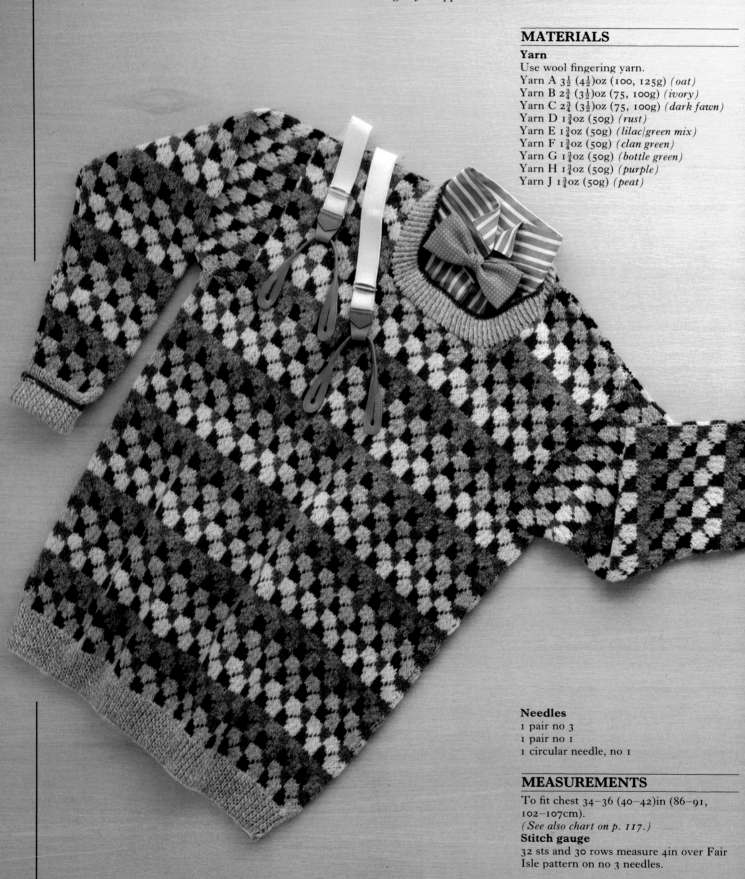

MATERIALS

Yarn
Use wool fingering yarn.
Yarn A 3½ (4½)oz (100, 125g) *(oat)*
Yarn B 2¾ (3½)oz (75, 100g) *(ivory)*
Yarn C 2¾ (3½)oz (75, 100g) *(dark fawn)*
Yarn D 1¾oz (50g) *(rust)*
Yarn E 1¾oz (50g) *(lilac/green mix)*
Yarn F 1¾oz (50g) *(clan green)*
Yarn G 1¾oz (50g) *(bottle green)*
Yarn H 1¾oz (50g) *(purple)*
Yarn J 1¾oz (50g) *(peat)*

Needles
1 pair no 3
1 pair no 1
1 circular needle, no 1

MEASUREMENTS

To fit chest 34–36 (40–42)in (86–91,
102–107cm).
(See also chart on p. 117.)
Stitch gauge
32 sts and 30 rows measure 4in over Fair
Isle pattern on no 3 needles.

BACK

**With no 1 needles and yarn A, cast on 136 (150) sts. Work 2 (2¼)in in k1, p1 twisted rib, increasing in the last (wrong-side) row as follows: rib 2 (3) sts, *rib 6 (5) sts, rib twice into next st; repeat from * 17 (23) more times, rib 8 (3) sts – 154 (174) sts in all.

Change to no 3 needles and work pattern from chart, reading odd (knit) rows from right to left and even (purl) rows from left to right. Repeat the basic 10 pattern sts (1–10) fifteen (seventeen) times and work the extra 4 sts (11–14) indicated at the end of knit rows and at the beginning of purl rows. Continuing in pattern, work straight until you have worked the 30 rows of the pattern chart four times and the back measures approximately 17¾ (18)in from the cast-on edge.

Shape armholes: Continuing in pattern, bind off 12 (15) sts at the beginning of the next 2 rows (rows 1 and 2 of fifth working of the pattern chart) – 130 (144) sts**. Continuing in pattern work straight until you have worked row 10 (14) of the seventh working of the pattern chart and armhole measures 9 (9½)in from start of armhole shaping.

Shape shoulders: Continuing in pattern, bind off 15 (17) sts at the beginning of the next 2 rows. Then bind off 13 (14) sts at the beginning of the next 4 rows. Transfer the remaining 48 (54) sts to a spare needle or stitch holder.

FRONT

Work front as for back from ** to ** – 130 (144) sts. Continuing in pattern work straight until you have worked row 8 of the sixth working of the pattern chart and front measures approximately 22½ (22¾)in from cast-on edge.

Shape neck: Continuing in pattern, on the next row, work the first 47 (53) sts of the row and slip these 47 (53) sts on to a spare needle or stitch holder; bind off the next 36 (38) sts in the row, then work the remaining 47 (53) sts in pattern. Continue in pattern on these last 47 (53) sts, decreasing one st at the neck edge on the next 6 rows – 41 (47) sts. Then work these 41 (47) sts straight in pattern until you have worked row 10 (14) of the sixth working of the pattern chart and right front measures approximately 9 (9½)in from start of armhole shaping.

Shape shoulder: Continuing in pattern bind off 15 (17) sts at the beginning of the next row. Then bind off 13 (14) sts at the beginning of the 2 alternate rows.

With wrong side of the work facing, rejoin yarn to the first 47 (53) sts at the neck edge. Work left shoulder and neck shaping to match right side, reversing all shapings.

SLEEVES

With no 1 needles and yarn D, cast on 60 (68) sts and work one row in k1, p1 twisted rib in yarn D. Join in yarn A and work a further 4in in twisted rib in yarn A, increasing on the last wrong-side row as follows: rib 0 (1), *rib 7 (5) sts, rib twice into the next st, rib 7 (5) sts; repeat from * 3 (5) more times, rib 0 (1) – 64 (74) sts in all.

Change to no 3 needles and work Fair Isle pattern from chart, repeating sts 1–10 six (seven) times across the row and working the extra 4 sts (11–14) indicated at the end of knit rows and at the beginning of purl rows. Shape sides of sleeve by increasing one st at each end of the 3rd and every following 4th row, until there are 106 (116) sts on the needle, taking the extra sts into the pattern as they are made. Then increase one st at each end of every 3rd row until there are 142 (148) sts on the needle. Continuing in pattern, work straight until you have worked row 16 (24) of the fifth working of the pattern chart and the sleeve measures approximately 21¾ (22¾)in from cast-on edge. Bind off fairly loosely across row – this bound-off edge should measure 18½ (19)in to fit around armhole. Make another sleeve in the same way.

NECKBAND

Join front to back at shoulders. Using the circular no 1 needle and yarn A, beginning at the left shoulder seam, pick up and knit 39 (43) sts down left side of neck, then 36 (38) sts across front bound-off edge, 39 (43) sts up the right side of the neck, and finally the 48 (54) sts on the spare needle at the back – 160 (178) sts altogether. Work 10 rounds in twisted rib in yarn A. Join in yarn D and work one round in rib in yarn D. Bind off in rib in yarn D.

FINISHING

Press all pieces lightly from the wrong side, avoiding ribbing. Join front to back at side seams. Join underarm sleeve seams, leaving 1½ (2)in of seam unstitched at the top of the seam. Pin top of sleeve into top of armhole, and pin the unstitched section of the sleeve seam across the straight bound-off edge at the base of the armhole. Sew in place and repeat for other sleeve. Press seams lightly from wrong side.

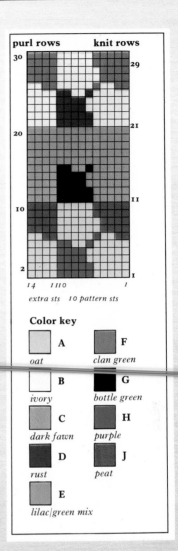

purl rows   **knit rows**

14 11 10   1

extra sts   10 pattern sts

Color key

	A		F
	oat		*clan green*
	B		G
	ivory		*bottle green*
	C		H
	dark fawn		*purple*
	D		J
	rust		*peat*
	E		
	lilac/green mix		

SQUARES ON BLACK

A striking geometric design of small boxes of color bounded with black makes this peplum jacket a smart and unusual garment. The pattern incorporates bands of black garter stitch.

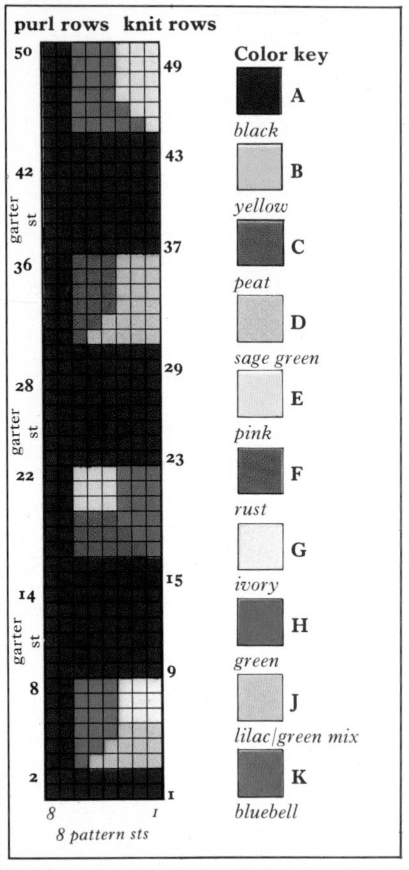

purl rows
knit rows
50
49
43
42
garter st
37
36
29
28
garter st
23
22
15
14
garter st
9
8
2
1
8
1
8 pattern sts
Color key
A black
B yellow
C peat
D sage green
E pink
F rust
G ivory
H green
J lilac/green mix
K bluebell

MATERIALS

Yarn
Use wool fingering yarn.
Yarn A $10\frac{1}{2}$oz (300g) *(black)*
Yarn B 1oz (25g) *(yellow)*
Yarn C 1oz (25g) *(peat)*
Yarn D 1oz (25g) *(sage green)*
Yarn E $1\frac{3}{4}$oz (50g) *(pink)*
Yarn F 1oz (25g) *(rust)*
Yarn G 1oz (25g) *(ivory)*
Yarn H $1\frac{3}{4}$oz (50g) *(green)*
Yarn J 1oz (25g) *(lilac/green mix)*
Yarn K $1\frac{3}{4}$oz (50g) *(bluebell)*
Needles
1 pair no 3
1 pair no 1
1 crochet hook size C
Notions
1 button

MEASUREMENTS

To fit bust 32 (34, 36)in (81, 86, 91cm). *(See also chart on p. 117.)*
Stitch gauge
32 sts and 34 rows measure 4in over Fair Isle pattern on no 3 needles.

BACK

Peplum skirt
With no 1 needles and yarn A, cast on 272 (288, 304) sts. Work 6 rows in st st in yarn A. Then knit 2 rows to form hemline. Change to no 3 needles and work 8 rows in st st in yarn A, starting with a knit row.
Now work Fair Isle pattern from chart, reading odd (knit) rows from right to left and even (purl) rows from left to right, except for rows 9–16, 23–30, 37–44 inclusive which are all knit rows forming wide bands of garter stitch. Repeat the 8 pattern sts 34 (36, 38) times across the rows. Continue in pattern until you have worked row 2 (8, 8) of the second working of the pattern chart and the work measures approx. $6\frac{3}{4}$ ($7\frac{1}{2}$, $7\frac{1}{2}$)in from hemline.
Decrease for waist across next row as follows: (yarn A), k2 tog right across row – 136 (144, 152) sts. Change to no 1 needles and work 9 rows in k1, p1 twisted rib.
Change to no 3 needles and st st and continue pattern from row 3 (15, 15) of the second working of the pattern chart, until you have completed row 14 (28, 32) of the third working of the pattern chart and back measures approximately 7 ($7\frac{1}{2}$, $7\frac{3}{4}$)in from top of waistband.
Shape armholes: Continuing in pattern, bind off 8 sts at the beginning of the next 2 rows. Then k2 tog at each end of the next 9 rows – 102 (110, 118) sts. Now work straight in pattern until you have completed row 32 of the fourth working of chart (row 50 of fourth working, row 8 of fifth working) and armhole measures approximately $7\frac{1}{2}$ ($7\frac{3}{4}$, $8\frac{3}{4}$)in from start of armhole shaping.
Shape shoulders: Continuing in pattern, bind off 8 sts at the beginning of the next 4 rows; then bind off 5 (6, 7) sts at the beginning of the next 6 rows. Transfer the remaining 40 (42, 44) sts to a spare needle or stitch holder.

FRONTS

Left front
With no 1 needles and yarn A, cast on 120 (128, 136) sts. Work 6 rows in st st in yarn A. Then knit 2 rows to form hemline. Change to no 3 needles and work 8 more rows in st st in yarn A, starting with a knit row.
Now work Fair Isle pattern from chart, repeating the 8 pattern sts 15 (16, 17) times across the rows. Continue in pattern until you have completed row 2 (8, 8) of the second working of the pattern chart and work measures approximately $6\frac{3}{4}$ ($7\frac{1}{2}$, $7\frac{1}{2}$)in from hemline. Then decrease for waist as follows: *for the smaller size,* (k2 tog, k3 tog) four times, (k2 tog) forty times, (k3 tog, k2 tog) four times; *for the medium size,* k2 tog right across row; *for the larger size,* k4, (k2 tog) sixty-four times, k4 – 56 (64, 72) sts.
Waistband: Change to no 1 needles and work 9 rows in k1, p1 twisted rib in yarn A.
Change to no 3 needles and st st and work Fair Isle pattern from chart, beginning at row 3 (15, 15) of the second working of the pattern chart. Continue in pattern until you have completed row 14 (28, 32) of the third working of the pattern chart and the front measures approximately 7 ($7\frac{1}{2}$, $7\frac{3}{4}$)in from the top of the waistband.
Shape armhole: Continuing in pattern, bind off 4 (6, 7) sts at the beginning of the next row. Then work one row straight. K2 tog at the armhole edge on the next 7 (9, 10) rows – 45 (49, 55) sts. Now continue in pattern without further shaping until you have completed row 11 (29, 33) of the fourth working of the pattern chart.
Shape neck: With wrong side facing, bind off 3 (3, 4) sts at the beginning of the next row. Then k2 tog at the neck edge on every row until 31 (34, 37) sts remain. Work straight in pattern until you have worked row 32 of the fourth working of the chart (row 50 of the fourth working of the chart, row 8 of the fifth working of the chart), and armhole measures approximately $7\frac{1}{2}$ ($7\frac{3}{4}$, $8\frac{3}{4}$)in from the start of the armhole shaping.
Shape shoulder: Bind off 8 sts at the beginning of next and following alternate row; bind off 5 (6, 7) sts at the beginning of the following 3 alternate rows.

Right front
Work in the same way as left front, matching pattern, but reversing shapings.

SLEEVES

With no 1 needles and yarn A, cast on 62 (62, 64) sts and work $2\frac{1}{4}$in in k1, p1 twisted rib, increasing across the last (wrong-side) row as follows: rib 10 (10, 8) sts, *make one st, rib one st; repeat from * to last 11 (11, 9) sts; make one st, rib to end of row – 104 (104, 112) sts.
Change to no 3 needles and, starting at row 37 (43, 43) of chart, work straight in pattern until you have worked row 14 (28, 32) of the third working of the chart and the sleeve measures approximately $16\frac{1}{4}$ (17, $17\frac{1}{4}$)in from cast-on edge.
Shape top of sleeve: Continuing in pattern, bind off 8 sts at the beginning of the next 2 rows. Then k2 tog at each end of the next and every following alternate row, 7 (10, 12) times. Work 13 (15, 15) rows straight in pattern. K2 tog at each end of the next and following alternate row, 11 (8, 8) times. Purl one row. Bind off remaining sts fairly tightly. Make another sleeve in the same way.

FRONT BANDS

Begin by joining fronts to back at shoulders.

Left front

With no 1 needles and yarn A, pick up and knit 189 (189, 197) sts down front opening edge as far as hemline. Work 9 rows in k1, p1 twisted rib in yarn A, increasing one st at the neck edge on rows 4 and 8. Bind off in rib.

Right front

Beginning at hemline, with right side facing, pick up and knit 189 (189, 197) sts up front opening edge to start of neck shaping. Work to correspond with left front band.

NECKBAND

With right side facing, using no 1 needles and yarn A, starting at beginning of neck shaping on right front and leaving front bands free, pick up and knit 117 (119, 121) sts around the neck as far as the start of neck shaping on left front, including the sts on the stitch holder at the back of the neck. Work 8 (10, 10) rows in st st in yarn A, starting with a purl row. Then knit 2 rows to form foldline of neckband. Work a further 8 (10, 10) rows in st st. Bind off.

FINISHING

Press all pieces lightly from wrong side avoiding ribbing. Join side and sleeve seams. Sew in sleeves, easing fullness at top of sleeves to fit armholes. Turn under the 6 rows of st st around hem to inside, following garter stitch hemline, and slip stitch inner cast-on edge in position on inside. Oversew edges of hem at each side of front opening to jacket fronts. Turn in the 8 (10) rows of st st around neckband to inside, following garter stitch foldline, and slip stitch inner bound-off edge in position around neck. Oversew the two edges of neckband together on either side of front opening. Crochet a chain loop for button (see p. 141) and sew in position at right front waistband. Sew a button to left band to match. Press all seams from wrong side.

COPPER DIAMONDS

*A loose fitting crew neck sweater. The subtle blue and beige stripes
are brought out with specks of copper yarn, but these could be replaced
with Shetland yarn for a softer effect.*

MATERIALS

Yarn

Use wool fingering yarn unless otherwise
indicated.

Yarn A 2¾oz (75g) *(blue/orange mix)*
Yarn B 2¾oz (75g) *(blue/fawn mix)*
Yarn C 1¾oz (50g) *(mid-blue mix)*
Yarn D 1¾oz (50g) lurex *(copper)*
Yarn E 1¾oz (50g) *(mid-brown mix)*

Yarn F 1¾oz (50g) *(oat)*
Yarn G 1oz (25g) *(bright blue)*
Yarn H 1oz (25g) *(rust/blue mix)*
Yarn J 1oz (25g) *(tan)*

Needles

1 pair no 3
1 pair no 1

MEASUREMENTS

To fit chest 33 (36, 39, 42)in (84, 91,
99, 107cm).
(See also chart on p. 117.)

Stitch gauge

30 sts and 32 rows measure 4in over Fair
Isle pattern on no 3 needles.

BACK

**With no 1 needles and yarn A, cast on 118 (130, 142, 152) sts. Work $1\frac{1}{2}$ (2, 2, $2\frac{1}{4}$)in in k1, p1 twisted rib in yarn A, increasing across the last wrong-side row as follows: rib 6 (4, 2, 8) sts, *rib twice into the next st, rib 7 (8, 9, 8) sts; repeat from * 13 (13, 13, 15) more times – 132 (144, 156, 168) sts. Change to no 3 needles and st st and work Fair Isle pattern from chart, reading odd (knit) rows from right to left and even (purl) rows from left to right. Repeat the 12 pattern sts indicated on chart 11 (12, 13, 14) times across each row. Continuing in pattern, work straight until you have worked row 52 (56, 64, 64) of the second working of the pattern chart and the back measures approximately $16\frac{1}{4}$ (17, $17\frac{3}{4}$, 18)in from the cast-on edge.

Shape armholes: Bind off 8 (12, 12, 16) sts at the beginning of the next 2 rows – 116 (120, 132, 136) sts remain**. Then work armhole edges straight, continuing in pattern until you have worked row 50 (58, 66, 4) of the third (third, third, fourth) working of the pattern chart, and the back measures approximately $23\frac{1}{2}$ ($24\frac{3}{4}$, 26, $27\frac{1}{4}$)in from cast-on edge.

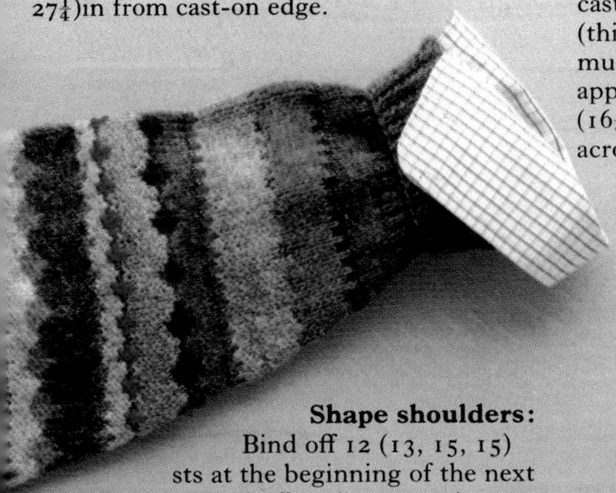

Shape shoulders: Bind off 12 (13, 15, 15) sts at the beginning of the next 2 rows. Bind off 12 (12, 13, 14) sts at the beginning of the following 4 rows. Leave remaining 44 (46, 50, 50) sts on a spare needle.

FRONT

Work as for back from ** to ** – 116 (120, 132, 136) sts. Continuing in pattern, work straight until you have completed row 34 (40, 46, 52) of the third working of chart, and front measures approximately 20 ($20\frac{3}{4}$, 22, $22\frac{3}{4}$)in from cast-on edge.

Shape neck: On the next (right-side) row, work the pattern across the first 42 (44, 48, 50) sts in the row, bind off the next 32 (32, 36, 36) sts and then work the pattern across the remaining 42 (44, 48, 50) sts in the row. Now shape neck edge on these last 42 (44, 48, 50) sts by decreasing one st at the (inner) neck edge on the next 6 (7, 7, 7) rows – 36 (37, 41, 43) sts remain. Then work straight until you have completed row 50 (58, 66, 4) of the third (third, third, fourth) working of the pattern chart and front measures the same as the back from cast-on edge – approximately $23\frac{1}{2}$ ($24\frac{3}{4}$, 26, $27\frac{1}{4}$)in.

Shape shoulder: Bind off 12 (13, 15, 15) sts at the beginning of the next row. Work 1 row. Then bind off 12 (12, 13, 14) sts at the beginning of the following 2 alternate rows.
With wrong side of work facing, rejoin the yarn to the remaining 42 (44, 48, 50) sts of the left side of neck. Work left neck edge and shoulder to correspond with right neck edge and shoulder, reversing shapings.

SLEEVES

With no 1 needles and yarn A, cast on 58 (58, 60, 60) sts. Work $3\frac{1}{4}$ ($3\frac{1}{2}$, $3\frac{1}{2}$, $3\frac{1}{2}$)in in k1, p1 twisted rib in yarn A.
Change to no 3 needles and st st and work Fair Isle pattern from chart, beginning at row 1 as before, *at the same time* shaping the sides by increasing one st at each end of the 3rd and every following 4th row, until there are 128 (128, 136, 144) sts on the needle. Take the extra sts into the pattern as they are made. When there are 128 (128, 136, 144) sts on the needle, work straight until the sleeve measures approximately 20 ($20\frac{1}{2}$, $20\frac{3}{4}$, $21\frac{1}{4}$)in from cast-on edge. Bind off right across row (this bound-off edge must measure approximately $16\frac{1}{4}$ ($16\frac{1}{4}$, 17 $17\frac{3}{4}$)in across to fit armhole.
Make another sleeve in the same way.

NECKBAND

Join right shoulder seam.
With right side of work facing, using no 1 needles and yarn A, beginning at the left shoulder, pick up and knit 36 (36, 38, 38) sts down left side of neck, 32 (32, 34, 34) sts across center-front, 36 (36, 38, 38) sts up right side of neck and the 44 (46, 50, 50) sts on spare needle at back of neck – 148 (150, 160, 160) sts in all. Work 13 rows in k1, p1 twisted rib in yarn A. Bind off in rib in yarn A.

FINISHING

Press all pieces from the wrong side, avoiding ribbing. Join left shoulder seam and side seams. Join underarm sleeve seam, leaving $\frac{3}{4}$ ($1\frac{1}{2}$, $1\frac{1}{2}$, 2)in unstitched at the top of seam. Pin sleeve into armhole, pinning unstitched section of sleeve seam across straight bound-off edge at bottom of armhole. Sew in place. Repeat for other sleeve. Press seams from wrong side.

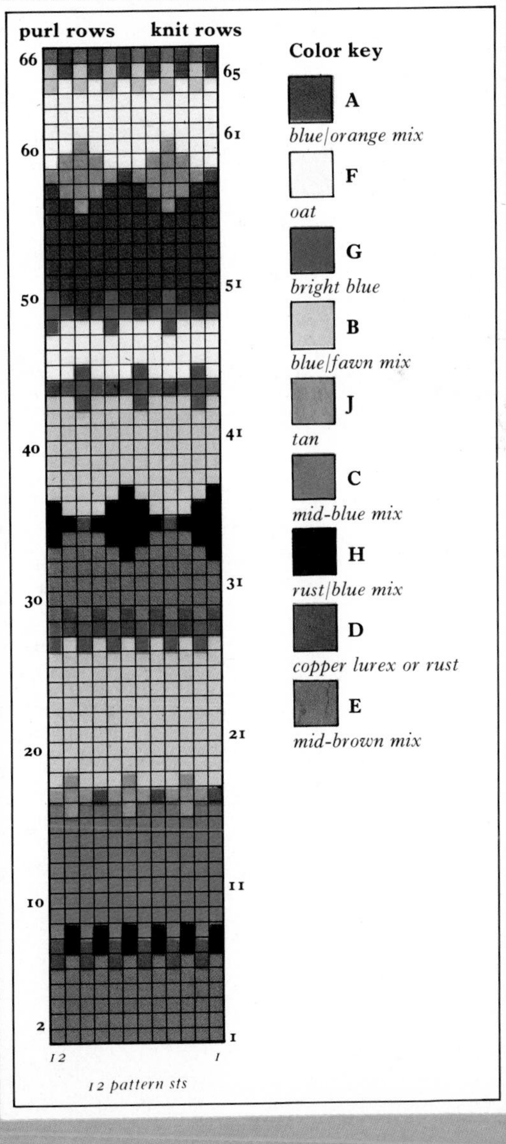
purl rows
knit rows
66
65
61
60
51
50
41
40
31
30
21
20
11
10
2
1
12
1
12 pattern sts
Color key
A
blue/orange mix
F
oat
G
bright blue
B
blue/fawn mix
J
tan
C
mid-blue mix
H
rust/blue mix
D
copper lurex or rust
E
mid-brown mix

MAURICE

Men's or women's Fair Isle button-down vest with striped rib back.
The shawl collar is worked separately and sewn over
the top of the front bands.

MATERIALS

Yarn
Use wool fingering yarn.
Yarn A 2¾oz (75g) *(blue/white mix)*
Yarn B 1oz (25g) *(peat)*
Yarn C 1oz (25g) *(lilac/green mix)*
Yarn D 1¾oz (50g) *(pale green mix)*
Yarn E 1¾oz (50g) *(dark fawn)*
Yarn F 1oz (25g) *(rust/blue mix)*
Yarn G 1oz (25g) *(pale lilac mix)*
Yarn H 1¾oz (50g) *(rust)*
Yarn J 1oz (25g) *(rust mix)*
Yarn K 1oz (25g) *(pale pink mix)*

Needles
1 pair no 3
1 pair no 2
1 pair no 1

Notions
5 buttons

MEASUREMENTS

To fit chest 34 (38, 40)in (86, 97, 102cm).
(See also chart on p. 117.)

Stitch gauge
32 sts and 32 rows measure 4in over Fair
Isle pattern on no 3 needles.

FRONTS

Pocket linings
Begin by making the pocket linings as
follows; with no 2 needles and yarn A,
cast on 28 (30, 32) sts. Work 2¼in in st st
ending with a purl row. Leave sts on a
spare needle and repeat for other pocket.

Left front
With no 1 needles and yarn A, cast on
68 (72, 80) sts. Work 2in in k1, p1 twisted
rib in yarn A, increasing across the last
(wrong-side) row as follows: *purl 16 (11,
19) sts, purl twice into the next st; repeat
from * 3 (5, 3) more times – 72 (78,
84) sts.
Change to no 3 needles and st st and
work Fair Isle pattern from chart, reading
odd (knit) rows from right to left and even
(purl) rows from left to right. Work the
pattern across knit rows as follows: *for the
small size* (34in), repeat sts *1–12* six
times; *for the medium size* (38in), repeat
sts *1–12* six times and then work sts *1–6*
once to complete row; *for the large size*
(40in), work sts *1–12* seven times. Work
purl rows in reverse. Continue thus in
pattern until you have completed row 18
(20, 20) of the pattern chart.

Pocket: Introduce pocket in row 19 (21,
21) as follows: work the first 22 (24, 26)
sts in row, slip the next 28 (30, 32) sts on
to a spare needle and in their place work
the pattern across the 28 (30, 32) sts of
one pocket lining on spare needle; work
the pattern to the end of the row.
Continue straight in pattern until you have
completed row 76 (4, 8) of the first
(second, second) working of the pattern
chart and front measures approximately
11½ (11¾, 12½)in from cast-on edge.
Shape armhole and neck edge: Bind
off 14 (15, 16) sts at the beginning of the
next row, then work pattern to last 2 sts,
k2 tog. Continuing in pattern, decrease
one st at the armhole edge on the next 15
(15, 17) rows – 29 (30, 33) sts should have
been decreased in all – then work armhole
edge straight. *At the same time,* decrease
one st at the neck edge on every following
5th (4th, 4th) row after the first decrease
on row 1 (5, 9), until you have decreased
13 (16, 18) sts at neck edge – 30 (32, 33)
sts remain. Now work straight until you
have worked row 72 (4, 16) of the second
(third, third) working of the pattern chart
and the front measures approximately 20
(21¾, 22½)in from cast-on edge.

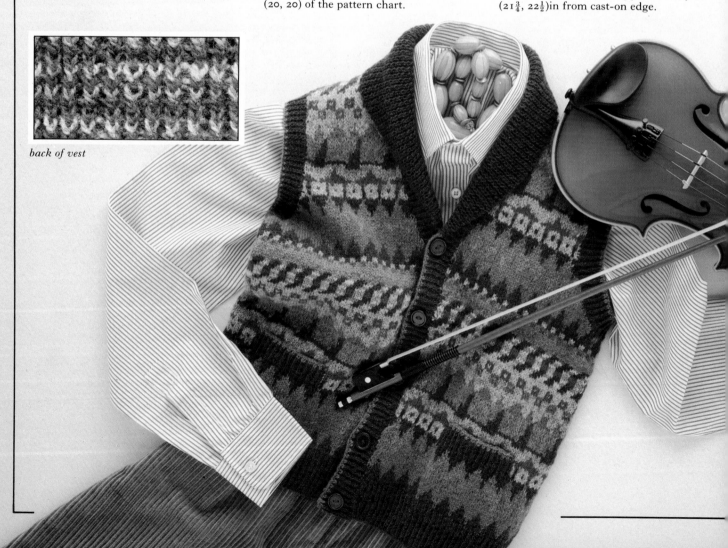

back of vest

Shape shoulder: Continuing in pattern, bind off 10 (12, 11) sts at the beginning of the next row. Then bind off 10 (10, 11) sts at the beginning of the following 2 alternate rows.

Right front
Work as for left front, reversing pocket, armhole, neck and shoulder shapings.

BACK

With no 1 needles and yarn A, cast on 144 (156, 168) sts. Work 2in in k1, p1 twisted rib, ending on a wrong-side row. Change to no 2 needles and continue to work entire back in twisted rib in the following five-color stripe sequence:

Row 1: Yarn A
Row 2: Yarn D
Row 3: Yarn H
Row 4: Yarn J
Row 5: Yarn E

Continue repeating rows 1–5 up the back, carrying yarns not in use up the sides of the work, until back measures approximately 11½ (11¾, 12½)in from cast-on edge, ending with a wrong-side row.
Shape armholes: Continuing in rib, bind off 4 (5, 6) sts at the beginning of the next 2 rows. Then k2 tog at each end of the next 16 (17, 18) rows – 104 (112, 120) sts remain. Then work straight in striped rib until back measures the same as the front from cast-on edge to start of shoulder shaping – approximately 20 (21¾, 22½)in – ending on a wrong-side row.
Shape shoulders: Continuing in striped rib, bind off 10 (12, 11) sts at the beginning of the next 2 rows. Then bind off 10 10, 11) sts at the beginning of the following 4 rows; divide the remaining 44 (48, 54) sts in half and transfer each half to a

needle or stitch holder.

Join fronts to back at shoulders.

FRONT BANDS

Right front
With no 1 needles and yarn A, with right side facing and beginning at lower edge, pick up and knit 93 (97, 101) sts up front opening edge to start of neck shaping; then pick up and knit a further 89 (93, 101) sts around the side of the neck including the 22 (24, 27) sts on first spare needle at back of neck. Work 3 rows in k1, p1 twisted rib in yarn A.
Buttonholes: Make 5 buttonholes in the 4th row of ribbing as follows: rib 4 sts, *bind off 3 sts, rib 18 (19, 20) sts; repeat from * three more times, bind off 3 sts, rib to end of row. Rib back along the next row casting on 3 sts directly over those bound off in the previous row. Work 4 more rows in rib in yarn A. Join in yarn B and work a further row in rib in yarn B. Bind off in rib in yarn B.

Left front
With right side facing, using no 1 needles and yarn D, beginning at the center-back of the neck rib the 22 (24, 27) sts from the remaining spare needle at the back of the neck and then pick up and knit a further 67 (69, 74) sts down to start of neck shaping and then 93 (97, 101) sts down front opening edge. Work to correspond with right front band, omitting buttonholes.

ARMHOLE BANDS

With right side facing, using no 1 needles and yarn A, pick up and knit 142 (150, 166) sts around one armhole. Work 9 rows of twisted rib in yarn A. Join in yarn B and work a further row in rib in yarn B. Bind off in rib in yarn B. Repeat for other armhole.

POCKET TOPS

With right side facing, using no 1 needles and yarn A, knit across the 28 (30, 32) sts for one pocket on spare needle. Work 7 rows in twisted rib in yarn A. Join in yarn B and work a further row of rib in yarn B. Bind off in rib in yarn B. Repeat for other pocket top.

SHAWL COLLAR

With no 2 needles and yarn A, cast on 191 (195, 201) sts. Work 9 rows in k1, p1 twisted rib. Continue in rib and shape collar by binding off 2 sts at the beginning of the next 24 rows. Then bind off 6 sts at the beginning of the following 16 rows – 47 (51, 57) sts remain. Bind off in rib.

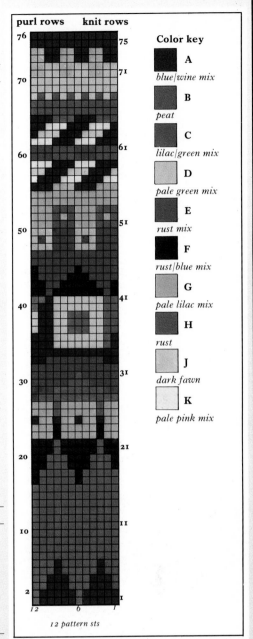

purl rows   knit rows

Color key

A
blue/wine mix

B
peat

C
lilac/green mix

D
pale green mix

E
rust mix

F
rust/blue mix

G
pale lilac mix

H
rust

J
dark fawn

K
pale pink mix

12 pattern sts

FINISHING

Press pieces lightly from the wrong side, avoiding ribbing. Join fronts to back at side seams. Join front bands together at center-back. Sew the three free sides of each pocket lining to the back of the vest fronts. Sew down the sides of each pocket top. Pin center of shaped collar piece to the center-back of neck, inside the ribbed front band and then pin the rest of the edge of the collar around the neck edge to start of neck shaping on each side. Stitch collar in position and then fold it over so that it covers the ribbed border. Catch down at front edges to hold in position. Press collar lightly to hold fold. Sew on five buttons to left front band to match buttonholes. Press seams lightly from wrong side.

FLOWERS

WALLFLOWERS

This boat neck cotton sweater with repeating Wallflower motifs is interspersed with bands of écru Turkish stitch. The wide ribbing at the sleeve and neck is bordered with a contrasting yarn.

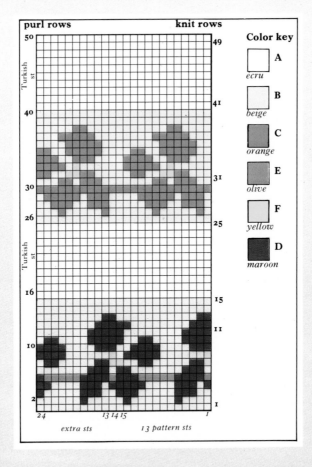

purl rows   knit rows

Color key

A
ecru

B
beige

C
orange

E
olive

F
yellow

D
maroon

extra sts   *13 pattern sts*

as follows: (row 16) k1, *yfwd, sl 1, k1, pass slipped st over; repeat from * to last st; k1. Work 9 more rows in the same way (see also p. 130 for Turkish stitch). Now work the next 15 rows of Wallflower pattern from chart as before starting at row 26. Then work rows 41–50 in Turkish stitch to complete one working of pattern chart. Work rows 1–40 inclusive again. The work should now measure approximately 13¾ (14½)in from cast-on edge.
Shape armholes: Continuing in pattern (row 41, Turkish stitch) bind off 10 (12) sts at the beginning of the next 2 rows – 124 (130) sts. Then work straight until you have completed row 25 of the third working of the pattern chart.
Change to no 0 needles and yarn A and work 4¼in in k1, p1 twisted rib, to form ribbing for boat neck. Change to yarn E and work a further row in twisted rib in yarn E. Bind off in rib in yarn E.
Make another piece in the same way.

SLEEVES

With no 0 needles and yarn E, cast on 60 sts. Work one row of k1, p1 twisted rib in yarn E. Change to yarn A and continue in twisted rib for 4in, increasing across the last (wrong-side) row as follows: *rib 2, rib twice into next st; repeat from * 19 more times – 80 sts.
Change to no 3 needles and work pattern from chart, repeating the basic 13 pattern sts (*1–13*) six times across the row and working the extra 2 sts (*14–15*) at the end of knit rows and at the beginning of purl rows. *At the same time,* shape sides by increasing one st at each end of the 3rd and every following 4th row until there are 134 sts on the needle, taking the extra sts into the pattern as they are made. Then work straight in pattern until you have completed row 25 of the third working of the pattern chart, and the sleeve measures approximately 19¼in from cast-on edge. Bind off right across row.
Make another sleeve in the same way.

FINISHING

Press all pieces lightly from wrong side avoiding ribbing. Join front to back at side seams. Join each sleeve seam leaving 1½in at top of seam unstitched. Overlap 1½in of front neck ribbing over back neck ribbing and hold each side with a pin. Sew the ribbings together from shoulder edge to point 1½in in from shoulder edge on each side, sewing just underneath the edge of the front ribbing so that stitches are invisible. Pin sleeves into armholes, pinning each side of unstitched section of sleeve seam across straight bound-off edge at bottom of armholes. Sew sleeves in position. Press seams from wrong side.

MATERIALS

Yarn
Use No. 8 cotton yarn.
Yarn A 12¼oz (350g) *(écru)*
Yarn B 5¼oz (150g) *(beige)*
Yarn C 3½oz (100g) *(orange)*
Yarn D 3½oz (100g) *(maroon)*
Yarn E 1¾oz (50g) *(olive)*
Yarn F 1¾oz (50g) *(yellow)*
Needles
1 pair no 3
1 pair no 0

BACK and FRONT

Work the front and back in the same way. With no 0 needles and yarn A, cast on 128 (136) sts. Work 2¾ (3½)in in k1, p1 twisted rib in yarn A increasing across the last (wrong-side) row as follows: *rib 4 (3) sts, rib twice into the next st, rib 3 sts; repeat from * 15 (17) more times – 144 (154) sts.
Change to no 3 needles and st st and work Wallflower pattern from chart, reading odd (knit) rows from right to left and even (purl) rows from left to right. Work the pattern across knit rows as follows: repeat the basic 13 pattern sts indicated on chart (*1–13*) eleven times across row *for both sizes,* and then work st *14 for the smaller size,* and sts *14–24 for the larger size,* to finish row. Work purl rows in reverse starting with the extra sts. Work rows 1–15 of the chart. Then work the next 10 rows (16–25) in Turkish stitch

MEASUREMENTS

To fit chest 36 (38)in (91, 97cm).
(See also chart on p. 118.)
Stitch gauge
31 sts and 32 rows measure 4in over Wallflowers pattern on no 3 needles.

IRIS

A pretty feminine cardigan of yellow and purple Irises,
bordered with mohair. The cardigan has a moss stitch collar
and front pockets.

MATERIALS

Yarn
Use wool fingering yarn unless otherwise
indicated.
Yarn A 3½oz (100g) *(pale lilac mix)*
Yarn B 2¾oz (75g) *(lilac/green mix)*
Yarn C 1oz (25g) *(violet)*
Yarn D 1oz (25g) *(purple)*
Yarn E 1oz (25g) *(sage green)*
Yarn F 1oz (25g) *(wine)*
Yarn G 1oz (25g) *(pale yellow)*
Yarn H 1oz (25g) *(yellow)*
Yarn K 1oz (25g) lurex *(gold)*
Yarn L 3½oz (100g) mohair *(wine mix)*

Needles
1 pair no 3
1 pair no 2
1 pair no 1
1 pair no 0

Notions
7 buttons

MEASUREMENTS
To fit bust 34 (36)in (86, 91cm).
(See also chart on p. 118.)

Stitch gauge
30 sts and 36 rows measure 4in over Fair
Isle pattern on no 3 needles.

BACK

With no 1 needles and yarn B, cast on
124 (130) sts. Work 2 (2¼)in in k1, p1
twisted rib in yarn B, increasing across the
last (wrong-side) row as follows: rib 2 sts,
*rib twice into the next st, rib 9 (8) sts;
repeat from * 11 (13) more times, rib 2 sts
– 136 (144) sts.
Change to no 3 needles and st st and
work pattern from chart, reading odd
(knit) rows from right to left and even
(purl) rows from left to right. Work the
pattern across knit rows as follows: *for the
smaller size* (34in), repeat sts 1–16, eight
times across the row and then work sts
1–8 once to complete the row; *for the
larger size* (36in), repeat sts 1–16, nine

times across the row. Work purl rows in
reverse. Continuing in pattern, work
straight until you have completed row 22
of the chart. Now work rows 23–28
inclusive in reversed st st in mohair as
follows: row 23, knit; row 24, knit; row
25, purl; row 26, knit; row 28, purl.
Then continue in pattern from row 29
to the end of row 50. Work rows 51–56
in reversed st st in the same way as rows
23–28. Repeat chart until you have
worked row 36 (second working) and back
measures approximately 11¾ (12¼)in from
the cast-on edge.
Shape armholes: Continuing in pattern,
bind off 6 (8) sts at the beginning of the
next 2 rows. Then decrease one st at each

end of every row
until 100 (108) sts remain.
Work straight in pattern until
you have worked row 50 (54) of the
third working of chart and back measures
approximately 20 (20½)in from cast-on edge.
Shape shoulders: Bind off 6 sts at the
beginning of the next 4 rows. Then bind
off 6 (7) sts at the beginning of the next 6
rows; bind off remaining 40 (42) sts.

FRONTS

Pocket linings
Begin by making pocket linings. With
no 2 needles and yarn B, cast on 28 (30)
sts. Work 2½in in st st, ending with a knit
row. Leave the sts on a spare needle and
work another lining in the same way.

Left front
With no 1 needles and yarn B, cast on
54 (58) sts. Work 2 (2¼)in in k1, p1 twisted
rib, increasing across last (wrong-side) row
as follows: rib 3 (1) sts, *rib 5 (6) sts, rib
twice into next st; repeat from * 7 more
times, rib 3 (1) sts – 62 (66) sts.

Change to no 3 needles and st st and work pattern from chart. Work the pattern across knit rows as follows: *for the smaller size,* repeat sts *1–16,* three times, then work sts *1–14* once to complete the row; *for the larger size,* repeat sts *1–16* four times then work sts *1–2* once to complete the row. Work purl rows in reverse. Continue thus in pattern until you have worked row 20 of the chart.

Pocket: Introduce pocket in row 21 as follows: work the first 17 (18) sts in the row, bind off the next 28 (30) sts, then continue the pattern to end of row. On the next row (row 22), work the pattern across the first 17 (18) sts of row and then

continue in pattern across the 28 (30) sts of one pocket lining on spare needle; then work pattern to end of row. Continue in pattern from row 23 of chart until you have worked row 36 of the second working of the chart and the front measures approximately 11¾ (12¼)in from cast-on edge.

Shape armholes: Continuing in pattern, bind off 8 (10) sts at the beginning of the next row. Then k2 tog at armhole edge on the next 10 (8) rows – 44 (48) sts remain. Now work straight until you have completed row 29 (33) of the third working of the chart and front measures approximately 17 (18½)in from cast-on edge.

Shape neck: Continuing in pattern, bind off 3 sts at the beginning of the next row; then k2 tog at the neck edge on the next 11 (12) rows – 30 (33) sts remain. Work straight in pattern, until you have worked row 50 (54) of the third working of the chart and the front measures approximately 20 (20½)in from cast-on edge.

Shape shoulder: Bind off 6 sts at the beginning of the next and following alternate row. Bind off 6 (7) sts at the beginning of the following 3 alternate rows.

Right front
Work in the same way as left front, but reverse pocket, armhole, neck and shoulder shapings.

SLEEVES

With no 1 needles and yarn B, cast on 62 sts. Work 2 (2¼)in in k1, p1 twisted rib, increasing across the last wrong-side row as follows: rib 10 sts, rib twice into the next 42 sts, rib 10 sts – 104 sts. Change to no 3 needles and st st and work pattern from chart, beginning on row 23 of the chart. Work rows 23 to 29 inclusive in reversed st st as before. Then work the pattern across knit rows as

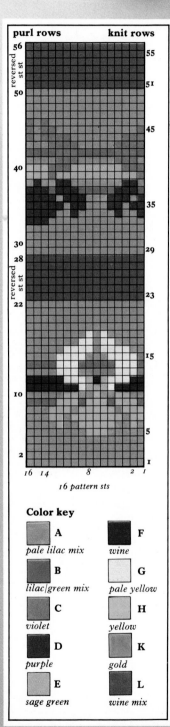

purl rows   **knit rows**

reversed st st

reversed st st

16 14   8   2 1

16 pattern sts

Color key

A *pale lilac mix*		F *wine*
B *lilac/green mix*		G *pale yellow*
C *violet*		H *yellow*
D *purple*		K *gold*
E *sage green*		L *wine mix*

follows: repeat sts *1–16* six times across the row and then work sts *1–8* once to complete the row. Work purl rows in reverse. Continue in pattern until you have worked row 36 of the third working of the chart and sleeve measures approximately 16¼ (16½)in from cast-on edge.

Shape top of sleeve: Continuing in pattern, bind off 8 sts at the beginning of the next 2 rows; then k2 tog at each end of the next and every following alternate row, ten times – 68 sts. Now work 17 (19) rows straight. Then k2 tog at each end of the next and every following alternate row five times. K2 tog at each end of the following 7 rows – 44 sts remain. Bind off. Make another sleeve in the same way.

FRONT BANDS

Right front
With no 1 needles and yarn B, with right side of work facing and beginning at lower edge, pick up and knit 159 (165) sts up front opening edge to start of neck shaping. Work 5 rows in k1, p1 twisted rib.
Buttonholes: Make 7 buttonholes in the 6th row of ribbing as follows: rib 4 sts, *bind off 3 sts, rib 22 (23) sts; repeat from * five more times, bind off 3 sts, rib 2 sts. Rib back across next row, casting on 3 sts over those bound off in previous row. Work 4 more rows in rib, then bind off.

Left front
Beginning at start of neck shaping pick up and knit 159 (165) sts down the front opening edge. Work to correspond with right front band but omit buttonholes.

COLLAR

With no 0 needles and yarn B, cast on 39 (43) sts and work the collar in moss stitch (i.e. work every row k1, p1 to last st, k1. Cast on 5 sts at the beginning of the next 10 rows after the first row. Then cast on 7 (8) sts at the beginning of the following 2 rows – 103 (109) sts. Work a further 2¼in in moss st. Bind off in moss st.

POCKET TOPS

With right side facing, no 1 needles and yarn B, pick up and knit 28 (30) sts across bound-off edge of one pocket. Work 10 rows in k1, p1 twisted rib; bind off. Work other pocket top in same way.

FINISHING

Press all pieces lightly from wrong side, avoiding ribbing. Join shoulder and side and sleeve seams. Pin and sew sleeves into armholes, gathering top of sleeves to fit. Pin shaped edge of collar around neck between inner edges of front bands. Sew in position with a flat seam sewn from the under side. Sew down sides of pocket tops and linings. Sew on buttons.

MARIGOLD

*Yellow Marigolds interspersed with bands of mohair
worked in reverse stockinette stitch. The vest has front pockets
and the back is worked in striped rib.*

MATERIALS

Yarn

Use wool fingering yarn unless otherwise
indicated.

Yarn A 2¾oz (75g) *(brown-green mix)*
Yarn B 1¾oz (50g) *(rust)*
Yarn C 1oz (25g) *(yellow)*
Yarn D 1oz (25g) *(dark orange mix)*
Yarn E 1oz (25g) lurex *(copper)*
Yarn F 1¾oz (50g) *(chocolate)*
Yarn G 1oz (25g) *(clan green)*
Yarn H 1¾oz (50g) mohair *(brown mix)*

Needles

1 pair no 3
1 pair no 2
1 pair no 1

Notions

5 buttons

MEASUREMENTS

To fit chest 32 (34, 38)in (81, 86, 96cm).
(See also chart on p. 118.)

Stitch gauge

32 sts and 30 rows measure 4in over Fair
Isle pattern on no 3 needles.

FRONTS

Pocket linings

With no 1 needles and yarn A, cast on
28 (32, 36) sts. Work 2¾in in st st in yarn
A, ending with a purl row. Leave sts on a
spare needle or stitch holder. Repeat for
other pocket lining.

Left front

**With no 1 needles and yarn A, cast on
60 (66, 72) sts. Work 2in in k1, p1 twisted
rib, increasing 6 sts evenly across the last

back of vest

(wrong-side) row, by working twice into every 10th (11th, 12th) st, 6 times – 66 (72, 78) sts**.

Change to no 3 needles and st st and work Fair Isle pattern from chart, reading odd (knit) rows from right to left and even (purl) rows from left to right. Work the pattern across the knit rows as follows: repeat the basic 16 pattern sts (1–16) four times across row *for all sizes,* and then work sts 1–2 (1–8, 1–14) once to finish the row. Work purl rows in reverse, working the extra sts at the beginning of the row. Continue in pattern until you have worked row 20 of the pattern chart.

Pocket: Introduce pocket in row 21 as follows: knit the first 19 (20, 21) sts of row in pattern, then slip the next 28 (32, 36) sts on to a spare needle or stitch holder and in their place continue to work the

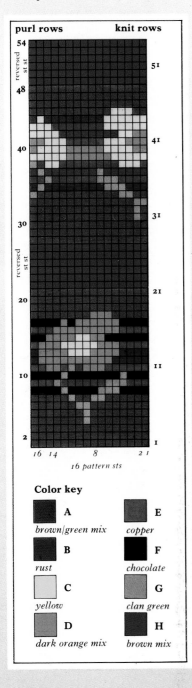

purl rows **knit rows**

reversed st st

54
51
48
41
40
31
30
21
20
11
10
2 1

16 14   8   2 1

16 pattern sts

Color key

	A		E
	brown/green mix		*copper*
	B		F
	rust		*chocolate*
	C		G
	yellow		*clan green*
	D		H
	dark orange mix		*brown mix*

pattern across the 28 (32, 36) sts of one pocket lining piece on spare needle; continue in pattern to end of row. Work rows 22–27 of chart in reversed st st in mohair as follows: row 22, knit; row 23, knit; row 24, purl; row 25, knit; row 26, purl; row 27, knit. Continue to work rows 28–48 in pattern from chart, then work rows 49–54 in reversed st st in mohair as follows: row 49, purl; row 50, purl; row 51, knit; row 52, purl; row 53, knit; row 54, purl. The 54 rows of one complete pattern chart have now been worked.

Continue in pattern until you have completed row 14 (18, 20) of the second working of pattern and front measures approx. 11 (11½, 11¾)in from cast-on edge.

Shape armhole and neck: At the beginning of the next row, bind off 8 (10, 12) sts and then work pattern across to the last 2 sts: k2 tog. Continuing in pattern, decrease one st at the armhole edge on the next 12 (14, 16) rows. Then work armhole edge straight. *At the same time,* decrease one st at the neck edge on every following 4th row after the first decrease, 8 (9, 13) times in all. Then decrease one st at neck edge on every following 3rd row until 26 (28, 30) sts remain. Then work neck edge straight in pattern until you have completed row 28 of the third working of pattern chart. Work a few rows straight in st st and yarn A only (to avoid having broken pattern) until front measures approx. 20½ (21¼, 22½)in from cast-on edge.

Shape shoulder: Bind off 10 sts at the beginning of the next right-side row. Then bind off 8 (9, 10) sts at the beginning of the following 2 alternate rows.

Right front

Work in same way as for left front from ** to **. Change to no 3 needles and work pattern from chart, repeating the basic 16 pattern sts four times across the rows and the extra 2 (8, 14) sts at the end of knit rows and at the beginning of purl rows as before. Work to correspond with left front, taking in remaining pocket lining and reversing neck, armhole and shoulder shapings.

BACK

With no 1 needles and yarn A, cast on 128 (140, 152) sts. Work 2in in k1, p1 twisted rib in yarn A, increasing across the last (wrong-side) row by working twice into every 32nd (35th, 38th) st, four times – 132 (144, 156) sts.

Change to no 2 needles and work entire back in twisted rib, in the following three-color stripe sequence:

Row 1: Yarn A
Row 2: Yarn B
Row 3: Yarn F

Continue working back straight, repeating rows 1–3 until back measures approximately 11 (11½, 11¾)in from cast-on edge, ending on a wrong-side row.

Shape armholes: Bind off 3 (4, 6) sts at the beginning of the next 2 rows; then k2 tog at each end of every row until 100

(108, 116) sts remain. Then work straight until back measures the same as the fronts from the start of the armhole shaping to the start of the shoulder shaping – approximately 20½ (21¼, 22½)in.

Shape shoulders: On next right-side row, bind off 10 (10, 11) sts at beginning of this and next row. Bind off 9 (10, 11) sts at beginning of next 4 rows. Divide remaining 44 (48, 50) sts in half and transfer each half to a spare needle or stitch holder.

Join fronts to back at shoulders.

FRONT BANDS

Right front

With no 1 needles and yarn A, beginning at lower edge, pick up and knit 89 (93, 97) sts up front opening edge as far as start of neck shaping; then pick up 88 (92, 97) sts around the neck edge to center-back, including the 22 (24, 25) sts on the first spare needle. Work 3 rows in k1, p1 twisted rib in yarn A.

Buttonholes: Make five buttonholes in the 4th row of ribbing as follows: rib 4 sts, *bind off 3, rib 17 (18, 19); repeat from * 3 more times, bind off 3 sts and rib to end. Then rib back across the next row, casting on 3 sts directly over those bound off in previous row. Work 4 more rows in rib in yarn A; then work one row in rib in yarn B. Bind off in rib in yarn B.

Left front

Beginning at the center-back, with yarn A, rib the 22 (24, 25) sts on the spare needle and then pick up and knit 66 (68, 72) sts around neck edge to start of neck shaping, then 89 (93, 97) sts down front to lower edge. Work to correspond with right front band, omitting buttonholes.

ARMHOLE BANDS

With no 1 needles and yarn A, pick up and knit 148 (154, 160) sts around one armhole. Work to correspond with left front band in k1, p1 twisted rib. Repeat for other armhole.

POCKETS

Pocket tops

With no 1 needles and yarn A, rib across the 28 (32, 36) sts of one pocket on the spare needle. Work to correspond with left front band.

FINISHING

Press Fair Isle pieces lightly from wrong side, avoiding ribbing. Join fronts to back at sides. Join ribbing at back of neck. Sew down the sides of pocket tops and sew the three sides of each pocket lining to the wrong side of vest fronts. Sew buttons to left front band. Press seams lightly from wrong side.

PURPLE PANSY

Warm and loose-fitting, this long one-size sweater
can be worn as a sweater dress. The neck is worked in silver lurex yarn
for a more decorative effect.

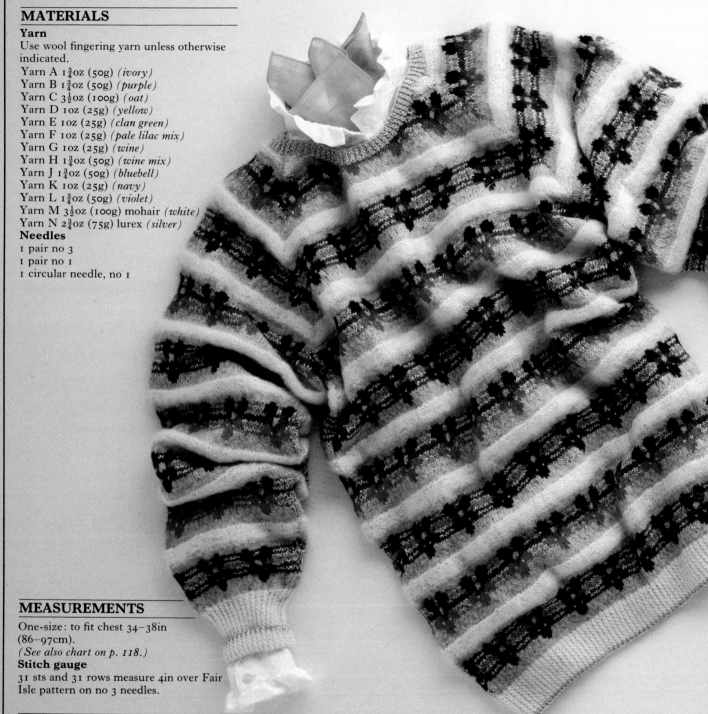

MATERIALS

Yarn
Use wool fingering yarn unless otherwise
indicated.
Yarn A 1¾oz (50g) *(ivory)*
Yarn B 1¾oz (50g) *(purple)*
Yarn C 3½oz (100g) *(oat)*
Yarn D 1oz (25g) *(yellow)*
Yarn E 1oz (25g) *(clan green)*
Yarn F 1oz (25g) *(pale lilac mix)*
Yarn G 1oz (25g) *(wine)*
Yarn H 1¾oz (50g) *(wine mix)*
Yarn J 1¾oz (50g) *(bluebell)*
Yarn K 1oz (25g) *(navy)*
Yarn L 1¾oz (50g) *(violet)*
Yarn M 3½oz (100g) mohair *(white)*
Yarn N 2¾oz (75g) lurex *(silver)*

Needles
1 pair no 3
1 pair no 1
1 circular needle, no 1

MEASUREMENTS

One-size: to fit chest 34–38in
(86–97cm).
(See also chart on p. 118.)

Stitch gauge
31 sts and 31 rows measure 4in over Fair
Isle pattern on no 3 needles.

BACK

With no 1 needles and yarn N, cast on
156 sts. Work 1 row in k1, p1 twisted rib
in yarn N. Join in yarn A and continue in
twisted rib for 2in in yarn A.
Change to no 3 needles and st st and
work Pansy pattern from chart, reading
odd (knit) rows from right to left and even
(purl) rows from left to right. Repeat the
basic 16 pattern sts (1–16) indicated on
chart nine times across the row and work
the extra 12 sts (17–28) at the end of knit
and at the beginning of purl rows. Work
rows 1–20 inclusive from chart. Then
work rows 21–26 in reversed st st in yarn
M as follows: row 21, knit; row 22, knit;
row 23, purl; row 24, knit; row 25, purl;
row 26, knit. Continue in pattern from
rows 27–46 and then work rows 47–52 in
yarn M in reversed st st as follows: row
47, purl; row 48, purl; row 49, knit; row
50, purl; row 51, knit; row 52, purl. You
have now completed the 52 rows of the
pattern chart. Continue repeating the
pattern chart until you have worked row
40 of the third working of the chart and
the back measures approximately 20in
from the cast-on edge.

Shape armhole: Continuing in pattern, shape raglan edge as follows: bind off 5 sts at the beginning of the next 2 rows. *Decrease one st at each end of the next 3 rows; work one row straight. *Repeat from * to * sixteen more times – 70 rows in all. Bind off the remaining 44 sts (4 complete patterns and 6 rows of the fifth should have been worked in all).

FRONT

Work as for back until beginning of armhole shaping, casting on 156 sts and working to the end of row 40 of the third working of the pattern chart.

Shape armhole: Continuing in pattern, shape raglan edge as follows: bind off 5 sts at the beginning of the next 2 rows. *Decrease one st at each end of the next 3 rows; work one row straight. Repeat from * 10 more times – 80 sts. Then decrease one st at each end of the next 2 rows – 76 sts.

Shape neck: Continuing in pattern (row 36 of the fourth working of the pattern chart), shape neck as follows, *at the same time* continuing to shape raglan edge:

Row 1: K2 tog, k42 sts, turn. Put remaining sts on to a spare needle.
Row 2: Bind off 11 sts, purl to end (32 sts).
Row 3: K2 tog, knit to end.
Row 4: Bind off 4 sts, purl to last 2 sts, p2 tog.
Row 5: K2 tog, knit to end.
Row 6: Bind off 4 sts, purl to end.
Row 7: K2 tog, knit to end.
Row 8: Bind off 2 sts, purl to last 2 sts, p2 tog.
Row 9: K2 tog, knit to end.
Row 10: Bind off 2 sts, purl to end.
Row 11: K2 tog, knit to end.
Row 12: Bind off 2 sts, purl to last 2 sts, p2 tog.
Row 13: K2 tog, knit to end.
Row 14: Bind off 2 sts, purl to end.
Row 15: K2 tog, knit to end.
Row 16: Bind off 2 sts, purl to end.
Row 17: K2 tog, knit to end.
Row 18: Bind off 2 sts. Fasten off.
Rejoin wool at neck edge. Work other side of neck to match, reversing all shapings at neck edge and raglan edge.

SLEEVES

Right sleeve

With no 1 needles and yarn N, cast on 66 sts. Work one row in k1, p1 twisted rib in yarn N. Change to yarn A and continue in twisted rib for 3¼in, increasing across the last wrong-side row as follows: rib 8 sts, *make one st, rib 2 sts; repeat from * across row to the last 8 sts; make one st, rib 8 sts – 92 sts.

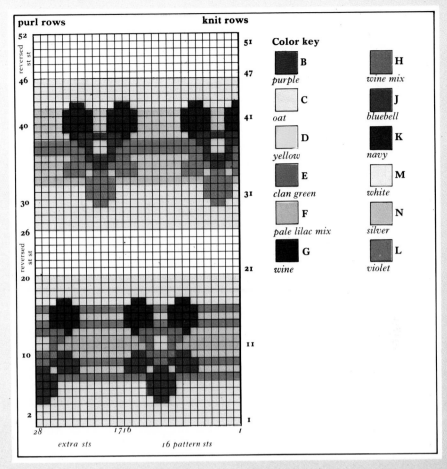

purl rows   knit rows

Color key

B purple
C oat
D yellow
E clan green
F pale lilac mix
G wine

H wine mix
J bluebell
K navy
M white
N silver
L violet

extra sts   *16 pattern sts*

Change to no 3 needles and st st and work Pansy pattern from chart repeating sts 1–16 five times across the row and working sts 17–28 at the end of the row on knit rows; work purl rows in reverse. Increase one st at each end of the 7th and every following 6th row, 20 times in all, taking the extra sts into the pattern as they are made – 132 sts after 121 rows. Then work straight until you have completed row 40 of the third working of the pattern chart and the sleeve measures approximately 21¼in from the cast-on edge.

Shape sleeve top: Continuing in pattern, bind off 6 sts at the beginning of the next 2 rows. *Decrease one st at each end of the next 3 rows. Work one row straight. Repeat from * thirteen more times – 36 sts. Then decrease one st at each end of the next 2 rows** – 32 sts. With right side of work facing starting at row 49 of the fourth working of the pattern chart, shape the top of the sleeve over the next 10 rows as follows:

Row 1: Bind off 11 sts; knit to end.
Row 2: P2 tog, purl to end.
Row 3: Bind off 5 sts, knit to last 2 sts, k2 tog.
Row 4: P2 tog, purl to end.
Row 5: Bind off 3 sts, knit to last 2 sts, k2 tog.
Row 6: P2 tog, purl to end.
Row 7: Bind off 2 sts, knit to last 2 sts, k2 tog.
Row 8: P2 tog, purl to end – 5 sts.
Row 9: Bind off 2 sts, knit to end.
Row 10: P2 tog, p1: bind off.

Left sleeve

Work as for right sleeve to ** (32 sts).
Shape top of sleeve: With right side facing, starting at row 49 of the fourth working of chart, shape top of the left sleeve as follows:

Row 1: Knit to end.
Row 2: Bind off 11 sts, purl to last 2 sts, p2 tog.
Row 3: K2 tog, knit to end.
Row 4: Bind off 5 sts, purl to last 2 sts, p2 tog.
Row 5: Knit to end.
Row 6: Bind off 3 sts, purl to last 2 sts, p2 tog.
Row 7: K2 tog, knit to end.
Row 8: Bind off 2 sts, purl to last 2 sts, p2 tog.
Row 9: Knit to end (5 sts).
Row 10: Bind off 2 sts, purl one st, p2 tog. Bind off.

NECKBAND

Join sleeves to front and back at raglan edges. Using the circular no 1 needles and yarn N, with right side of the work facing, pick up and knit 176 sts around neck edge. Work 8 rounds in k1, p1 twisted rib in yarn N. Bind off in rib.

FINISHING

Press pieces lightly on wrong side, avoiding ribbing. Join underarm seams of sleeves and side seams. Press seams.

ROSES

*Romantic Roses in pink and blue on an écru ground
broken up with bands of gray Turkish stitch
form the pattern for this pretty cotton cardigan.*

MATERIALS

Yarn
Use No. 8 cotton yarn.
Yarn A 10½oz (300g) *(écru)*
Yarn B 5¼oz (150g) *(pale gray)*
Yarn C 1¾oz (50g) *(pale blue)*
Yarn D 1¾oz (50g) *(mid-blue)*
Yarn E 1¾oz (50g) *(brown)*
Yarn F 1¾oz (50g) *(pink)*
Yarn G 1¾oz (50g) *(deep pink)*

Needles
1 pair no 3
1 pair no 1

Notions
8 buttons
1yd hat elastic

MEASUREMENTS
To fit bust 34–35 (36–37)in (86–89,
91–94cm).
(See also chart on p. 118.)

Stitch gauge
32 sts and 38 rows measure 4in over
Rose pattern on no 3 needles.

BACK
With no 1 needles and yarn A, cast on
124 (134) sts. Work 2in in k1, p1 twisted
rib in yarn A, increasing across the last
(wrong-side) row as follows: rib 2 (4) sts,
*rib 3 sts, rib twice into the next st, rib 2
(3) sts; repeat from * 19 (17) times, rib 2
(4) sts – 144 (152) sts.
Change to no 3 needles and st st and
work Rose pattern from chart, reading
odd (knit) rows from right to left and even
(purl) rows from left to right. Work the
pattern across knit rows as follows: *for the
small size,* work sts *1–12,* twelve times; *for
the large size,* work sts *1–12,* twelve times
and then work sts *1–8* once to finish row.
Work purl rows in reverse. Continue thus
in the pattern until you have worked row
14 of the chart. Then work rows 15–24
inclusive in Turkish st in yarn B as
follows: k1, *yfwd, slip 1, k1, psso; repeat
from * to last st, k1. Repeat this row
nine times more. Then work rows 25–38
of the chart in st st in pattern and work
rows 39–48 in Turkish st as for rows 15–
24. You have now completed the 48 rows
of the pattern chart. Continue in pattern
until you have worked row 24 (28) of third
working of chart and back measures
approx. 14½ (15)in from cast-on edge.
Shape armholes: Continuing in pattern,
bind off 10 (12) sts at the beginning of the
next 2 rows – 124 (128) sts. Then work
straight until you have worked row 8 (16)
of the fifth working of the pattern chart
and front measures 22½ (23¼)in from cast-
on edge.
Shape shoulders: Continuing in pattern,
bind off 13 (14) sts at the beginning of the

next 4 rows. Then bind off 12 sts at the
beginning of the following 2 rows. Bind
off the remaining 48 sts.

FRONTS

Left front
With no 1 needles and yarn A, cast on
58 (62) sts. Work 2in in k1, p1 twisted
rib in yarn A, increasing across the last
wrong-side row as follows: rib 5 (1) sts,
*rib 2 sts, rib twice into the next st, rib 2
(3) sts; repeat from * 9 more times, rib 3
(1) sts – 68 (72) sts.
Change to no 3 needles and st st and
work pattern from chart. Work pattern
across knit rows as follows: *for the small
size,* repeat sts *1–12* five times across row
and then work sts *1–8* once; *for the large
size,* repeat sts *1–12* six times across the
rows. Work purl rows in reverse. Continue
thus in pattern until you have worked row
24 (28) of the third working of the pattern
chart and front measures approximately
14½ (15)in from cast-on edge.
Shape armhole: Continuing in pattern,
bind off 10 (12) sts at the beginning of the
next row – 58 (60) sts. Then work straight
in pattern until you have worked row 29
(37) of the fourth working of the pattern
chart and the armhole measures approximately 5 (5½)in from the start of the armhole shaping.
Shape neck: Continuing in pattern, bind
off 4 sts at the beginning of the next
(wrong-side) row. Then decrease one st at
the neck edge on every row until 38 (40)
sts remain. Now work straight in pattern
until you have worked row 8 (16) of the
fifth working of the chart.
Shape shoulder: Bind off 13 (14) sts at
the beginning of the next and following
alternate row; then bind off 12 sts at the
beginning of the following alternate row.

Right front
Work as for left front, reversing all
shapings.

SLEEVES
With no 1 needles and yarn A, cast on
56 (60) sts. Work 4 (4¼)in in twisted rib
in yarn A, increasing across the last
(wrong-side) row as follows: rib 8 (10) sts,
*rib one st, rib twice into the next st;
repeat from * 19 more times, rib 8 (10)
sts – 76 (80) sts.
Change to no 3 needles and st st and
work pattern from chart as follows: *for the
small size,* repeat sts *1–12* six times and
then work sts *1–4* once to complete the
row; *for the large size,* repeat sts *1–12* six
times and then work sts *1–8* once to complete row. Work purl rows in reverse.
Continue in pattern, *at the same time*

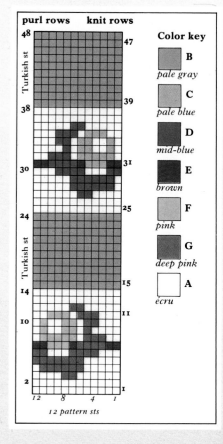

Color key

■ B	*pale gray*
■ C	*pale blue*
■ D	*mid-blue*
■ E	*brown*
■ F	*pink*
■ G	*deep pink*
□ A	*écru*

12 pattern sts

shaping the sides by increasing one st
each end of the 3rd and every
following 4th row, until there
are 130 (136) sts on
the needle. Take the
extra sts into the
pattern as they are
made. Then work
straight in pattern
until you have worked
row 20 (24) of the fourth
working of the pattern chart and
the sleeve measures approximately
20¾ (21¾)in from the cast-on edge. Bind off
right across row; this bound-off edge
should measure 16¼ (17)in to fit armhole.

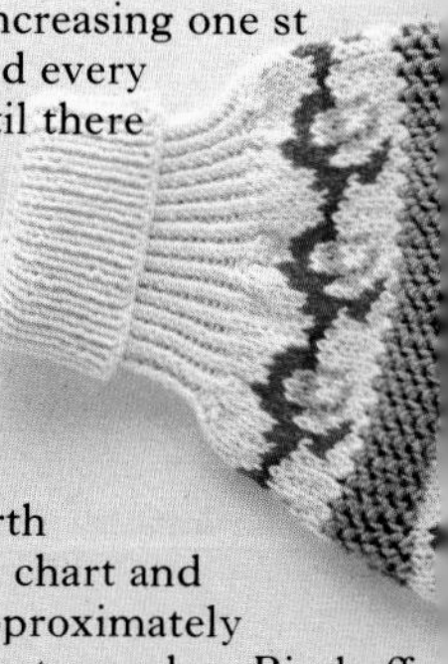

FRONT BANDS

Left front
With no 1 needles and yarn A, beginning at the start of the neck shaping with
right side facing, pick up and knit 155
(162) sts down left front opening edge to
lower edge. Work 9 rows of twisted rib in
yarn A. Join in yarn B and work a further
row in rib in yarn B, then bind off.

Right front
Starting at lower edge, pick up and knit
155 (162) sts up right front opening edge

as far as start of neck shaping. Work 3 rows in twisted rib in yarn A.

Buttonholes: Make 8 buttonholes in row 4 of ribbing as follows: rib 3 sts, *bind off 3 sts, rib 18 (19) sts; repeat from * six more times, then bind off 3 sts, rib 2 sts. Rib back along the next row (row 5), casting on 3 sts directly over those bound off in previous row. Work 4 more rows in rib in yarn A. Join in yarn B and work a further row in rib in yarn B. Bind off in rib in yarn B.

COLLAR

With no 1 needles and yarn A, cast on 109 (113) sts. Work one row in twisted rib. Continuing in twisted rib, increase one st at each end of the next and following 5 alternate rows. Then increase one st at each end of the following 6 rows – 133 (137) sts. Then work 4 (6) rows straight in rib. Now decrease one st at each end of the next 6 rows, and then decrease one st at each end of the following 6 alternate rows – 109 (113) sts. Work one row straight in rib. Bind off in rib.

FINISHING

Press pieces lightly from wrong side, avoiding ribbing and Turkish st bands. Join shoulder seams and side seams. Join underarm sleeve seams, leaving 1½ (2)in of the seam unstitched at the top of the seam. Pin the top of the sleeve into the top of the armhole, easing if necessary, and then pin each side of the unstitched section of sleeve seam across the straight bound-off edge at the bottom of the armhole. Sew sleeve in place and repeat for other sleeve. Pin cast-on edge of collar around neck edge, aligning it between inner cast-on edges of front bands. Sew in position and then fold the collar in half so that the bound-

off edge just overlaps this seam on inside of cardigan. Pin this edge in position and sew down neatly. Sew buttons on to left front band to correspond with button-holes. Cut the hat elastic to fit around top of hips and thread this length through the bottom of the welt from the wrong side, securing ends. Press seams lightly from wrong side.

DAISY

*White and yellow Daisies against a soft gray background,
broken up with bands of mohair. The vest back
is worked in striped rib and the beret is worked in the round.*

MATERIALS Hat

Yarn
Use wool fingering yarn unless otherwise
indicated.
Yarn A 1¾oz (50g) *(pale gray mix)*
Yarn B 1oz (25g) *(ivory)*
Yarn C 1oz (25g) *(yellow)*
Yarn D 1oz (25g) *(dark gray mix)*
Yarn E 1oz (25g) *(peat)*
Yarn F 1oz (25g) *(sage green)*
Yarn G 1¾oz (50g) lurex *(silver)*
Yarn H 1oz (25g) mohair *(pale gray)*

Needles
1 set of four *or* circular no 3
1 set of four *or* circular no 1

MEASUREMENTS

One-size; to fit an average head.
(See also chart on p. 118.)

Stitch gauge
32 sts and 32 rows measure 4in over Fair
Isle pattern on no 3 needles.

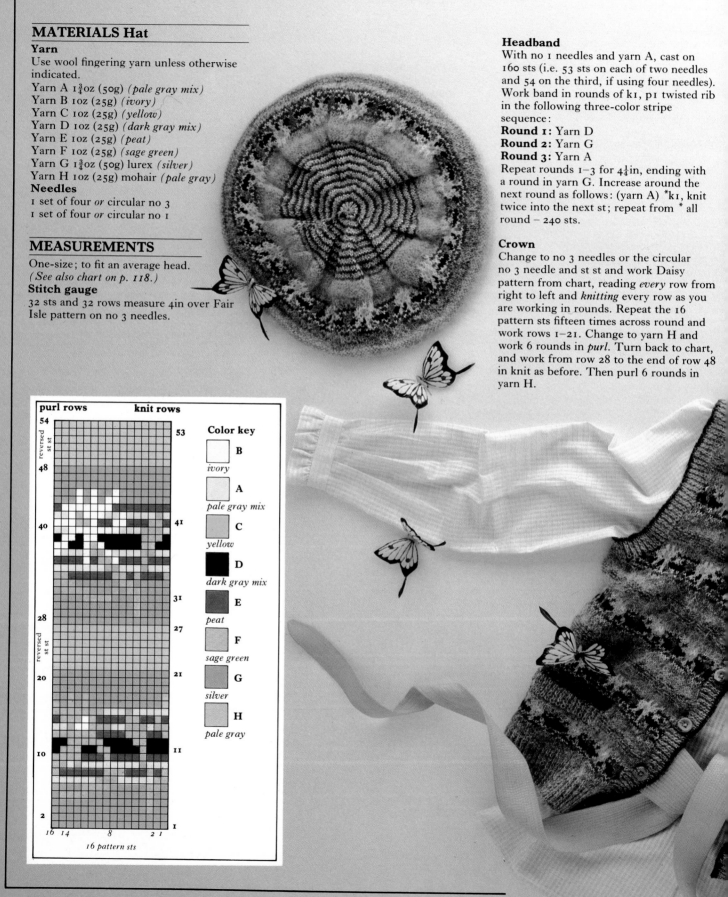

Headband
With no 1 needles and yarn A, cast on
160 sts (i.e. 53 sts on each of two needles
and 54 on the third, if using four needles).
Work band in rounds of k1, p1 twisted rib
in the following three-color stripe
sequence:
Round 1: Yarn D
Round 2: Yarn G
Round 3: Yarn A
Repeat rounds 1–3 for 4¼in, ending with
a round in yarn G. Increase around the
next round as follows: (yarn A) *k1, knit
twice into the next st; repeat from * all
round – 240 sts.

Crown
Change to no 3 needles or the circular
no 3 needle and st st and work Daisy
pattern from chart, reading *every* row from
right to left and *knitting* every row as you
are working in rounds. Repeat the 16
pattern sts fifteen times across round and
work rows 1–21. Change to yarn H and
work 6 rounds in *purl*. Turn back to chart,
and work from row 28 to the end of row 48
in knit as before. Then purl 6 rounds in
yarn H.

Color key

B	*ivory*	
A	*pale gray mix*	
C	*yellow*	
D	*dark gray mix*	
E	*peat*	
F	*sage green*	
G	*silver*	
H	*pale gray*	

purl rows   knit rows

16 pattern sts

Shape crown: Change back to the three-color stripe sequence of yarns D, G and A used for headband and decrease for crown as follows:
Round 1: (Yarn D) *k8, slip 1, k1, pass slipped st over (psso); repeat from * all round – 216 sts.
Rounds 2 and 3: (Yarns G and A) Work straight.
Round 4: (Yarn D) *k7, slip 1, k1, psso; repeat from * all round – 192 sts.
Rounds 5 and 6: (Yarns G and A) Work straight.
Round 7: (Yarn D) *k6, slip 1, k1, psso; repeat from * all round – 168 sts.
Rounds 8 and 9: (Yarns G and A) Work straight.
Continue decreasing in this way, decreasing 24 sts in each decrease round and working 2 rounds straight in between, until you have worked the round: *k1, slip 1, k1, psso; repeat from * all round – 48 sts. Work 2 more rounds straight. **On the next round, k2 tog all round – 24 sts. Work 2 rounds straight. Repeat from ** 2 more times – 6 sts. Break yarn leaving about a 6in end. Thread this end through the 6 sts; draw up and secure.

FINISHING

Fold headband in half to inside and pin inner edge in position. Slip stitch this edge to main body of hat. Darn in any loose ends. Press hat flat at first round of mohair to give tam o'shanter shape.

MATERIALS Vest

Yarn
Use wool fingering yarn.
Yarn A 2¾oz (75g) *(pale gray mix)*
Yarn B 1oz (25g) *(ivory)*
Yarn C 1oz (25g) *(yellow)*
Yarn D 1¾oz (50g) *(dark gray mix)*
Yarn E 1¾oz (50g) *(peat)*
Yarn F 1oz (25g) *(sage green)*
Yarn G 1oz (25g) lurex *(silver)*
Yarn H 1oz (25g) mohair *(pale gray)*

Needles
1 pair no 3
1 pair no 2
1 pair no 1

Notions
5 buttons

MEASUREMENTS

To fit chest 32 (34, 38)in (81, 86, 96cm).
(See also chart on p. 118.)

Stitch gauge
32 sts and 32 rows measure 4in over Fair Isle pattern on no 3 needles.

FRONTS

Pocket linings
Begin by making both pocket linings as follows: with no 2 needles and yarn A, cast on 28 (32, 36) sts and work 2¾in in st st, ending with a purl row. Leave sts on a spare needle or stitch holder. Repeat for other pocket lining.

Left front
With no 1 needles and yarn A, cast on 66 (72, 78) sts. Work 2in in k1, p1 twisted rib in yarn A.
Change to no 3 needles and st st and work Daisy pattern from chart, reading odd (knit) rows from right to left and even (purl) rows from left to right. Work the pattern across the rows as follows: *for the small size (32in)*, work sts *1–16* four times and then work sts *1–2* once; *for the medium size (34in)*, work sts *1–16* four times, then work sts *1–8* once; *for the large size (38in)*, work sts *1–16* four times, then work sts *1–14* once. Work purl rows in reverse, working the extra sts at the beginning of the rows and reading from left to right. Continue in pattern, until you have worked row 20 of the pattern chart.

Pocket: Introduce pocket in row 21 as follows: continuing in pattern, work the pattern across the first 19 (20, 21) sts in the row, then slip the next 28 (32, 36) sts on to a spare needle or stitch holder and in their place continue to work the pattern across the 28 (32, 36) sts of one pocket

lining on spare needle; then work pattern across remaining 19 (20, 21) sts in row. Work the next 6 rows in reversed st st in yarn H as follows: row 22, purl; row 23, purl; row 24, knit; row 25, purl; row 26, knit; row 27, knit.
Then work Daisy pattern again from row 28 to the end of row 48. Work the next 6 rows in reversed st st in yarn H as follows: row 49, knit; row 50, knit; row 51, purl; row 52, knit; row 53, purl; row 54, knit.
You have now completed the 54 rows of the first working of the pattern chart. Continue in pattern until you have worked row 26 (30, 34) of the second working of chart and front measures approximately 11¾ (12¼, 12½)in from cast-on edge.
Shape armhole and neck: Bind off 10 (12, 14) sts at the beginning of the next row, then work across row in pattern to the last 2 sts; k2 tog. Continuing in pattern, decrease one st at the armhole edge on the next 14 (15, 16) rows. Then work armhole edge straight. *At the same time,* continue to decrease one st at the neck edge on every following 4th row after the first decrease on row 27 (31, 35), until 26 (28, 30) sts remain on the needle. Then work neck edge straight until you have completed row 36 (44, 52) of the third working of the pattern chart and front measures approximately 19¾ (20½, 20¾)in from the cast-on edge.
Shape shoulder: Bind off 8 (8, 10) sts at the beginning of the next (right-side) row. Then bind off 9 (10, 10) sts at the beginning of the following 2 alternate rows.

Right front
Work as for left front, but reverse pocket, armhole, neck and shoulder shapings.

BACK

With no 1 needles and yarn A, cast on 128 (140, 152) sts. Work 2in in k1, p1 twisted rib in yarn A, increasing 4 sts evenly across the last wrong-side row by working twice into every 32nd (35th, 38th) st, 4 times – 132 (144, 156) sts.

back of vest

DAISY

Change to no 2 needles and continue to work entire back in twisted rib in the following three-color stripe sequence:
Row 1: Yarn D
Row 2: Yarn E
Row 3: Yarn A
Repeat rows 1–3 up back without shaping until work measures approximately 11¾ (12¾, 12½)in from cast-on edge and matches the fronts from cast-on edge to start of armhole shaping, ending on a wrong-side row.
Shape armholes: Bind off 3 (4, 6) sts at the beginning of the next 2 rows, then k2 tog at each end of every row until 100 (104, 108) sts remain. Then work armhole edges straight until the back measures the same as the fronts from cast-on edge to start of shoulder shaping – approximately 19¾ (20½, 20¾)in – ending on a wrong-side row.
Shape shoulders: Bind off 8 (8, 10) sts at the beginning of the next 2 rows. Then bind off 9 (10, 10) sts at the beginning of the following 4 rows. Divide the remaining 48 (50, 52) sts in half and transfer each half to a spare needle or stitch holder.

Join fronts to back at shoulders.

FRONT BANDS

Right front
With no 1 needles and yarn A, beginning at hem edge and with right side of work facing, pick up and knit 93 (97, 101) sts up right front opening edge, as far as start of neck shaping; then pick up and knit a further 89 (93, 97) sts around the neck to the center-back, including the 24 (25, 26) sts on the first spare needle – 182 (190, 198) sts in all. Work 3 rows in k1, p1 twisted rib in yarn A.
Buttonholes: Make 5 buttonholes in the 4th row as follows: rib 4 sts, *bind off 3 sts, rib 18 (19, 20) sts; repeat from * 3 more times, bind off 3 sts and rib to end of row. Rib back along the next row (5th row of ribbing), casting on 3 sts directly over those bound-off in the previous row. Work a further 4 rows in twisted rib in yarn A. Then join in yarn D and work one row twisted rib in yarn D. Bind off in rib in yarn D.

Left front
With no 1 needles and yarn A, beginning at the center-back of the neck and with right side facing rib the 24 (25, 26) sts on the remaining spare needle, then pick up and knit 65 (68, 71) sts round neck edge to start of neck shaping; then pick up and knit 93 (97, 101) sts down front opening edge to hem. Work to correspond with right front band, omitting buttonholes.

ARMHOLE BANDS

With right side facing, using no 1 needles and yarn A, pick up and knit 144 (152, 160) sts around one armhole. Work 9 rows in k1, p1 twisted rib in yarn A. Join in yarn D and work a further row in rib in yarn D. Bind off in rib in yarn D. Repeat for other armhole.

POCKET TOPS

With right side facing, using no 1 needles and yarn A, rib the 28 (32, 36) sts of one pocket on spare needle. Work to correspond with left front band. Repeat for other pocket.

FINISHING

Press all pieces lightly from the wrong side, avoiding ribbing. Join side seams. Join ribbing at back of neck with a flat seam. Sew down sides of pocket tops and sew pocket linings to backs of vest fronts. Sew on five buttons to left front band to correspond with buttonholes.

MATERIALS
Yarn
Use No. 8 cotton yarn.
Yarn A 5¼oz (150g) *(écru)*
Yarn B 1¾oz (50g) *(purple*
Yarn C 1¾oz (50g) *(bluebell)*
Yarn D 1¾oz (50g) *(pale green)*
Yarn E 1¾oz (50g) *(pink)*
Yarn F 1¾oz (50g) *(deep pink)*
Yarn G 3½oz (100g) *(beige)*
Needles
1 pair no 3
1 pair no 0
Notions
1yd shirring or hat elastic

MEASUREMENTS

To fit bust 32 (34)in (81, 86cm).
(See also chart on p. 119.)
Stitch gauge
32 sts and 32 rows measure 4in over Fair Isle pattern on no 3 needles.

BACK and FRONT

Work the back and the front in the same way.
With no 0 needles and yarn A, cast on 120 (126) sts. Work 2 (2¼)in in k1, p1 twisted rib.
Change to no 3 needles and st st and work Sweet pea pattern from chart, reading odd (knit) rows from right to left and even (purl) rows from left to right. Work the pattern across the rows as follows: *for the smaller size* (34in), repeat the basic 14 pattern sts (*1–14*), eight times across the row and then work sts *1–8* once to finish the row; *for the larger size* (36in), work sts *1–14*, nine times across the row. Work purl rows in reverse. Continue thus until you have worked row 14 of the pattern chart. Then work the next 10 rows in Turkish st in yarn A only as follows (see also p. 130): k1, *yfwd, slip 1, k1, psso; repeat from * to last st, k1. Work rows 16–24 inclusive in the same way as row 15. Then work rows 25–38 in Sweet pea pattern from chart and rows 39–48 in Turkish st in the same way as rows 15–24. You have now completed the 48 rows of the first working of the pattern chart. Work rows 1–38 of pattern chart again. Change to no 0 needles and work 2in in k1, p1 twisted rib in yarn A, ending with a wrong-side row, to form top welt. Join in yarn C and work another row in twisted rib. Bind off in rib in yarn C.

SHOULDER STRAPS

With no 0 needles and yarn A, cast on 112 (116) sts. Work 1¼in in k1, p1 twisted rib in yarn A. Then bind off in rib in yarn A. Make another strap in the same way.

SWEET PEAS

*Pretty pink and purple Sweet peas are worked in bands
against an écru ground in this close-fitting cotton summer camisole.
Bands of Turkish stitch separate the pattern.*

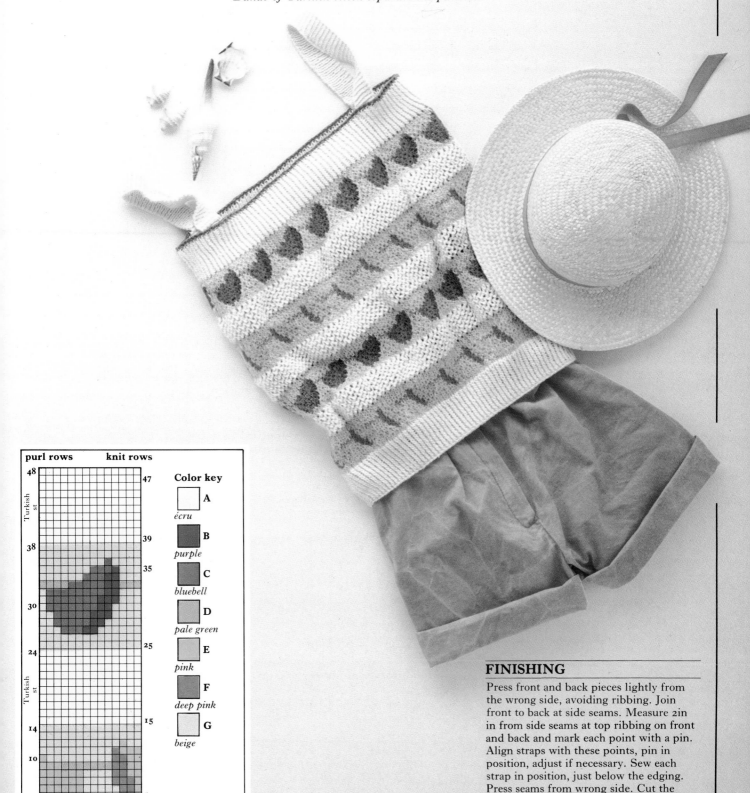

purl rows   **knit rows**

48	47
38	39
	35
30	
24	25
14	15
10	
2	5
	1

Turkish st

14   8   1

14 pattern sts

Color key

☐ **A**	*écru*
◼ **B**	*purple*
◼ **C**	*bluebell*
◼ **D**	*pale green*
◼ **E**	*pink*
◼ **F**	*deep pink*
☐ **G**	*beige*

FINISHING

Press front and back pieces lightly from
the wrong side, avoiding ribbing. Join
front to back at side seams. Measure 2in
in from side seams at top ribbing on front
and back and mark each point with a pin.
Align straps with these points, pin in
position, adjust if necessary. Sew each
strap in position, just below the edging.
Press seams from wrong side. Cut the
length of shirring or hat elastic to fit
waist and thread it through the bottom
edge of the hem welt from the wrong side,
taking care that it does not show through
on the right side, securing it firmly at
side seam.

PRETTY PANSIES

Delicate pink and purple Pansies on an ivory ground
with bands of white mohair running in between the pattern.
The cardigan has three-quarter length sleeves pleated into the armholes.

MATERIALS

Yarn
Use wool fingering yarn unless otherwise indicated.
Yarn A 4½oz (125g) *(ivory)*
Yarn B 1oz (25g) *(pale yellow)*
Yarn C 1oz (25g) *(pale lilac mix)*
Yarn D 1oz (25g) *(powder blue)*
Yarn E 1oz (25g) *(wine mix)*
Yarn F 1oz (25g) *(lilac/green mix)*
Yarn G 1oz (25g) *(clan green)*
Yarn H 1oz (25g) *(pale pink mix)*
Yarn J 3½oz (100g) mohair *(white)*
Yarn K 1¾oz (50g) lurex *(silver)*

Needles
1 pair no 3
1 pair no 2
1 pair no 0

Notions
5 pearl buttons

MEASUREMENTS

One-size: to fit bust 34–36in (86–91cm).
(See also chart on p. 119.)

Stitch gauge
30 sts and 30 rows measure 4in over Fair Isle pattern on no 3 needles.

BACK

With no 0 needles and yarn A, cast on 128 sts. Work 2in in k1, p1 twisted rib, increasing on the last wrong-side row as follows: *rib 7, rib twice into the next st; repeat from * 16 more times – 144 sts. Change to no 3 needles and st st and work Pansy pattern from chart, reading odd (knit) rows from right to left and even (purl) rows from left to right. Repeat the 16 pattern sts nine times across the rows. Continue in pattern until you have worked row 20 of the pattern chart. Change to yarn J (mohair) and work 6 rows of reverse st st as follows: row 21, knit; row 22, knit; row 23, purl; row 24, knit; row 25, purl; row 26, knit. Then continue to work pattern from chart from row 27, until you have worked row 46.
Change to yarn J again and work rows 47–52 as for rows 21–26. You have now completed the first working of the pattern chart. Continue to work pattern, until you have worked row 22 of the second working of the pattern chart, and the back measures approximately 11½in from cast-on edge.
Shape armholes: Continuing in pattern, bind off 8 sts at the beginning of the next 2 rows (rows 23 and 24). Then k2 tog at each end of every row until 108 sts remain. Now work straight until you have worked row 34 of the third working of the pattern chart and the back measures approximately 20in.
Shape shoulders: Continuing in pattern,
bind off 6 sts at the beginning of the next and following 3 rows. Then bind off 7 sts at the beginning of the next 6 rows. Divide the remaining 42 sts in half and transfer each half to a spare needle or stitch holder.

FRONTS

Pocket linings
Begin by making two pocket linings. With no 2 needles and yarn A, cast on 28 sts. Work 2¼in in st st in yarn A, ending with a purl row. Leave sts on spare needle. Repeat for other pocket lining.

Left front
With no 0 needles and yarn A, cast on 56 sts. Work 2in in k1, p1 twisted rib in yarn A, increasing across the last (wrong-side) row as follows: *rib 3 sts, rib twice into the next st, rib 3 sts; repeat from * seven more times – 64 sts.
Change to no 3 needles and st st and work Pansy pattern from chart as before, repeating the 16 pattern sts four times across each row. Continue in pattern until you have worked row 20 of pattern chart.
Pocket: Introduce pocket in the next row (row 21) as follows: work the first 18 sts in the row, slip the next 28 sts on to a spare needle or stitch holder and in their place, continue to work the pattern across the 28 sts of one pocket lining on spare needle; work pattern across the remaining 18 sts in the row. Continuing in pattern, work the front straight until you have completed row 12 of the second working of the pattern chart.
Shape neck and armhole edge: Continuing in pattern, work across the next row to the last 2 sts; k2 tog. Then decrease one st at the neck edge on every following 5th row, thirteen times in all, keeping in pattern. *At the same time,* when you have completed row 22 of the second working of the pattern chart and the front measures approximately 11½in, shape armhole as follows: bind off 8 sts at the beginning of the next row (row 75). Then decrease one st at the armhole edge on the following 10 rows. Now work armhole edge straight, but continue decreasing one st at the neck edge on every 5th row until 33 sts remain. Then work straight in pattern until you have completed row 34 of the third working of the pattern chart.
Shape shoulders: Bind off 6 sts at the beginning of the next and following alternate row. Then bind off 3 sts at the beginning of the following 3 alternate rows.

Right front
Work as for left front, reversing pocket, neck, armhole and shoulder shapings.

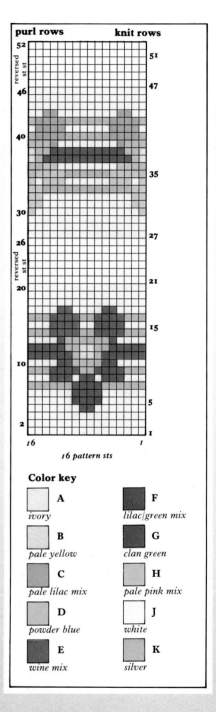

purl rows   knit rows

16 pattern sts

Color key

A *ivory*		F *lilac/green mix*	
B *pale yellow*		G *clan green*	
C *pale lilac mix*		H *pale pink mix*	
D *powder blue*		J *white*	
E *wine mix*		K *silver*	

SLEEVES

With no 0 needles and yarn G, cast on 66 sts and work one row in k1, p1 twisted rib in yarn G.

Join in yarn A and continue in rib for 2¾in, increasing across the last (wrong-side) row as follows: rib 10 sts, rib twice into each of the next 46 sts, rib 10 sts – 112 sts in all.

Change to no 3 needles and st st and work straight in pattern from chart, repeating the 16 pattern sts seven times across the rows. Work from chart until you have completed row 22 of the second working of the pattern chart, and sleeve measures approximately 12¼in.

Shape top: Continuing in pattern, bind off 8 sts at ̇e beginning of the next 2 rows. Then k2 tog at each end of the next and every alternate row, until 76 sts remain on the needle. Work 17 rows straight in pattern. K2 tog at each end of the next and every following alternate row, seven times in all; then k2 tog at each end of the next 9 rows – 42 sts remain. Bind off remaining sts, taking every 10th and 11th st in row together. This wide sleeve top will be gathered into the armhole later. Make another sleeve in the same way.

Join fronts to back at shoulders.

FRONT BANDS

Right front

With no 0 needles and yarn A, beginning at lower edge, pick up and knit 89 sts up front opening edge to start of neck shaping; then pick up and knit a further 113 sts around neck to center-back, including the 21 sts on the first spare needle. Work 3 rows in k1, p1 twisted rib in yarn A.

Buttonholes: Make 5 buttonholes in row 4 of ribbing as follows: rib 4 sts, *bind off 3 sts, rib 17 sts; repeat from * three more times, bind off 3 sts and rib to end of row. On the next row (row 5) rib back, casting on 3 sts directly over those bound off in previous row. Work 4 more rows of rib in yarn A. Join in yarn G, and work one row of rib in yarn G. Bind off in rib in yarn G.

Left front

Starting at the center-back and with yarn A, rib the 21 sts on the remaining spare needle; then pick up and knit 89 sts around neck edge to start of neck shaping, and a further 89 sts down front opening to lower edge. Work left front band to correspond with right front band, but omit buttonholes.

POCKETS

Pocket tops

With right side of work facing, using no 0 needles and yarn A, rib across the 28 sts of one pocket on spare needle. Work 7 more rows in k1, p1 twisted rib in yarn A. Join in yarn G and work a further row in twisted rib in yarn G. Bind off in rib in yarn G. Repeat for other pocket.

FINISHING

Press all pieces lightly from wrong side avoiding ribbing. Join fronts to back at side seams. Join sleeve seams. Pin sleeves into each armhole, pleating fullness around top of sleeve as you pin in position. Sew sleeves into armholes as before. Join front bands at center-back of neck with flat seam. Sew down sides of pocket tops and pocket linings. Sew on the 5 buttons to left front band to correspond with buttonholes.

ETHNIC

CACTUS

Prickly Cacti against desert shades are the theme of this sleeveless men's or women's V-neck vest. The back, welts, armholes and neckband are worked in striped rib.

MEASUREMENTS

To fit chest 35 (38, 41, 44)in (89, 97, 104, 112cm).
(See also chart on p. 119.)

Stitch gauge

32 sts and 32 rows measure 4in over Cactus pattern on no 3 needles.

MATERIALS

Yarn

Use wool fingering yarn.

Yarn A 1¾ (1¾, 2¾, 2¾)oz (50, 50, 75, 75g) *(clan green)*

Yarn B 1¾ (1¾, 2¾, 2¾)oz (50, 50, 75, 75g) *(bottle green)*

Yarn C 1¾oz (50g) *(peat)*

Yarn D 1¾oz (50g) *(pale green mix)*

Yarn E 1oz (25g) *(dark fawn)*

Yarn F 1oz (25g) *(oat)*

Yarn G 1oz (25g) *(pale gray mix)*

Yarn H 1oz (25g) *(flax)*

Yarn J 1oz (25g) *(blue/wine mix)*

Yarn K 1oz (25g) *(red/blue mix)*

Needles

1 pair no 3

1 pair no 2

1 pair no 1

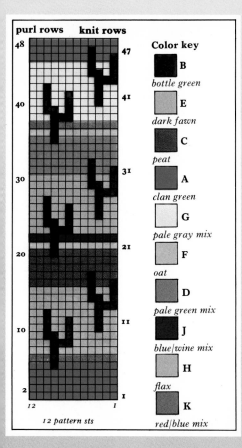

purl rows   knit rows

48
47

40
41

30
31

20
21

10
11

2
1

12   *1*

12 pattern sts

Color key

B
bottle green

E
dark fawn

C
peat

A
clan green

G
pale gray mix

F
oat

D
pale green mix

J
blue/wine mix

H
flax

K
red/blue mix

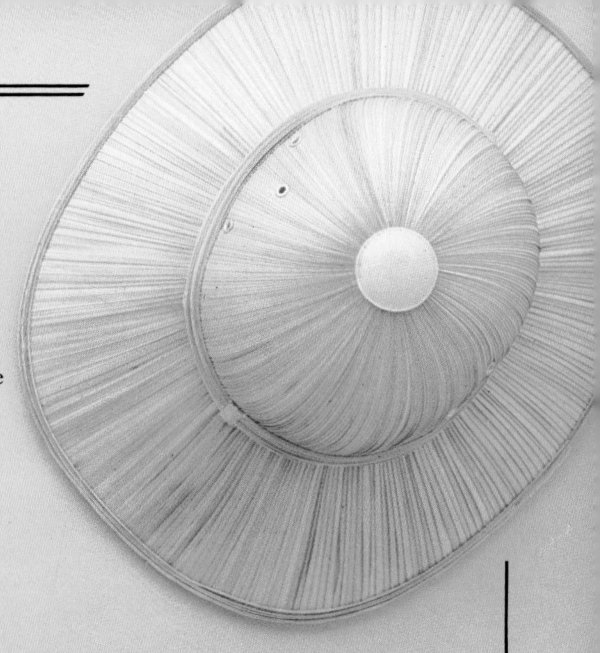

next row straight. K2 tog at the beginning of the next row, then work to end. Work the next row straight. K2 tog at the beginning of the next row, work to last 2 sts, k2 tog**. Repeat from ** to ** until 33 (36, 41, 43) sts remain. Work the next row straight. K2 tog at the beginning of the next row, then work to end. Work the next row straight. Now work the armhole edge straight, but continue to decrease one st at the neck edge on the next and every following 4th row as before, until 24 (27, 30, 33) sts remain. Work straight in pattern until you have completed row 22 (30, 38, 46) of the fourth working of the pattern chart and the left front measures approximately 22 (23¼, 24, 25¼)in from cast-on edge.

Shape shoulder: Continuing in pattern, bind off 8 (9, 10, 11) sts at the beginning of the next and following 2 alternate rows. Rejoin yarn to the remaining 59 (64, 69, 74) sts of front at neck edge. K2 tog at the beginning of the next row, then knit 55 (60, 65, 70) sts, k2 tog.
Work the next row straight. Work across the next row to the last 2 sts, k2 tog. Work the next row straight. K2 tog at the beginning of next row, work pattern to last 2 sts, k2 tog. Repeat from ** to ** until 33 (36, 41, 43) sts remain. Finish right side to correspond with left side, reversing all shapings.

FRONT

With no 1 needles and yarn A, cast on 136 (148, 160, 172) sts. Work 2in in k1, p1 twisted rib in the following three-color stripe sequence:
Row 1: Yarn D
Row 2: Yarn C
Row 3: Yarn A
Continue repeating rows 1–3 for 2in, ending with a row in yarn A. Change to yarn D and increase across this row as follows: purl 0 (2, 0, 2) sts, *purl twice into the next st, purl 16 (17, 19, 20) sts; repeat from * seven more times, purl 0 (2, 0, 2) sts – 144 (156, 168, 180) sts. Change to no 3 needles and st st and work pattern from chart, reading odd (knit) rows from right to left and even (purl) rows from left to right. Repeat the 12 pattern sts on chart, 12 (13, 14, 15) times across the row. Continuing in pattern, work straight until you have completed row 44 (48, 4, 8) of the second (second, third, third) working of the pattern chart and the front measures approximately 13½ (13¾, 14¼, 14½)in from the cast-on edge.
Shape armholes and neck: Continuing in pattern, bind off 13 (14, 15, 16) sts at the beginning of the next 2 rows – 118 (128, 138, 148) sts remain. Now divide for 'V'-neck. On the next row, k2 tog, k55 (60, 65, 70) sts, k2 tog; then turn leaving the remaining sts in row on a spare needle or stitch holder. Now work the left side of the front on these 56 (61, 66, 71) sts as follows, continuing in pattern: **work the

BACK

With no 1 needles and yarn A, cast on 144 (156, 168, 180) sts. Work 2in in k1, p1 twisted rib following the same three-color stripe sequence as for front welt, ending with a row in yarn A.
Change to no 2 needles and continue to work entire back in striped twisted rib, repeating rows 1–3 and carrying yarns not in use up the sides of the work, until back measures approximately 13½ (13¾, 14¼, 14½)in from cast-on edge, ending with a wrong-side row.
Shape armholes: Continuing in striped rib, bind off 8 (10, 12, 14) sts at the beginning of the next 2 rows. Then k2 tog at each end of the next and every following alternate row until 100 (108, 116, 124) sts remain. Now work straight until back measures approximately 22 (23¼, 24, 25¼)in from the cast-on edge.
Shape shoulders: Continuing in striped rib, bind off 8 (9, 10, 11) sts at the beginning of the next 6 rows. Leave the remaining 52 (54, 56, 58) sts on a spare needle or stitch holder.

NECKBAND

Join right shoulder seam. With no 1 needles and yarn A, beginning at the left shoulder seam and with right side facing, pick up and knit 72 (76, 80, 84) sts down the side of the neck to center and mark with colored thread; then pick up 2 sts from the center-front and mark again with colored thread; pick up and knit 72 (76, 80, 84) sts up right side of neck and finally

knit the 52 (54, 56, 58) sts from the spare needle at the back of the neck. Work neckband in k1, p1 twisted rib in the same three-color stripe sequence as before, shaping the neckband as follows: on the next row rib around back and down side of neck to last 2 sts before marker; slip 1, k1, psso, k2, k2 tog and then rib to end. On the next row, rib back down left side of neck to last 2 sts before marker, slip 1, k1, psso, k2, k2 tog, rib to end. Repeat these 2 rows three more times. Then bind off in rib in yarn A, still decreasing as before.

ARMBANDS

Join left shoulder seam and neckband. With right side facing, using no 1 needles and yarn A, pick up and knit 164 (170, 176, 182) sts around one armhole. Work 8 rows in twisted rib following the same three-color stripe sequence as before. Bind off in rib in yarn A. Repeat for other armhole.

FINISHING

Press front lightly from wrong side, avoiding ribbing. Join side seams and press seams lightly.

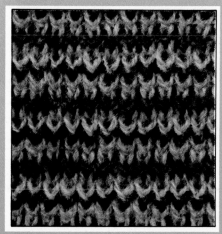

back of vest

DOUBLE DUTCH

*A one-size crew neck sweater with patterned front and back
and plain sleeves. The pattern is derived from Delft tile designs.*

MATERIALS

Yarn

Use wool fingering yarn.
Yarn A 8oz (225g) *(navy)*
Yarn B 5¼oz (150g) *(ivory)*
Yarn C 1oz (25g) *(crimson)*

Needles

1 pair no 3
1 pair no 1

MEASUREMENTS

One-size: to fit chest 38in (97cm).
(See also chart on p. 119.)

Stitch gauge

30 sts and 30 rows measure 4in over Delft pattern on no 3 needles; 31 sts and 32 rows measure 4in over plain st st.

BACK

**With no 1 needles and yarn A, cast on 136 sts. Work 2in in k1, p1 twisted rib in yarn A. Increase across the next wrong-side row as follows: rib 5 sts, *rib 5 sts, rib twice into the next st; repeat from * 19 more times, rib 11 sts – 156 sts.
Change to no 3 needles and st st and work Delft pattern from chart, reading odd (knit) rows from right to left and even (purl) rows from left to right. Repeat the 78 pattern sts indicated on chart, twice across the row. Continue in pattern until you have worked row 38 of the second working of the pattern chart and the back measures approximately 17¾in from the cast-on edge.**

Shape armholes: Bind off 12 sts at the beginning of the next 2 rows. Then work straight in pattern until you have worked row 18 of the third working of the pattern chart, and the work measures approximately 25½in from the cast-on edge.

Shape shoulders: With right side facing, bind off 15 sts at the beginning of the next 2 rows. Then bind off 13 sts at the beginning of the next 4 rows. Leave the remaining 50 sts on a spare needle.

FRONT

Work front as for back from ** to ** completing row 38 of the second working of the pattern chart.

Shape armholes: Bind off 12 sts at the beginning of the next 2 rows – 132 sts. Then work straight in pattern until you have completed row 72 of the second working of the pattern chart and the front measures approximately 22in from the cast-on edge.

Shape neck: Work the first 48 sts of row 73 on chart, bind off the next 36 sts, and then work the pattern across the remaining 48 sts of the row. Continuing in pattern on these last 48 sts of the row, decrease one st at the neck edge on the next 7 rows – 41 sts remain. Then work straight in pattern until you have worked row 18 of the third working of the pattern chart and the right front shoulder edge measures approximately 25½in from the cast-on edge.

Shape shoulder: Continuing in pattern, bind off 15 sts at the beginning of the next row. Then bind off 13 sts at the beginning of the following 2 alternate rows. Rejoin yarn to the 48 sts of left front at neck edge on spare needle. Work left side of neck and left shoulder to correspond with right side, reversing shapings.

SLEEVES

With no 1 needles and yarn A, cast on 62 sts. Work 4in in k1, p1 twisted rib in yarn A, ending on a right-side row. Increase across the next (wrong-side) row as follows: rib 10 sts, rib twice into each of the next 42 sts, rib 10 sts – 104 sts in all. Change to no 3 needles and knit one row in yarn C. Rejoin yarn A and continue to work sleeve in st st and yarn A only, starting with a purl row and shaping sides by increasing one st at each end of the next (after the purl row) and every following 7th row until there are 132 sts on the needle. Then work straight until the sleeve measures 22in from the cast-on edge. Bind off right across row.
Make another sleeve in the same way.

NECKBAND

Join right shoulder seam only.
With right side of work facing, using no 1 needles and yarn A, beginning at the left shoulder, pick up and knit 31 sts down left side of neck, 30 sts across center-front bound-off edge, 31 sts up right side of neck and 50 sts across back of neck – 142 sts in all. Work 13 rows in k1, p1 twisted rib in yarn A. Join in yarn C and work a further row of twisted rib in yarn C. Bind off in rib in yarn C.

FINISHING

Press all pieces lightly from the wrong side avoiding ribbing. Join left shoulder seam and neckband and both side seams. Then join underarm sleeve seams, leaving the last 1½in at top of seam unstitched. Pin top of sleeve into top of armhole and pin each side of the unstitched section of the sleeve seam across the straight bound-off edge at the bottom of the armhole. Sew in place and repeat for other sleeve. Press seams lightly from wrong side.

purl rows — knit rows

78 pattern sts

Color key

■ **A** □ **B**
navy *ivory*

NAVAJO

*An interesting pattern deriving from an Indian design,
using geometric shapes against a plain ground.
The back of the vest is worked in plain rib.*

MATERIALS

Yarn

Use wool fingering yarn.

Yarn A 5¼ (5¼, 6¼)oz (150, 150, 175g) *(oat)*

Yarn B 1oz (25g) *(rust)*

Yarn C 1oz (25g) *(black)*

Yarn D 1oz (25g) *(mustard)*

Yarn E 1oz (25g) *(lilac/green mix)*

Yarn F 1oz (25g) *(olive mix)*

Needles

1 pair no 3

1 pair no 2

1 pair no 1

Notions

5 buttons

MEASUREMENTS

To fit chest 32 (34, 38)in (81, 86, 96cm).
(See also chart on p. 119.)

Stitch gauge

32 sts and 34 rows measure 4in over Fair
Isle pattern on no 3 needles.

FRONTS

Left front

With no 1 needles and yarn A, cast on
66 (72, 78) sts. Work 2in in k1, p1 twisted
rib in yarn A.

Change to no 3 needles and st st and
work Fair Isle pattern from chart, reading
odd (knit) rows from right to left and even
(purl) rows from left to right. Work the
pattern across knit rows as follows: *for the
small size (32in)*, work sts *1–40* once, then
work sts *1–26* once; *for the medium size
(34in)*, work sts *1–40* once, then work sts
1–32 once; *for the large size (38in)*, work
sts *1–40* once, then work sts *1–38* once.
Work purl rows in reverse. Continue in
pattern until the end of row 12 on chart.

Pocket: Introduce pocket in row 13
(right-side row) as follows: work the first
19 (20, 21) sts of row in pattern, bind off
the next 28 (32, 36) sts, and then continue
to work pattern to end of row. On the
next row, work the first 19 (20, 21) sts of
row in pattern, then cast on 28 (32, 36) sts
directly over those bound off and then work
pattern to end of row. Continue straight in
pattern until you have worked row 32 (36,
40) of the second working of the pattern
chart and the front measures approximately 12½ (13, 13¾)in from cast-on edge.

Shape armholes and neck: Bind off 10
(12, 14) sts at the beginning of the next
(right-side) row and then work the pattern
across row to the last 2 sts; k2 tog. Continuing in pattern, decrease one st at the
armhole edge on the next 14 (14, 16) rows,
and then work armhole edge straight. *At
the same time,* decrease one st at the neck
edge on every following 4th row after the

first decrease on row 33 (37, 41) until 26
(28, 30) sts remain. Then work neck edge
straight until you have worked row 48 (56,
62) of the third working of the pattern
chart and front measures approximately
21¾ (22½, 23½)in from cast-on edge.

Shape shoulder: Continuing in pattern
*(for the larger size, continue in plain st st
in yarn A only)*, bind off 10 sts at the
beginning of the next (right-side) row;
then bind off 8 (9, 10) sts at the beginning
of the following 2 alternate rows.

Right front

Work as for left front and reverse pocket,
armhole, neck and shoulder shapings.

BACK

With no 1 needles and yarn A, cast on
128 (140, 152) sts. Work 2in in k1, p1
twisted rib, increasing to 132 (144, 156)
sts across the last (wrong-side) row by
working twice into every 32nd (35th, 38th)

st in the row, four times.

Change to no 2 needles and continue to
work entire back in twisted rib in yarn A.
Work until back measures same as front
from cast-on edge to start of armhole
shaping – approximately 12½ (13, 13¾)in –
ending on a wrong-side row.

Shape armholes: Bind off 4 (6, 8) sts at
the beginning of the next 2 rows. Then
k2 tog at each end of every row until 100
(106, 112) sts remain. Work straight until
back measures the same as the fronts from
cast-on edge to start of shoulder shaping –
approximately 21¾ (22½, 23½)in – ending
on a wrong-side row.

Shape shoulders: With right side facing,
bind off 10 (11, 11) sts at the beginning of
the next 2 rows. Then bind off 9 (9, 10) sts
at the beginning of the following 4 rows.
Divide the remaining 44 (48, 50) sts in
half and transfer each half to a spare
needle or stitch holder.

Join fronts to back at shoulders.

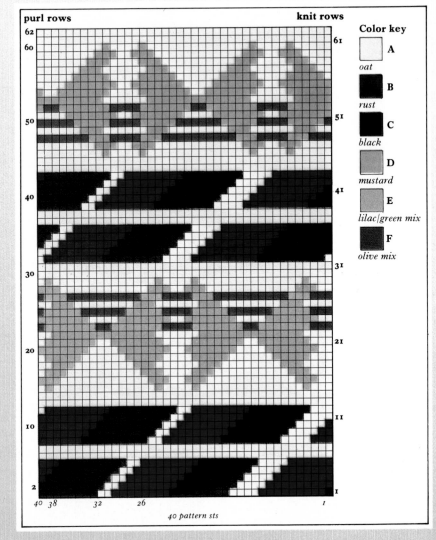

purl rows   knit rows

40 pattern sts

Color key

- A *oat*
- B *rust*
- C *black*
- D *mustard*
- E *lilac/green mix*
- F *olive mix*

FRONT BANDS

Right front

With right side of the work facing and using no 1 needles and yarn A, beginning at hem edge, pick up and knit 97 (101, 105) sts up right front opening edge, as far as start of neck shaping; then pick up and knit a further 80 (84, 88) sts around neck opening edge as far as center-back, including the 22 (24, 25) sts on the first spare needle – 177 (185, 193) sts in all. Work 3 rows in k1, p1 twisted rib in yarn A.

Buttonholes: Make five buttonholes in the next row (row 4) as follows: rib 4 sts, *bind off 3 sts, rib 19 (20, 21) sts; repeat from * 3 more times, then bind off 3 sts and rib to end of row. Rib back along next row, casting on 3 sts directly over those bound off in previous row. Work 4 more rows in rib in yarn A. Join in yarn C and work 1 row in rib in yarn C. Bind off in rib in yarn C.

Left front

Beginning at the center-back of the neck, using no 1 needles and yarn A, rib the 22 (24, 25) sts on the remaining spare needle; then pick up and knit 58 (60, 63) sts around neck edge to start of neck shaping and then a further 97 (101, 105) sts down front opening edge to hem edge. Work to correspond with right front band, but omit buttonholes.

ARMHOLE BANDS

With no 1 needles and yarn A, and with right side of work facing, pick up and knit 147 (155, 163) sts around one armhole. Work to correspond with left front band. Repeat for other armhole.

POCKETS

Pocket tops

With right side of work facing and using no 1 needles and yarn A, pick up and knit 28 (32, 36) sts along the lower bound-off edge of one pocket slit. Work to correspond with left front band. Repeat for lower bound-off edge of other pocket slit.

Pocket linings

Holding work upside down and with right side facing, using no 2 needles and yarn A, pick up and knit 28 (32, 36) sts across the remaining cast-on edge of one pocket slit behind pocket top. Starting with a purl row, work in st st and yarn A, until the lining measures 2¾in. Bind off. Repeat for other pocket.

FINISHING

Press all pieces lightly from wrong side, avoiding ribbing. Join fronts to back at side seams. Join ribbing at center-back of neck and underarm points with flat seams. Sew down pocket linings to wrong side of fronts and sew down sides of pocket tops. Sew on five buttons to left front band to correspond with buttonholes.

PIERROT

Clownish colors speckled over alternating stripes make this cotton cardigan an ideal summer garment. The cardigan buttons to the neck and has a shaped, ribbed collar and front pockets.

MATERIALS

Yarn
Use No. 8 cotton yarn.
Yarn A 8¾oz (250g) *(écru)*
Yarn B 5¼oz (150g) *(pale blue)*
Yarn C 1¾oz (50g) *(lilac)*
Yarn D 1¾oz (50g) *(bluebell)*
Yarn E 1¾oz (50g) *(deep pink)*
Yarn F 3½oz (100g) *(yellow)*
Yarn G 1¾oz (50g) *(purple)*

Needles
1 pair no 3
1 pair no 1

Notions
8 buttons
1yd narrow hat elastic

MEASUREMENTS

To fit bust 34 (36)in (86, 91cm).
(See also chart on p. 120.)

Stitch gauge
32 sts and 32 rows measure 4in over Fair Isle pattern on no 3 needles.

BACK

With no 1 needles and yarn A, cast on 124 (134) sts. Work 2in in k1, p1 twisted rib, increasing across the last (wrong-side) row as follows: rib 2 (4) sts, *rib 3 sts, rib twice into the next st, rib 2 (3) sts; repeat from * 19 (17) more times, rib 2 (4) sts – 144 (152) sts in all.
Change to no 3 needles and st st and work pattern from chart, reading odd ((knit) rows from right to left and even (purl) rows from left to right. Work the pattern across knit rows as follows: *for the smaller size (34in)*, work the 24 pattern sts (*1–24*), six times across the row; *for the larger size (36in)*, work sts *1–24* six times across the row and then work sts *1–8* once to finish the row. Work purl rows in reverse, working sts *8–1* at the beginning of the row for the larger size. Continuing in pattern work straight until you have completed row 12 (16) of the fourth working of the pattern chart and the back measures approximately 12¼ (12½)in from the cast-on edge.
Shape armholes: Continuing in pattern, bind off 10 (13) sts at the beginning of the next 2 rows – 124 (126) sts. Then work straight until you have worked row 24 of the sixth working of the pattern chart (row 8 of the seventh working of the pattern chart) and the back measures approximately 19¾ (20½)in from the cast-on edge.
Shape shoulders: Continuing in pattern, bind off 13 (14) sts at the beginning of the next 4 rows. Then bind off 12 sts at the beginning of the following 2 rows. Bind off the remaining sts across back of neck.

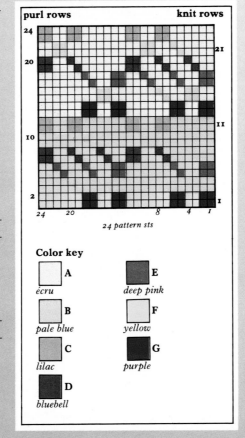

purl rows · knit rows · 24 · 21 · 20 · 10 · 11 · 2 · 1 · 24 · 20 · 8 · 4 · 1 · *24 pattern sts*

Color key

A *écru*		E *deep pink*	
B *pale blue*		F *yellow*	
C *lilac*		G *purple*	
D *bluebell*			

FRONTS

Pocket linings
Begin by making the pocket linings as follows: with no 1 needles and yarn A, cast on 28 (32) sts. Work 2¼in in st st in yarn A, ending with a knit row. Leave the sts on a spare needle and make another lining in the same way.

Left front
With no 1 needles and yarn A, cast on 58 (62) sts. Work 2in in k1, p1 twisted rib in yarn A, increasing across the last wrong-side row as follows: rib 5 (1) sts, *rib 2 sts, rib twice into the next st, rib 2 (3) sts; repeat from * nine more times, rib 3 (1) sts – 68 (72) sts.
Change to no 3 needles and st st and work pattern from chart, reading knit rows from right to left and purl rows from left to right. Work the pattern across knit rows as follows: *for the smaller size (34in)*, work sts *1–24* twice then work sts *1–20* to finish the row; *for the larger size (36in)*, work sts *1–24* three times across the row. Work purl rows in reverse. Continue thus in pattern until you have worked row 12 of the chart.

Pocket:
Introduce the pocket in row 13 as follows: continuing in pattern, work the first 20 sts of the row, bind off the next 28 (32) sts and then work the pattern across the remaining 20 sts in the row. On the next row, work the pattern across the first 20 sts, then continue in pattern across the 28 (32) sts of one pocket lining on spare needle, and then work the pattern to the end of the row.
Continuing in pattern, work straight until you have completed row 12 (16) of the fourth working of the pattern chart, and front measures the same as the back from cast-on edge to start of armhole shaping – approximately 12¼ (12½)in.

continued on p. 73

MATERIALS Jacket

Yarn
Use wool fingering yarn unless otherwise
indicated.
Yarn A 2¾oz (75g) *(wine)*
Yarn B 1¾oz (50g) *(olive)*
Yarn C 2¾oz (75g) lurex *(copper)*
Yarn D 1¾oz (50g) *(mustard)*
Yarn E 2¾oz (75g) *(pale lilac mix)*
Yarn F 1¾oz (50g) *(fawn)*
Yarn G 2¾oz (75g) *(peat)*
Yarn H 1¾oz (50g) *(chocolate)*
Yarn K 1¾oz (50g) *(dark wine mix)*

Needles
1 pair no 3
1 pair no 1
1 crochet hook, size C

Notions
1 button

MEASUREMENTS
To fit chest 34 (36, 38)in (86, 91, 97cm).
(See also chart on p. 120.)

Stitch gauge
31 sts and 32 rows measure 4in over Fair
Isle pattern on no 3 needles.

continued on p. 72.

STERLING ZIG-ZAG

*Subtle shades of Shetland yarn, enhanced with specks of copper
make this peplum skirted jacket an ideal garment for winter evenings.
The one-size camisole top is worked entirely in striped rib
following the same colors as the rib in the jacket.*

MATERIALS Camisole

Yarn
Use wool fingering yarn unless otherwise
indicated.
Yarn A 1¾oz (50g) *(peat)*
Yarn B 1¾oz (50g) *(wine)*
Yarn C 1¾oz (50g) lurex *(copper)*

Needles
1 pair no 2

MEASUREMENTS

One-size: to fit bust 34in (86cm).
(See also chart on p. 120.)

Stitch gauge
36 sts and 36 rows measure 4in over
pattern on no 2 needles.

BACK

**With no 2 needles and yarn B, cast on
120 sts. Work the entire back in k1, p1
twisted rib in the following three-color
stripe sequence:
Row 1: Yarn A
Row 2: Yarn C
Row 3: Yarn B
Continue repeating rows 1–3 up the back,
carrying yarn not in use up the sides of
the work, until back measures 11½in from
cast-on edge**. Bind off in rib in yarn B.

FRONT

Work as for back from ** to **. Then
divide for the shaped top as follows: on
the next (right-side) row, rib the first 60
sts of row and then turn, leaving the
remaining 60 sts on a spare needle or
stitch holder. Continue in rib on these
first 60 sts, decreasing one st at each end
of the next and every following alternate
row, 27 times in all – 6 sts remain.
Continuing in striped rib on these 6 sts,
work 14¼in to form shoulder strap. Bind
off. Shape the remaining 60 sts on spare
needle in the same way, continuing on
into strap as before. Bind off.

FINISHING

Darn in any loose ends at the sides. Join
side seams. Measure a point 3¼in in from
each side seam and mark with a pin. Pin
shoulder straps in position at each pin
point, adjust if necessary and then sew in
position. Do not press the camisole.

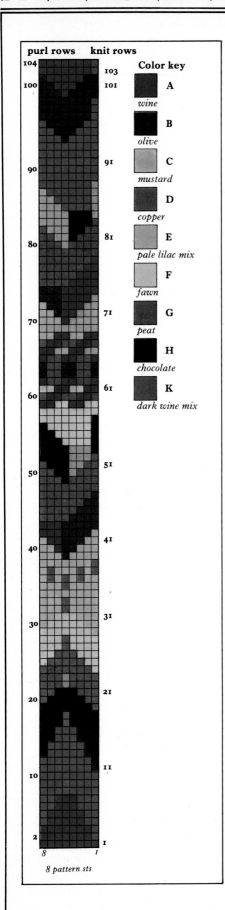

purl rows   knit rows

104	103
100	101
90	91
80	81
70	71
60	61
50	51
40	41
30	31
20	21
10	11
2	1

8   1

8 pattern sts

Color key

A
wine

B
olive

C
mustard

D
copper

E
pale lilac mix

F
fawn

G
peat

H
chocolate

K
dark wine mix

BACK

With no 1 needles and yarn K, cast on 272 (288, 304) sts. Work 9 rows in k1, p1 twisted rib in the following three-color sequence, starting with a wrong-side row:

Rows 1, 4, 7: Yarn G
Rows 2, 5, 8: Yarn D
Rows 3, 6, 9: Yarn A

Carry yarns not in use up the sides of the work. Change to no 3 needles and st st and work Fair Isle pattern from chart, reading odd (knit) rows from right to left and even (purl) rows from left to right. Repeat the 8 pattern sts 34 (36, 38) times across the rows. Continue in pattern until you have worked row 54 (58, 62) of the chart. With right side facing, decrease for waist as follows: k2 tog right across row – 136 (144, 152) sts.

Waistband: Change to no 1 needles and work rows 1–9 of striped rib as before. Then work rows 1–2 again. Change to no 3 needles and st st and continue in Fair Isle pattern from row 55 (59, 63) of the first working of the chart until you have completed row 14 (22, 30) of the second working of the chart and the back measures approximately $7\frac{3}{4}$ ($8\frac{3}{4}$, $9\frac{1}{2}$)in from the top of the waistband.

Shape armholes: Continuing in pattern bind off 8 sts at the beginning of the next 2 rows. Then decrease one st at each end of every row until 102 (110, 118) sts remain. Work straight in pattern until you have worked row 76 (88, 100) of the second working of the pattern chart and the armhole measures approximately $7\frac{1}{2}$ ($7\frac{3}{4}$, $8\frac{3}{4}$)in from start of armhole shaping.

Shape shoulders: Continuing in pattern, bind off 8 sts at the beginning of the next 4 rows. Then bind off 5 (6, 7) sts at the beginning of the following 6 rows. Leave the remaining 40 (42, 44) sts on a spare needle or stitch holder.

FRONTS

Left front

With no 1 needles and yarn A, cast on 124 (132, 140) sts. Work rows 1–9 of striped rib as before.

Change to no 3 needles and st st and work pattern from chart, repeating sts 1–8 15 (16, 17) times across and then working sts 1–4 to finish the rows. Continue in pattern until you have completed row 54 (58, 62) of the chart. On the next row, decrease for waist as follows: k2 tog right across row – 62 (66, 70) sts.

Waistband: Change to no 1 needles and work rows 1–9 of striped rib as before, starting on a wrong-side row. Then work rows 1–2 of rib again.

Change to no 3 needles and st st and continue in pattern from row 55 (59, 63) of the first working of the chart until you have worked row 14 (22, 30) of the second working of the chart and front measures approximately $7\frac{3}{4}$ ($8\frac{3}{4}$, $9\frac{1}{2}$)in from the top of the waistband.

Shape armhole: Continuing in pattern, bind off 8 sts at the beginning of the next (right-side) row. Then decrease one st at the armhole edge on every row until 45 (49, 53) sts remain. Then work straight in pattern for the next 32 (36, 40) rows, ending at the neck edge.

Shape neck: Continuing in pattern, bind off 3 sts at the beginning of the next (wrong-side) row. Then k2 tog at the neck edge on every row until 31 (34, 38) sts remain. Work straight in pattern until you have worked row 76 (88, 100) of the second working of the pattern chart and armhole measures approximately $7\frac{1}{2}$ ($7\frac{3}{4}$, $8\frac{3}{4}$)in from start of armhole shaping.

Shape shoulder: Continuing in pattern, bind off 8 sts at the beginning of the next and following alternate row three times. Work one row straight. Then bind off 7 (5, 7) sts at the beginning of the next row. *For the two larger sizes,* work one row purl, then bind off the remaining 5 (7) sts.

Right front

Work as for left front but reverse all shapings.

SLEEVES

With no 1 needles and yarn A, cast on 62 (62, 64) sts. Work 24 rows in striped rib as before, repeating rows 1–3 eight times, then work rows 1 and 2 again. Increase across the next (wrong-side) row as follows: (yarn A) purl 10 (10, 8) sts, *make one st, rib one st; repeat from * to last 11 (11, 9) sts, make one st, purl to end of row – 104 (104, 112) sts.

Change to no 3 needles and st st and work Fair Isle pattern from chart, beginning at row 3 (7, 11) of chart. Continue in pattern until you have worked row 14 (22, 30) of the second working of the pattern chart and the sleeve measures approximately 17 ($17\frac{1}{4}$, $17\frac{3}{4}$)in from the cast-on edge.

Shape top of sleeve: Bind off 8 sts at the beginning of the next 2 rows. Then k2 tog at each end of the next and every following alternate row 7 (10, 10) times. Work 13 (17, 16) rows straight. K2 tog at each end of the next and every following row, 10 (8, 6) times. Purl one row. Bind off remaining sts. Repeat for other sleeve.

FRONT BANDS

Begin by joining the fronts to the back at shoulders.

Left front

With no 1 needles and yarn A, and with right side facing, pick up and knit 171 (181, 191) sts down left front opening edge, from start of neck shaping to bottom edge of ribbing. Work rows 1–9 of striped rib as before. Bind off in rib in yarn A.

Right front

Beginning at bottom edge pick up and knit 171 (181, 191) sts as far as start of neck shaping. Work to correspond with left front band.

PIERROT

NECKBAND

With right side facing, using no 1 needles and yarn A, starting at inner (picked-up) edge of right front band, pick up and knit 97 (99, 101) sts around neck edge as far as inner edge of left front band, including the sts on spare needle at back of neck. Work rows 1–9 of striped rib as before. Then bind off in rib in yarn A.

FINISHING

Press all pieces lightly from wrong side, avoiding ribbing. Join both side seams and sleeve seams. Sew in sleeves, gathering fullness around top of sleeve, to fit armhole. Crochet a chain loop for button and sew to left front band at waistband. Sew on button to right front band to match. Press all seams.

Shape armhole: Continuing in pattern, bind off 10 (13) sts at the beginning of the next row. Then work armhole edge straight until you have worked row 21 of the fifth working of the pattern chart (row 7 of the sixth working of the chart) and armhole measures $4\frac{1}{4}$ ($4\frac{3}{4}$)in from the start of armhole shaping.
Shape neck: Continuing in pattern, bind off 4 sts at the beginning of the next (wrong-side) row, then decrease one st at the neck edge on the following 16 (15) rows – 38 (40) sts remain. Then work straight in pattern until you have completed row 24 of the sixth working of the pattern chart (row 8 of the seventh working of the pattern chart) and the front measures the same as the back from cast-on edge to start of shoulder shaping – approximately $19\frac{3}{4}$ ($20\frac{1}{2}$)in.
Shape shoulder: Continuing in pattern, bind off 13 (14) sts at the beginning of the next and the following alternate row. Work one row straight and then bind off 12 sts at the beginning of the next row.

Right front
Work as for left front, but reverse pocket, armhole, neck and shoulder shapings.

SLEEVES

With no 1 needles and yarn A, cast on 56 (60) sts. Work $4\frac{1}{4}$in in k1, p1 twisted rib increasing across the last (wrong-side) row as follows: rib 8 (10) sts, *rib one st, rib twice into the next st; repeat from * 19 more times, rib 8 (10) sts – 76 (80) sts. Change to no 3 needles and st st and work pattern from chart, beginning with row 13 (1) of the chart. *For the smaller size* (34in), starting at row 13 so that pattern matches at armhole, repeat sts *1–24* three times across the row and then work sts *1–4* (inclusive) to finish the row; *for the larger size* (36in), repeat sts *1–24* three times across the row and then work sts *1–8* once to finish the row. Work purl rows in reverse. Continuing in pattern shape side edges by increasing one st at each end of the 15th (3rd) row and every following fourth row until there are 130 (136) sts on the needle, taking the extra sts into the pattern as they are made. Then work straight in pattern until you have completed row 12 (24) of the sixth (fifth) working of the pattern chart. (It is the sixth working of the pattern chart for the smaller size because you have worked rows 15–24 of the first pattern, then 4 complete patterns, then rows 1–12 of the sixth.) Bind off right across row; this bound-off edge should measure $16\frac{1}{4}$ (17)in to fit armhole.
Make another sleeve in the same way.

FRONT BANDS

Right front
With no 1 needles and yarn A, and with right side of work facing, beginning at lower edge, pick up and knit 141 (148) sts up right front opening edge to start of neck shaping. Work 5 rows in twisted rib in yarn A.
Buttonholes: Make 8 buttonholes in the next row as follows: rib 3 sts, *bind off 3 sts, rib 16 (17) sts; repeat from * six more times, bind off 3 sts, rib 2 sts. Rib back along the next row, casting on 3 sts directly over those bound off in the previous row. Work 4 more rows of twisted rib in yarn A. Bind off in rib.

Left front
Work as for right front but begin at start of neck shaping and omit buttonholes.

COLLAR

With no 1 needles and yarn A, cast on 109 (113) sts. Work one row in twisted rib in yarn A. Continuing in rib in yarn A, increase one st at each end of the next and following 5 alternate rows. Then increase one st at each end of the next 6 rows – 133 (137) sts. Work 4 (6) rows straight in rib. Then decrease one st at each end of the next 6 rows, then decrease one st at each of the following 6 alternate rows – 109 (113) sts. Work a further row in rib in yarn A; then bind off in rib.

POCKETS

Pocket tops
With right side of work facing, using no 1 needles and yarn A, pick up and knit 28 (32) sts along lower bound-off edge of one pocket slit. Work 8 rows in twisted rib in yarn A, then bind off in rib. Repeat for other pocket.

FINISHING

Press all pieces lightly from wrong side, avoiding ribbing. Join side and shoulder seams. Join each sleeve seam, leaving $1\frac{1}{2}$ (2)in unstitched at the top of the seam. Pin straight edge around top of sleeve into top of armhole, and pin each side of the unstitched sleeve seam across the straight bound-off edge at the bottom of the armhole. Sew in place and repeat for other sleeve. With right side facing, pin cast-on, shaped edge of collar around neck edge, beginning and ending at start of front bands. Sew in position. Fold the collar in half so that bound-off, shaped edge just covers the first seam. Pin and sew in position. Sew down sides of pocket tops and sew around each pocket lining on wrong side. Sew on 8 buttons to left front band to match buttonholes. Cut elastic to fit around bottom of cardigan and thread through cast-on edge of welt from wrong side; secure ends of elastic.

CHITIMACHA

A men's or women's vest with a double thickness shawl collar.
A section of the pattern is used to border the pockets and armholes
and the front edges are self-faced.

MATERIALS

Yarn
Use wool fingering yarn.
Yarn A 3½oz (100g) *(rust)*
Yarn B 1oz (25g) *(mustard)*
Yarn C 1oz (25g) *(jade mix)*
Yarn D 1¾oz (50g) *(oat)*
Yarn E 3½oz (100g) *(black)*

Needles
1 pair no 3
1 pair no 2
1 pair no 1

Notions
5 buttons (leather)

MEASUREMENTS

To fit chest 34–36 (40–42)in (86–91,
102–106cm).
(See also chart on p. 120.)

Stitch gauge
30 sts and 32 rows measure 4in over Fair
Isle pattern on no 3 needles.

BACK

With no 1 needles and yarn E, cast on
120 (130) sts. Work 1½in in k1, p1 twisted
rib in yarn E, increasing 10 sts across the
last (wrong-side) row *for the larger size
only*, by working twice into every 13th st –
120 (140) sts.
Change to no 3 needles and st st and
work Fair Isle pattern from chart, reading
odd (knit) rows from right to left and even
(purl) rows from left to right. Work the
pattern across knit rows as follows: *for the
smaller size*, repeat sts 1–40 three times;
for the larger size, repeat sts 1–40 three
times and then work sts 1–20 once to
complete row. Work purl rows in reverse.
At the same time, shape the sides by
increasing one st at each end of the 5th
and every following 4th row until there
are 140 (160) sts on the needle, taking the
extra sts into the pattern as they are made.
Work straight in pattern until you have
worked row 14 (30) of the second working
of the chart and back measures approximately 10¼ (12¼)in from cast-on edge.
Shape armholes: Continuing in pattern,
bind off 16 sts at the beginning of the next
2 rows. Then decrease one st at each end
of the next 3 rows – 102 (122) sts. Now
work straight until you have completed
row 18 (46) of the third working of chart
and back measures approximately 9
(10¾)in from start of armhole shaping.
Shape shoulders: Bind off 6 (8) sts at the
beginning of the next 6 rows; then bind off
6 sts at the beginning of the following 2
rows – 54 (62) sts remain.
Shape collar: Work 12 rows straight in
pattern on these 54 (62) sts. Increase one
st at each end of next and every following
alternate row until there are 74 (82) sts on
the needle – 19 rows. Decrease one st at
each end of every following alternate row
until 56 (64) sts remain – 18 rows.
Decrease one st at each end of next row.
Work 12 rows straight. Bind off.

FRONTS

Right front
With no 1 needles and yarn E, cast on
80 (90) sts. Work 4 rows in k1, p1 twisted
rib in yarn E.
Buttonholes: Work the first buttonhole as

follows: on the next (right-side) row rib 6
sts, bind off 4 sts, rib 12 sts and bind off 4
sts; rib to end of row. On the next row,
rib to the last 25 sts, cast on 4 sts directly
over those bound off in previous row, rib
12 sts, cast on 4 sts and rib to end of row.
Continue in k1, p1 twisted rib in yarn E
until welt measures 1½in from cast-on edge.
Change to no 3 needles and st st and
work Fair Isle pattern from chart. Work
the pattern across knit rows as follows:
for the smaller size, work sts 1–40 twice;
for the larger size, work sts 1–40 twice and
then work sts 1–10 once to complete row.
Work purl rows in reverse. Increase one

st at the side seam edge on the 5th and every following 4th row, ten times in all, until there are 90 (100) sts on the needle, taking the extra sts into the pattern as they are made. *At the same time,* on row 15 (19) of the first working of the pattern chart, work the second buttonhole and the pocket opening as follows: continuing in pattern, work the first 6 sts of the row, then bind off 4 sts, work the next 10 sts, bind off 4 sts and then work pattern to the last 20 (26) sts in row. Turn and work back across next 32 sts in purl in yarn A. Turn again, join in yarn C, and work pocket lining on these 32 sts. Work 5in in st st in yarn C, ending with a knit row, so forming pocket lining. Now continue in pattern across the last 20 (26) sts of row 15 (19) from where you broke off to work pocket lining. To finish buttonhole, on the next row – row 16 (20) – work back along row in pattern until beginning of first bound-off buttonhole edge (last 24 sts in row). Cast on 4 sts directly over those bound off in row 15 (19), work the next 10 sts in pattern, cast on 4 sts over the next bound-off edge and then work the remaining 6 sts of row. Continuing in pattern, increase one st at the side edge on every 4th row until there are 90 (100) sts on needle. *At the same time,* make a buttonhole every 20 (24) rows, i.e. make third buttonhole on row 35 (43) of first working of the pattern chart, 4th buttonhole on row 55 (5) of first (second) working of chart, 5th buttonhole on row 13 (29) of the fifth working of chart. Work each buttonhole in the same way as row 15 (19), taking into account extra sts at side edge. *Meanwhile,* when there are 90 (100) sts on needle, work straight until you have completed row 13 (29) of the second working of chart and front measures approximately 10¼ (12¼)in from cast-on edge.

Shape armhole: Continuing in pattern, at the beginning of the next (wrong-side) row, bind off 16 sts and then work to end of row. Then decrease one st at the armhole edge on the next 3 rows – 71 (81) sts. Then work armhole edge straight.

Shape collar: Continuing in pattern, increase one st at the front edge on the next row – row 18 (34) of second working of pattern chart – and every following alternate row until there are 79 (89) sts on the needle. Then work straight until front measures approximately 9 (10¾)in, ending with a knit row, i.e. row 17 (45) of third working of chart.

Shape shoulder: Bind off 6 (8) sts at the beginning of the next and the following 2 alternate rows; then bind off 6 sts at the beginning of the following alternate row – 55 (59) sts. Bind off remaining sts.

Left front
Work as for right front but omit buttonholes and reverse pocket, armhole, collar

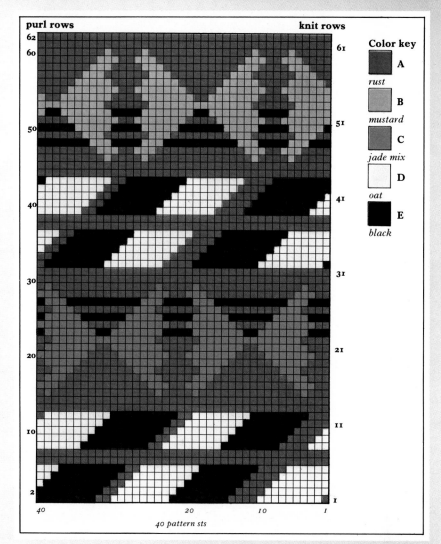

and shoulder shapings. When starting pocket lining on row 15 (19) work as follows: work the first 52 (58) sts of row in pattern; turn, purl back across the 32 sts of next row in yarn A; turn, join in yarn C and work 5in in st st, then complete pattern across remaining sts in row 15 (19) as before.

ARMHOLE BANDS

Join fronts to back at shoulders. With no 2 needles and yarn E, pick up 160 (180) sts around armhole. Work one row purl in yarn E. Turn back to chart. Work the pattern across knit rows as follows: *for the smaller size,* repeat sts 1–40 four times; *for the larger size,* repeat sts 1–40 four times, then work sts 1–20 once. Work rows 1–5 of chart. Change to yarn E and work a further row in purl in yarn E. Change to no 1 needles, work 9 rows in k1, p1 twisted rib in yarn E, to form facing. Bind off.

FINISHING

Using a bodkin or blunt needle, darn in any loose ends of yarn. Press all pieces lightly from the wrong side avoiding

ribbing. Sew side seams.

Armhole bands: Join bands at underarm points with a flat seam. Fold bands in half so that ribbing just shows at edge of armhole and pin and sew inner bound-off edge of ribbing in position around inside of armhole. Repeat for other armhole.

Front facings and buttonholes: Fold right front facing edge to inside so that buttonhole edges align and pin. Then sew this inner edge in position and oversew around the double bound-off edges of each buttonhole. Sew inner edge of left front facing in position, turning in the same amount of facing as for right front facing. Sew edges of back collar to top edge of shawl collar on right and left fronts with flat seams. Then fold entire collar over and pin and slip stitch inner edge in position inside. Oversew the sides of each pocket lining together, leaving linings free from main work. Sew on buttons to match buttonholes. Press.

WILLOW

*Chinese willow pattern in blue and white makes an ingenious
design for this simple vest. The back is worked in plain rib
and the ribbed bands are edged with navy yarn.*

MATERIALS

Yarn
Use wool fingering yarn.
Yarn A 5¼oz (150g) *(mid-blue mix)*
Yarn B 2¾oz (75g) *(ivory)*
Yarn C 1oz (25g) *(navy)*
Needles
1 pair no 3
1 pair no 1
Notions
5 buttons

MEASUREMENTS

To fit chest 36 (38)in (91, 97cm).
(See also chart on p. 120.)
Stitch gauge
32 sts and 32 rows measure 4in over
Willow pattern on no 3 needles.

FRONTS

Left front
With no 1 needles and yarn A, cast on
72 (77) sts. Work 2in in k1, p1 twisted
rib in yarn A.
Change to no 3 needles and work Willow
pattern from chart, reading odd (knit)
rows from right to left and even (purl)
rows from left to right. *For the smaller
size,* work sts 1–72 once and *for the larger
size,* work sts 1–77 once across knit rows.
Work purl rows in reverse. Continue to
work straight in pattern until you have
completed row 76 (80) of the pattern chart
and the front measures approximately
11½ (11¾)in from the cast-on edge.
Shape armhole and neck: Continuing
in pattern, bind off 10 (12) sts at the
beginning of the next row; then work
pattern across to the last 2 sts, k2 tog. Now
decrease one st at the armhole edge on the
next 21 rows and then work the armhole
edge straight. *At the same time,* continue
to decrease one st at the neck edge on
every following 4th row after the first
decrease on row 77 (81) until 27 (30) sts
remain. Then work straight in pattern
until you have completed row 62 (70) of
the second working of the pattern chart
and the front measures approximately 20
(20¾)in from the cast-on edge.
Shape shoulder: Continuing in pattern,
bind off 9 (10) sts at the beginning of the
next and following 2 alternate rows.

Right front
Work the same as left front, reversing
armhole, neck and shoulder shapings.

BACK

With no 1 needles and yarn A, cast on
148 (156) sts. Work 2in in k1, p1 twisted
rib in yarn A.
Change to no 3 needles and continue to

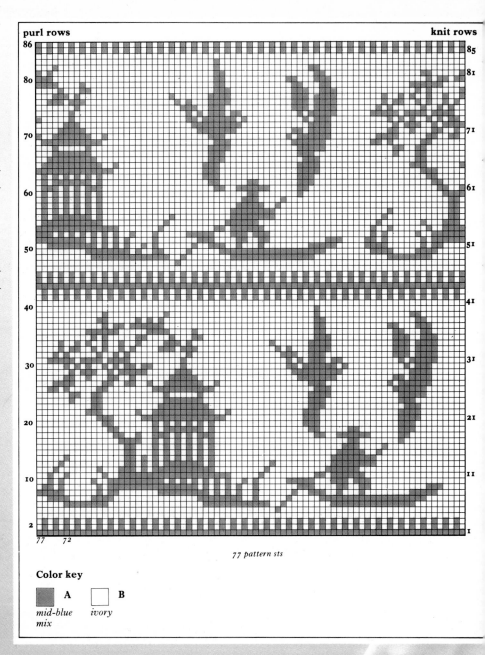

purl rows   knit rows

77 pattern sts

Color key

■ **A**
*mid-blue
mix*

□ **B**
ivory

work entire back in rib in A. Work straight
until back measures 11½ (11¾)in and matches
front from cast-on edge to start of armhole
shaping, ending on a wrong-side row.
Shape armholes: Bind off 6 sts at beginning of next 2 rows. K2 tog each end of
every row until 100 (108) sts remain. Work
straight until back matches fronts from
cast-on edge to start of shoulder shaping.
Shape shoulders: Bind off 9 (10) sts at
beginning of next 6 rows. Divide remaining 46 (48) sts in half. Leave each half on
a spare needle or stitch holder.
Join fronts to back at shoulders.

FRONT BANDS

Right front:

With right side of work facing, using no 1 needles and yarn A, beginning at the hem edge, pick up and knit 93 (97) sts up right front opening edge as far as start of neck shaping; then pick up and knit a further 100 (104) sts around neck to center-back, including the 23 (24) sts on the first spare needle. Work 3 rows in k1, p1 twisted rib.

Buttonholes: Make five buttonholes in the 4th row of ribbing as follows: rib 4 sts, *bind off 3 sts, rib 18 (19) sts; repeat from * three more times, bind off 3 sts, rib to end of row. Rib back along the 5th row of ribbing, casting on 3 sts directly over those bound off in the previous row. Work 4 more rows in rib in yarn A. Join in yarn C and work one more row in rib in yarn C. Bind off in rib in yarn C.

Left front

Work in the same way as for right front band, but begin at the center-back of neck with the remaining 23 (24) sts on spare needle and then pick up and knit 170 (177) sts to hem edge, and omit the buttonholes.

ARMBANDS

With right side of work facing, using no 1 needles and yarn A, pick up and knit 152 (160) sts around one armhole. Work 9 rows in twisted rib in yarn A. Join in yarn C and work a further row of rib in yarn C. Bind off in rib in yarn C. Repeat for other armhole.

FINISHING

Press fronts lightly from the wrong side, avoiding ribbing. Join fronts to back at side seams. Join ribbing at back of neck. Sew on buttons to left front band to correspond with buttonholes. Press seams lightly from wrong side.

ISLAMIC

A patterned vest with front pockets and striped rib back.
The pattern comes from old Islamic geometric designs
and is bordered here with chocolate brown and wine.

MATERIALS

Yarn
Use wool fingering yarn.
Yarn A 2¾ (2¾, 3½)oz (75, 75, 100g)
  (*chocolate*)
Yarn B 1¾oz (50g) (*peat*)
Yarn C 1¾oz (50g) (*wine*)
Yarn D 1oz (25g) (*powder blue*)
Yarn E 1oz (25g) (*ivory*)
Yarn F 1oz (25g) (*orange mix*)
Yarn G 1oz (25g) (*blue/orange mix*)
Yarn H 1¾oz (50g) (*lilac/green mix*)
Yarn J 1¾oz (50g) (*royal blue*)

Needles
1 pair no 3
1 pair no 2
1 pair no 1

Notions
5 buttons

MEASUREMENTS

To fit chest 32 (34, 38)in (81, 86, 96cm).
(*See also chart on p. 120.*)

Stitch gauge
32 sts and 32 rows measure 4in over Fair
Isle pattern on no 3 needles.

FRONTS

Pocket linings
Begin by making the pocket linings. With
no 2 needles and yarn A, cast on 28 (32,
36) sts and work 2¾in in st st, ending with
a purl row. Transfer the sts to a spare
needle or stitch holder. Make another
pocket lining in the same way.

Left front
**With no 1 needles and yarn A cast on
66 (72, 78) sts. Work 2in in k1, p1
twisted rib in yarn A**.
Change to no 3 needles and st st and
work Fair Isle pattern from chart, reading
odd (knit) rows from right to left and even
(purl) rows from left to right. Work the
pattern across knit rows as follows: *for the
small size* (32in), repeat sts *1–16* four
times across row and then work sts *1–2*
once; *for the medium size* (34in), repeat
sts *1–16* four times and then work sts *1–8*
once; *for the large size* (38in), repeat sts
1–16 four times and then work sts *1–14*
once. Work purl rows in reverse. Continue
in pattern until you have worked row 14
of the chart.
Pocket: Introduce pocket in row 15 as
follows: knit the first 19 (20, 21) sts of the
row, then transfer the next 28 (32, 36) sts
to a spare needle or stitch holder, and in
their place take into the pattern the 28
(32, 36) sts of one pocket lining on spare
needle; then work the remaining 19 (20,
21) sts of the row in pattern. Continuing
in pattern work straight until you have

worked row 28 (32, 36) of the second
working of the pattern chart and the front
measures approximately 11½ (11¾, 12½)in
from the cast-on edge.
Shape armhole and neck edge: At the
beginning of the next row, bind off 8 (10,
12) sts, then work in pattern to the last 2
sts; k2 tog. Continuing in pattern, decrease one st at the armhole edge on the
next 14 (16, 18) rows; then work armhole
edge straight. *At the same time,* continue
to decrease one st at the neck edge on
every following 4th row after the first
decrease on row 29 (33, 37), 8 (9, 13)
times. Then decrease one st on every
following 3rd row until 24 (26, 28) sts
remain. Work straight in pattern until you
have worked row 50 (6, 12) of the third
(fourth, fourth) working of the chart and
armhole measures approximately 8¾ (9,
9½)in from start of armhole shaping.
Shape shoulder: Continuing in pattern,
bind off 8 (10, 10) sts at the beginning of
the next row, then 8 (8, 9) sts at the beginning of the following 2 alternate rows.

Right front
Work welt as for front from ** to **.
Change to no 3 needles and st st and
work Fair Isle pattern from chart as
before. Work as for left front, introducing
remaining pocket lining and reversing all
shapings.

BACK

With no 1 needles and yarn A, cast on
132 (144, 156) sts. Work 2in k1, p1
twisted rib in yarn A.
Change to no 2 needles and continue to
work entire back in twisted rib, working
the following five-color stripe sequence:
Row 1: Yarn B
Row 2: Yarn C
Row 3: Yarn H
Row 4: Yarn J
Row 5: Yarn A
Carry yarns not in use up the sides of the
work and continue repeating these rows
1–5 until the back measures the same as
the front from the cast-on edge to the
start of the armhole shaping – approximately 11½ (11¾, 12½)in.
Shape armholes: Continuing in striped
rib, on the next right-side row, bind off
3 (4, 6) sts at the beginning of this and the
next row. Then k2 tog at each end of
every row until 100 (104, 108) sts remain.
Work straight until the back measures the
same as the front from beginning of armhole shaping to beginning of shoulder
shaping – approximately 8¾ (9, 9½)in.
Shape shoulders: Continuing in striped
rib, on the next right-side row, bind off 10
(11, 10) sts at the beginning of this and
the next row. Then bind off 9 (9, 10) sts at

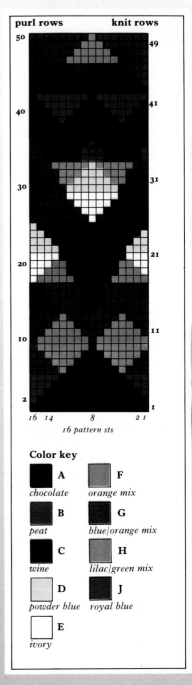

purl rows / knit rows

16 14   8   2 1
16 pattern sts

Color key

A *chocolate*   F *orange mix*
B *peat*   G *blue/orange mix*
C *wine*   H *lilac/green mix*
D *powder blue*   J *royal blue*
E *ivory*

the beginning of the following 4 rows.
Divide the remaining 44 (46, 48) sts in
half and transfer each half to a spare
needle or stitch holder.

Join fronts to back at shoulders.

FRONT BANDS

Right front

With no 1 needles and yarn A, beginning at hem edge, pick up and knit 93 (97, 101) sts up the front opening edge as far as the start of the neck shaping. Then continue to pick up and knit 81 (87, 93) sts around the neck edge as far as the center-back, including the 22 (23, 24) sts on the first spare needle – 174 (184, 194) sts in all. Work 3 rows of k1, p1 twisted rib in yarn A.

Buttonholes: Make five buttonholes in the 4th row of ribbing as follows: rib 4 sts, *bind off 3 sts, rib 18 (19, 20) sts; repeat from * 3 more times, bind off 3 sts and rib to end of row. On row 5 of ribbing, rib back, casting on 3 sts directly over each of the five bound-off stitches in the previous row. Then work 4 more rows in twisted rib in yarn A. Join in yarn C and work one row of twisted rib in yarn C. Bind off in rib in yarn C.

Left front

With no 1 needles and yarn A, beginning at the center-back of the neck, rib the 22 (23, 24) sts on the remaining needle, then pick up and knit 59 (64, 69) sts around neck to start of neck shaping and a further 93 (97, 101) sts down front opening edge to hem edge – 174 (184, 194) sts in all. Work 9 rows of twisted rib in yarn A. Join in yarn C, work one row of twisted rib and then bind off in rib in yarn C.

ARMHOLE BANDS

With no 1 needles and yarn A, and with right side facing, pick up and knit 144 (150, 156) sts around one armhole. Work 9 rows of twisted rib in yarn A. Change to yarn C and work one row of rib in yarn C. Bind off in rib in yarn C. Repeat for other armhole.

POCKETS

Pocket tops

With no 1 needles and yarn A, knit across the 28 (32, 36) sts of one pocket opening on spare needle. Then work 9 rows of twisted rib in yarn A. Change to yarn C and work a further row in twisted rib in yarn C. Bind off in rib in yarn C. Repeat for other pocket top.

FINISHING

Press fronts lightly from wrong side, avoiding ribbing. Sew ribbed borders together at center-back of neck. Join fronts to back at sides. Sew pocket linings to wrong side of vest fronts. Sew down sides of pocket tops. Sew 5 buttons to left front band to correspond with buttonholes. Press seams lightly from wrong side.

back of vest

LEAVES

A warm winter cardigan based on a Fair Isle pattern, inspired by autumn leaves and colors.

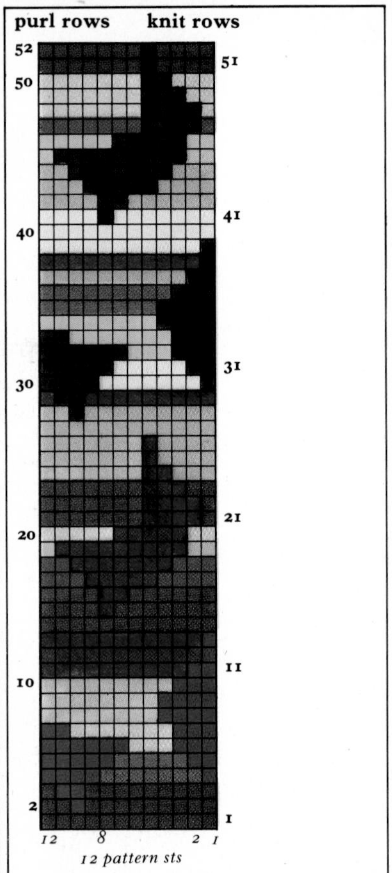

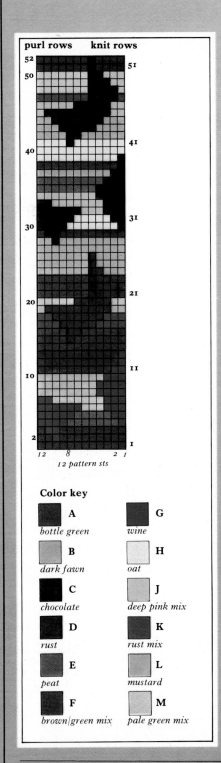

Color key

- **A** *bottle green*
- **B** *dark fawn*
- **C** *chocolate*
- **D** *rust*
- **E** *peat*
- **F** *brown/green mix*
- **G** *wine*
- **H** *oat*
- **J** *deep pink mix*
- **K** *rust mix*
- **L** *mustard*
- **M** *pale green mix*

MATERIALS

Yarn

Use wool fingering yarn.
Yarn A 3½oz (100g) *(bottle green)*
Yarn B 1oz (25g) *(dark fawn)*
Yarn C 1¾oz (50g) *(chocolate)*
Yarn D 1¾oz (50g) *(rust)*
Yarn E 1oz (25g) *(peat)*
Yarn F 1¾oz (50g) *(brown/green mix)*
Yarn G 1¾oz (50g) *(wine)*
Yarn H 1oz (25g) *(oat)*
Yarn J 1oz (25g) *(deep pink mix)*
Yarn K 1oz (25g) *(rust mix)*
Yarn L 1oz (25g) *(flax)*
Yarn M 1oz (25g) *(pale green mix)*

Needles

1 pair no 3
1 pair no 2
1 pair no 1

Notions

8 buttons

BACK

With no 1 needles and yarn A, cast on 123 (135) sts. Work 2 (2¼)in in k1, p1 twisted rib, increasing across the last (wrong-side) row as follows: rib 2 (8) sts, *rib 6 sts, rib twice into the next st; repeat from * 16 more times, rib 2 (8) sts – 140 (152) sts.

Change to no 3 needles and st st and work Fair Isle pattern from chart, reading odd (knit) rows from right to left and even (purl) rows from left to right. Work the pattern across knit rows as follows: *for the smaller size* (34in), repeat sts *1–12* eleven times across the row and then work sts *1–8* once to complete row; *for the larger size* (36in), repeat sts *1–12* twelve times across the row and then work sts *1–8* once to complete row. Work purl rows in reverse. Continuing thus in pattern work straight until you have completed row 40 of the second working of the pattern chart and the back measures approximately 13½ (13¾)in from the cast-on edge.

Shape armholes: Continuing in pattern, bind off 10 (12) sts at the beginning of the next 2 rows – 120 (128) sts remain. Now work straight until you have worked row 52 of the third working of the pattern chart (row 4 of the fourth working of the pattern chart) and the back measures approximately 20¾ (22)in from the cast-on edge.

Shape shoulders: Continuing in pattern, bind off 13 (14) sts at the beginning of the next 4 rows. Then bind off 11 (12) sts at the beginning of the following 2 rows. Bind off the remaining 46 (48) sts.

FRONTS

Pocket linings

Begin by making both pocket linings as follows: with no 2 needles and yarn A, cast on 26 (28) sts. Work 2¼in in st st, ending with a purl row.

Left front

With no 1 needles and yarn A, cast on 60 (64) sts. Work 2in in k1, p1 twisted rib, increasing across the last (wrong-side) row as follows: rib 29 (30) sts, rib twice into each of the next 2 (4) sts, rib 29 (30) sts – 62 (68) sts.

Change to no 3 needles and st st and work Fair Isle pattern from chart. Work the pattern across knit rows as follows: *for the smaller size,* repeat sts *1–12* five times across and then work sts *1–2* once; *for the larger size,* work sts *1–12* five times across and then work sts *1–8* once. Work purl rows in reverse. Continue thus in pattern until you have worked row 13 of the chart.

Pocket: Introduce the pocket in row 14 as follows: work the first 18 (20) sts in row, bind off the next 26 (28) sts and then work the pattern to end of row. Work the pattern back across the first 18 (20) sts of the next row (row 15), then continue to work pattern across the 26 (28) sts of one pocket lining on spare needle, work pattern to end of row. Continuing in pattern, work straight until you have worked row 40 of the second working of the pattern chart and the front measures approximately 13½ (13¾)in from the cast-on edge.

Shape armhole: Continuing in pattern, bind off 10 (12) sts at the beginning of the next row – 52 (56) sts. Now work straight until you have completed row 27 (31) of the third working of the pattern chart and the front measures approximately 18½ (19¼)in from cast-on edge.

Shape neck: Continuing in pattern, bind off 3 sts at the beginning of the next (wrong-side) row. Then decrease one st at the neck edge on the next 12 (13) rows – 37 (40) sts remain. Now work straight until you have worked row 52 of the third working of the chart (row 4 of the fourth working of the chart) and the front measures approximately 20¾ (22)in from cast-on edge.

Shape shoulder: Continuing in pattern, bind off 13 (14) sts at the beginning of the next and following alternate row. Work one row straight, then bind off 11 (12) sts at the beginning of the next row.

Right front

Work in the same way as left front, but reverse pocket, armhole, neck and shoulder shapings.

SLEEVES

With no 1 needles and yarn A, cast on 62 (64) sts. Work 4 (4¼)in in k1, p1 twisted rib, increasing across the last (wrong-side) row as follows: rib 4 (2) sts, *rib twice into the next st, rib 2; repeat from * 17 (19) more times, rib 4 (2) sts – 80 (84) sts.

Change to no 3 needles and st st and work pattern from chart. Work the pattern across knit rows as follows: *for the smaller size,* repeat sts *1–12* six times and then

work sts *1–8* once to complete row; *for the larger size,* work sts *1–12* seven times. Continue thus in pattern, *at the same time,* shaping the sides by increasing one st at each end of the 3rd and every following 5th row until there are 128 (134) sts on the needle. Take the extra sts into the pattern as they are made. Then work straight in pattern until you have completed row 26 of third working of the chart and sleeve measures approximately 19¾ (20)in. Bind off right across row; this bound-off edge should measure 16¼ (17)in to fit armhole.

FRONT BANDS

Right front

With right side of work facing, using no 1 needles and yarn A, beginning at the lower edge, pick up and knit 149 (157) sts up right front opening edge to start of neck shaping. Work 5 rows in k1, p1 twisted rib.
Buttonholes: Make 8 buttonholes in the next row (row 6) as follows: rib 3 (4) sts, *bind off 3 sts, rib 17 (18) sts; repeat from * six more times, bind off 3 sts, rib 3 sts. Rib back along the next row (row 7), casting on 3 sts directly over those bound off in the previous row. Work a further 4 rows in rib. Bind off in rib.

Left front

In the same way, beginning at the start of the neck shaping, pick up and knit 149 (157) sts down left front opening edge to lower edge. Work band to correspond with right front band, but omit buttonholes.

COLLAR

With no 1 needles and yarn A cast on 115 sts. Work one row in k1, p1 twisted rib. Continuing in rib, increase one st at each end of the next and following 5 alternate rows – 127 sts. Now increase one st at each end of the next 6 rows – 139 sts. Work 4in straight in twisted rib. Then k2 tog at each end of the next 6 rows, then k2 tog at each end of the next and following 5 alternate rows – 115 sts. Work one row straight in rib; bind off in rib.

POCKETS

Pocket tops

With no 1 needles and yarn A, pick up and knit 26 (28) sts across the lower bound-off edge of one pocket. Work 10 rows in k1, p1 twisted rib; bind off in rib. Repeat for other pocket.

FINISHING

Press all pieces from wrong side, avoiding all ribbing. Join shoulder seams. Join sleeve seams, leaving 1½in unstitched at top of seam. Pin top of sleeve into top of armhole and pin each side of unstitched section of sleeve seam across straight bound-off edge at bottom of armhole. Sew in position and repeat for other sleeve. With right side facing pin the cast-on and shaped edge of collar around neck edge, fitting it between the inner edges of the front bands. Sew in place and then fold collar in half so that the bound-off and

shaped edge just covers the seam. Pin this edge in position and sew neatly around neck. Sew the three sides of each pocket lining to the back of the cardigan fronts and catch down the sides of the pocket tops. Sew on 8 buttons to left front band to correspond with buttonholes. Press seams.

MEASUREMENTS

To fit chest 34 (36)in (86, 91cm).
(See also chart on p. 121.)

Stitch gauge
32 sts and 32 rows measure 4in over Fair Isle pattern on no 3 needles.

MOSAIC

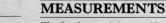

*Based on the same geometric Islamic pattern as the button-down vest,
this V-neck is ideal for both men and women.
The back is worked in striped rib.*

MATERIALS

Yarn

Use wool fingering yarn.

Yarn A 2¾oz (75g) *(navy)*
Yarn B 1¾oz (50g) *(rust)*
Yarn C 1¾oz (50g) *(olive)*
Yarn D 1 (1, 1¾)oz (25, 25, 50g) *(bottle green)*
Yarn E 1oz (25g) *(ivory)*
Yarn F 1oz (25g) *(mustard mix)*
Yarn G 1oz (25g) *(dark fawn)*
Yarn H 1oz (25g) *(sage green)*
Yarn J 1oz (25g) *(rust mix)*

Needles

1 pair no 3
1 pair no 2
1 pair no 0

MEASUREMENTS

To fit chest 36 (40, 44)in (91, 102, 112cm).
(See also chart on p. 121.)

Stitch gauge

31 sts and 30 rows measure 4in over Fair
Isle pattern on no 3 needles.

back of vest

FRONT

With no 0 needles and yarn A, cast on 130 (142, 152) sts. Work 2 (2, 2¼)in in k1, p1 twisted rib in yarn A, increasing across the last wrong-side row as follows: rib one st, *rib 8 (6, 5) sts, rib twice into the next st; repeat from * 13 (19, 23) more times, rib 3 (1, 7) sts – 144 (160, 176) sts in all. Change to no 3 needles and st st and work Fair Isle pattern from chart, reading odd (knit) rows from right to left and even (purl) rows from left to right. Repeat the 16 pattern sts indicated on chart 9 (10, 11) times across the rows. Continuing in pattern work front straight until you have worked row 42 (46, 46) of the second working of the pattern chart and the front measures approximately 13¾ (14½, 15)in from the cast-on edge.

Shape armholes and neck: Continuing in pattern, bind off 11 (13, 15) sts at the beginning of the next 2 rows. K2 tog at beginning of next row, work next 59 (65, 71) sts of row in the pattern. Turn, leaving remaining sts in row on a spare needle. Work back across these 60 (66, 72) sts in pattern. *On the next row, k2 tog, then work pattern to end. Work the pattern across the next row. K2 tog at the beginning of the next row, work pattern to the last 2 sts, k2 tog. Work the pattern across the next row*. Continuing in pattern, repeat the 4 rows from * to * until 33 (35, 41) sts remain. Work armhole edge straight but continue to k2 tog at neck edge on every 4th row as before until 27 (30, 33) sts remain. Work straight until completing row 14 (22, 30) of fourth working of chart and front measures approx. 23¼ (24½, 25½)in.
Shape shoulder: Bind off 9 (10, 11) sts at the beginning of the next and following 2 alternate rows.
Rejoin yarn to remaining sts on spare needle at neck edge and, continuing in pattern, shape right armhole and neck edge as follows: work the pattern across the next row to the last 2 sts, k2 tog. Work one row straight. **On the next row, work the pattern across to the last 2 sts, k2 tog. Work one row straight. K2 tog at the beginning of the next row, work pattern across to last 2 sts, k2 tog. Work one row straight.** Continuing in pattern, repeat these four rows from ** to **, until 33 (35, 41) sts remain. Finish to correspond with left shoulder, reversing all shapings.

BACK

With no 0 needles and yarn A, cast on 144 (160, 176) sts. Work 2 (2, 2¼)in in k1, p1 twisted rib in yarn A. Change to no 2 needles and continue to work entire back in twisted rib in the following three-color stripe sequence:
Row 1: Yarn B
Row 2: Yarn C
Row 3: Yarn A
Continue repeating rows 1–3 up the back, carrying yarns not in use up the sides of the work. Continue without shaping until back measures approximately 13¾ (14½, 15)in and matches the front from cast-on edge to start of armhole shaping, ending on a wrong-side row.
Shape armholes: Bind off 8 (10, 12) sts at the beginning of the next 2 rows. Then k2 tog at each end of every alternate row until 96 (106, 116) sts remain. Then work armhole edges straight until the back measures the same as the front from cast-on edge to start of shoulder shaping – approximately 23¼ (24½, 25½)in – ending on a wrong-side row.
Shape shoulders: Bind off 9 (10, 11) sts at the beginning of the next 6 rows. Leave the remaining 42 (46, 50) sts on a spare needle.

NECKBAND

Join right shoulder seam.
With no 0 needles and yarn A, beginning at the left shoulder and with right side of work facing, pick up and knit 70 (74, 80) sts down left side of neck to center of 'V'; mark this point with colored thread. Then pick up and knit 2 sts from center-front and mark again with colored thread. Then pick up and knit 70 (74, 80) sts up right side of neck and the 42 (46, 50) sts on spare needle around back of neck – 184 (194, 210) sts. Work the neckband in k1, p1 twisted rib in yarn A, decreasing each side of the 2 center-front sts as follows:
Row 1: Rib around back of neck and down right side of neck to within 2 sts of colored thread, slip 1, k1, psso, p2, k2 tog, rib up left side of neck to end.
Row 2: Rib down left side of neck to within 2 sts of colored thread, slip 1, k1, psso, k2, k2 tog, rib to end.
Repeat rows 1–2 four times, then work row 1 again. Join in yarn B and work one row in rib in yarn B as for row 2 above. Bind off in rib in yarn B.

ARMBANDS

Join left shoulder seam. With no 0 needles and yarn A, pick up and knit 172 (178, 186) sts around one armhole. Work 9 rows in twisted rib in yarn A. Join in yarn B and work a further row in rib in yarn B. Bind off in rib in yarn B. Repeat for other armhole.

FINISHING

Join both side seams, joining ribbing at underarm points. Press lightly.

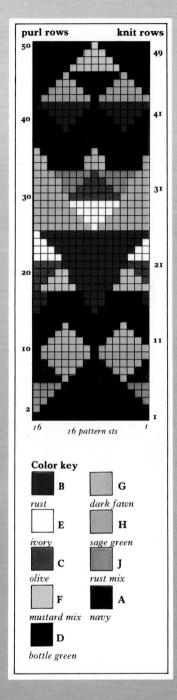

Color key

■ B	rust	□ G	dark fawn
□ E	ivory	▨ H	sage green
▨ C	olive	▨ J	rust mix
▨ F	mustard mix	■ A	navy
■ D	bottle green		

NURSERY

SUMMER SCOTTY

Black and white Scotties on a gray ground form the pattern for this short cotton cardie with three-quarter length sleeves.

MATERIALS

Yarn
Use No. 8 cotton yarn.
Yarn A 10½oz (300g) *(gray)*
Yarn B 3½oz (100g) *(black)*
Yarn C 3½oz (100g) *(white)*
Yarn D 1¾oz (50g) *(yellow)*
Yarn E 1¾oz (50g) *(lilac)*

Needles
1 pair no 3
1 pair no 2
1 pair no 0

Notions
5 buttons
1yd fine hat elastic

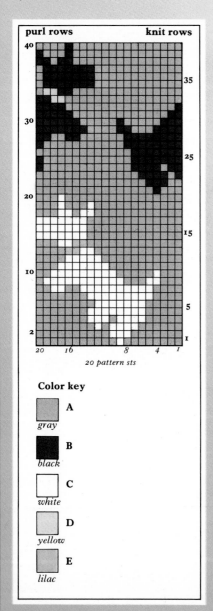

purl rows   knit rows

20 pattern sts

Color key

A
gray

B
black

C
white

D
yellow

E
lilac

MEASUREMENTS

To fit bust 34 (36)in (86, 91cm).
(See also chart on p. 121.)

Stitch gauge
30 sts and 30 rows measure 4in over Scotty pattern on no 3 needles.

BACK

With no 0 needles and yarn A, cast on 124 (128) sts. Work 2in in k1, p1 twisted rib, increasing across the last wrong-side row as follows: rib 2 (0) sts, *rib 9 (7) sts, rib twice into the next st; repeat from * 11 (15) more times, rib 2 (0) sts – 136 (144) sts.
Change to no 3 needles and st st and work Scotty pattern from chart, reading odd (knit) rows from right to left and even (purl) rows from left to right. Work the pattern across knit rows as follows: *for the smaller size* (34in), repeat the 20 pattern sts (1–20) six times across the row and then work sts 1–16 once to complete the row; *for the larger size* (36in), repeat sts 1–20 seven times and then work sts 1–4 once. Work purl rows in reverse. Continuing in pattern, work straight until you have worked row 30 of the second working of the pattern chart, and back measures approximately 11in from cast-on edge.
Shape armholes: Continuing in pattern, bind off 6 sts at the beginning of the next 2 rows. Then k2 tog at each end of every row until 100 (108) sts remain. Now work straight in pattern until you have worked row 6 (10) of the fourth working of the pattern chart and back measures approximately 18½ (19)in from cast-on edge.
Shape shoulders: Bind off 6 sts at the beginning of the next 4 rows. Then bind off 6 (7) sts at the beginning of the next 6 rows. Divide the remaining 40 (42) sts in half and transfer each half to a spare needle or stitch holder.

Pocket linings

Begin by making pocket linings. With no 2 needles and yarn A, cast on 26 (28) sts. Work 2¼in in st st ending with a purl row. Leave sts on a spare needle and make another lining in the same way.

Left front

With no 0 needles and yarn A, cast on 56 (60) sts. Work 2in in k1, p1 twisted rib increasing across the last wrong-side row as follows: rib 0 (2) sts, *rib 3 sts, rib twice into the next st, rib 3 sts; repeat from * seven more times, rib 0 (2) – 64 (68) sts.

FRONTS

Change to no 3 needles and st st and work the pattern from chart. Work the pattern across knit rows as follows: *for the smaller size* (34in), repeat sts 1–20 three times across the row and then work sts 1–4 to finish the row; *for the larger size* (36in), repeat sts 1–20 three times and then work sts 1–8 once. Work purl rows in reverse. Continue thus in pattern until you have worked row 20 of the chart.
Pocket: Introduce pocket in row 21 as follows: work the pattern across the first 19 (20) sts in the row, slip the next 26 (28) sts on to a spare needle or stitch holder and in their place work the pattern across the 26 (28) sts of one pocket lining on spare needle; continue pattern to end of row. Continue in pattern until you have worked row 22 of the second working of the pattern chart and front measures approximately 9¾in.
Shape neck: Work the pattern across the next row to the last 2 sts; k2 tog. Then work 3 rows straight. Now work these four rows again – 62 (66) sts.
Shape armhole: Continuing in pattern, bind off 6 sts at the beginning of the next row, work pattern to last 2 sts, k2 tog. Then continue to decrease one st at the neck edge on every following 4th row, 13 (14) more times. *At the same time*, decrease one st at the armhole edge on the next 12 rows – 40 (44) sts. Now work armhole edge straight, but continue to decrease one st at the neck edge on every 4th row after previous decrease, as before, 10 (11) more times – 30 (33) sts. Then work straight in pattern, until you have worked row 6 (10) of the fourth working of the pattern chart and the front measures approximately 18½ (19)in from cast-on edge.
Shape shoulder: Continuing in pattern, bind off 6 sts at the beginning of the next and following alternate row, then 6 (7) sts at the beginning of the following 3 alternate rows.

Right front

Work in the same way as left front, but reverse pocket, armhole, neck and shoulder shapings.

SLEEVES

With no 0 needles and yarn C, cast on 60 (64) sts. Work one row in k1, p1 twisted rib in yarn C. Join in yarn A and continue in rib for 2¾in, increasing across the last (wrong-side) row as follows: rib 10 (12) sts, rib twice into the next 40 sts, rib 10 (12) sts – 100 (104) sts.

Change to no 3 needles and st st and work pattern from chart as follows: *for the smaller size,* repeat sts *1–20* five times; *for the larger size,* repeat sts *1–20* five times and then work sts *1–4* once. Work purl rows in reverse. Continue to work straight in pattern until you have worked row 30 of the second working of the pattern chart and the sleeve measures approximately 11¾in from cast-on edge.

Shape top of sleeve: Continuing in pattern, bind off 6 (8) sts at the beginning of the next 2 rows. Then k2 tog at each end of the next and every following alternate row, ten times. Now work 14 (18) rows straight in pattern, and then k2 tog at each end of the next and every following alternate row 6 times. Then k2 tog at each end of the next 10 rows. Bind off the remaining 36 sts, to leave a wide edge which will be pleated into the armhole later.

Make another sleeve in the same way.

Join fronts to back at shoulders.

FRONT BANDS

Right front

With no 0 needles and yarn A, with right side of work facing and beginning at the lower edge, pick up and knit 81 sts up front opening edge as far as start of neck shaping; then pick up and knit a further 95 (99) sts around neck edge to center-back, including the 21 (22) sts on first spare needle – 176 (180) sts. Work 3 rows of k1, p1 twisted rib.

Buttonholes: Make five buttonholes in the 4th row of ribbing as follows: rib 4 sts, *bind off 3 sts, rib 15 sts; repeat from * three more times, bind off 3 sts, rib to end of row. Work back along the next row (5th row) in rib, casting on 3 sts directly over those bound off in the previous row. Work 3 further rows in rib in yarn A. Join in yarn C and work one row of rib in yarn C. Bind off in rib in yarn C.

Left front

With no 0 needles and yarn A, beginning at the center-back of neck with right side facing, rib the 21 (22) sts on remaining spare needle and then continue to pick up and knit 74 (77) sts around neck edge and a further 81 sts down front opening edge as far as hem edge. Work to correspond with right front band, omitting buttonholes.

POCKETS

Pocket tops

With no 0 needles and yarn A, with right side of work facing rib the 26 (28) sts of one pocket on spare needle. Work 9 rows in k1, p1 twisted rib in yarn A; join in yarn C and work a further row of rib in yarn C. Bind off in rib in yarn C.

FINISHING

Press all pieces lightly from wrong side, avoiding ribbing. Join fronts to back at side seams. Join both underarm sleeve seams. Pin one sleeve into one armhole, matching side and sleeve seams and pleating the fullness around the top of the sleeve to fit armhole. Sew sleeve into armhole and repeat for other sleeve. Sew down sides of pocket tops and sew the three free sides of each pocket lining to the back of cardigan fronts. Join ribbing at center-back. Sew on five buttons to left front band to correspond with buttonholes. Press seams lightly. Cut elastic to fit around bottom edge of cardigan and thread through the edge of the welt from wrong side, securing both ends.

BOYS ON BLUE

*A long-sleeved Shetland cardigan with ribbed collar
which uses the same running boys motif
as for the sweater, but here the ground is of pale blue mix.*

MATERIALS

Yarn
Use wool fingering yarn.
Yarn A 10½oz (300g) *(pale blue mix)*
Yarn B 1¾oz (50g) *(oat)*
Yarn C 1¾oz (50g) *(black)*
Yarn D 1oz (25g) *(red)*
Yarn E 1oz (25g) *(green)*
Yarn F 1oz (25g) *(mid-blue)*
Yarn G 1oz (25g) *(yellow)*
Yarn H 1oz (25g) *(rust)*
Yarn K 1oz (25g) *(royal blue)*

Needles
1 pair no 3
1 pair no 1

Notions
8 buttons

BACK

With no 1 needles and yarn A, cast on
127 (135) sts. Work 2in in k1, p1 twisted
rib in yarn A, increasing across the last
(wrong-side) row as follows: rib 4 (8) sts,
* rib 6 sts, rib twice into the next st;
repeat from * 16 more times, rib 4 (8) sts –
144 (152) sts.
Change to no 3 needles and st st and
work Boys pattern from chart, reading
odd (knit) rows from right to left and even
(purl) rows from left to right. Work the
pattern across knit rows as follows: *for the
smaller size* (34in), repeat sts *1–25* five
times across the row, then work sts *1–19*
once to complete row; *for the larger size*
(36in), repeat sts *1–25* six times, then
work sts *1–2* once to complete the row.
Work purl rows in reverse, working the
extra sts at the beginning of the row.
Continuing in pattern, work straight until
you have completed row 26 (30) of the
second working of the pattern chart and
the back measures approximately 14¼
(14½)in from the cast-on edge.
Shape armholes: Continuing in pattern,
bind off 10 (12) sts at the beginning of the
next 2 rows – 124 (128) sts. Then work
straight in pattern until you have worked
row 18 (26) of the third working of the
pattern chart, and the back measures
approximately 22½ (23¼)in.
Shape shoulders: Continuing in pattern,
bind off 14 sts at the beginning of the next
4 rows. Then bind off 11 (12) sts at the
beginning of the following 2 rows. Bind
off remaining 46 (48) sts.

FRONTS

Left front
With no 1 needles and yarn A, cast on
64 (68) sts. Work 2in in k1, p1 twisted
rib in yarn A, increasing across the last
(wrong-side) row as follows: rib 2 sts, *rib
11 (12) sts, rib twice into the next st;
repeat from * four more times, rib 2 (1)
sts – 69 (73) sts.

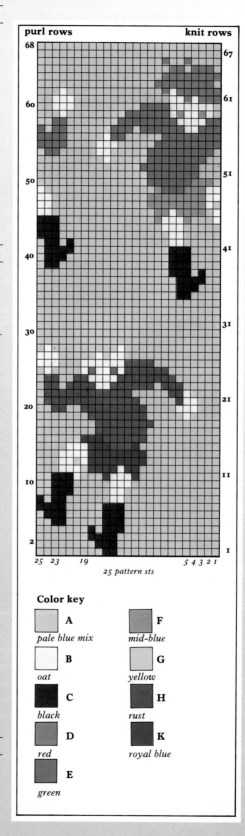

purl rows   knit rows

25 pattern sts

Color key

A *pale blue mix*		F *mid-blue*	
B *oat*		G *yellow*	
C *black*		H *rust*	
D *red*		K *royal blue*	
E *green*			

Change to no 3 needles and st st and
work Boys pattern from chart. Work
the pattern across knit rows as follows:
for the smaller size, work sts *5–25* once,
then work sts *1–25* once, and finish the
row with sts *1–23*; *for the larger size*,
work sts *3–25* once, then work sts *1–25*
twice. Work purl rows in reverse (i.e.
small size, work sts *23–1, 25–1, 25–5*;
large size, work sts *25–1* twice and *25–3*
once). Continuing in pattern, work
straight until you have worked row 26 (30)
of the second working of the pattern chart
and the front measures approximately 14¼
(14½)in from the cast-on edge.
Shape armhole: Continuing in pattern,
bind off 10 (12) sts at the beginning of the
next row – 59 (61) sts. Then work straight
in pattern until you have worked row 65
of the second working of the pattern chart
(row 5 of the third working of the pattern
chart) and front measures approximately
19¼ (20½)in from cast-on edge.
Shape neck: Bind off 4 sts at the beginning of the next row. Then k2 tog at the
neck edge on every following row, 16 (17)
times – 39 (40) sts remain. Now work
straight until you have worked row 18 (26)
of the third working of the pattern chart
and front measures approximately 22
(22¾)in from the cast-on edge.
Shape shoulder: Continuing in pattern,
bind off 14 sts at the beginning of the next
and following alternate row. Work one
row straight. Then bind off 11 (12) sts at
the beginning of the next row.

Right front
Work in the same way as left front,
but reverse armhole, neck
and shoulder shapings.

SLEEVES

With no 1 needles and yarn A, cast on 60 (64) sts. Work 4in in k1, p1 twisted rib, increasing across the last (wrong-side) row as follows: rib 0 (2) sts, *rib 3 sts, rib twice into the next st; repeat from * 14 (14) more times, rib 0 (2) sts – 75 (79) sts. Change to no 3 needles and st st and work Fair Isle pattern from chart. Work the pattern across knit rows as follows: *for the smaller size*, work sts 1–25 three times; *for the larger size*, work sts 1–25 three times and then work sts 1–4 to finish the row. Work purl rows in reverse. Continuing thus in pattern, shape the sides by increasing one st at each end of the 3rd and every following 4th row until there are 129 (135) sts on the needle. Take the extra sts into the pattern as they are made. Then work straight until you have worked row 66 of the second working of the pattern chart and the sleeve measures approximately 21¼in from the cast-on edge. Bind off right across; this bound-off edge should measure 16¼ (17)in to fit into armhole.

Make another sleeve in the same way.

FRONT BANDS

Right front

With no 1 needles and yarn A, beginning at the lower edge of right front with right side facing,

pick up and knit 143 (151) sts up front opening edge to start of neck shaping. Work 3 rows in k1, p1 twisted rib.
Buttonholes: Make 5 buttonholes in the fourth row of ribbing as follows: rib 4 (5) sts, *bind off 3 sts, rib 16 (17) sts; repeat from * six more times, bind off 3 sts, rib 3 sts. Rib back across row 5, casting on 3 sts directly over those bound off in the previous row. Work a further 4 rows in rib in yarn A. Join in yarn F and work one more row in yarn F. Bind off in rib in yarn F.

Left front

With right side of work facing, using no 1 needles and yarn A, beginning at the start of the neck shaping, pick up and knit 143 (151) sts down left front opening edge to hem edge. Finish to correspond with right front band, omitting buttonholes.

COLLAR

With no 1 needles and yarn A, cast on 113 (115) sts. Work one row in k1, p1 twisted rib. Continuing in rib in yarn A, increase one st at each end of the next and following 5 alternate rows. Then increase one st at each end of the next 6 rows – 137 (139) sts. Work 4 rows in rib without shaping. Now decrease one st at each end of the next 6 rows, then decrease one st at each end of the next and following 5 alternate rows. Work one row in rib. Bind off in rib.

FINISHING

Press all pieces lightly from wrong side, avoiding ribbing. Join fronts to back at side and shoulder seams. Join underarm sleeve seams, leaving 1¼ (1½)in unstitched at top of seam. Pin the bound-off edge around the top of the sleeve into the top of the armhole, and pin each side of the unstitched section of the sleeve seam across the straight bound-off edge at the base of the armhole. Sew sleeve in position and repeat for other sleeve.

Pin cast-on edge of collar around neck edge, starting and ending at the points where the front bands start. Stitch collar to neck and then fold the collar in half so that the bound-off edge just covers the seam of the cast-on edge. Pin in position and then slip neatly in place so that seam is covered. Sew buttons to left front band to correspond with buttonholes. Press seams lightly from wrong side.

MEASUREMENTS

To fit chest 34 (36)in (86, 91cm).
(See also chart on p. 121.)
Stitch gauge
32 sts and 30 rows measure 4in over Boys pattern on no 3 needles.

TEDDY·BEAR

Teddy-bears are the basis of this nursery pattern button-down vest.
The bears are worked against a plain ground which is bordered
with dark brown rib ; the back is worked in striped rib.

MEASUREMENTS

To fit chest 34 (36)in (86, 91cm).
(See also chart on p. 121.)

Stitch gauge

32 sts and 30 rows measure 4in over
Teddy-Bear pattern on no 3 nredles.

MATERIALS

Yarn

Use wool fingering yarn throughout.
Yarn A $2\frac{3}{4}$ ($3\frac{1}{2}$)oz (75, 100g) *(dark fawn)*
Yarn B $2\frac{3}{4}$ ($3\frac{1}{2}$)oz (75, 100g) *(chocolate)*
Yarn C 1oz (25g) *(red)*
Yarn D 1oz (25g) *(violet)*
Yarn E $1\frac{3}{4}$oz (50g) *(mid brown)*
Yarn F 1oz (25g) *(jade mix)*
Yarn G 1oz (25g) *(mid blue)*

Needles

1 pair no 3
1 pair no 2
1 pair no 1

Notions

5 × $\frac{5}{8}$in buttons

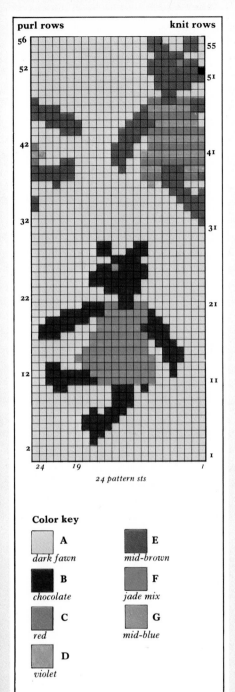

purl rows   knit rows

56   55
52   51
42   41
32   31
22   21
12   11
2   1

24   19   1

24 pattern sts

Color key

A *dark fawn*	E *mid-brown*
B *chocolate*	F *jade mix*
C *red*	G *mid-blue*
D *violet*	

FRONTS

Left front

With no 1 needles and yarn B, cast on 70 (76) sts. Work 2in in k1, p1 twisted rib in yarn B, increasing one st at each end of the final (wrong-side) row – 72 (78) sts. Change to no 3 needles and st st and work Teddy bear pattern from chart, reading odd (knit) rows from right to left and even (purl) rows from left to right. Work the pattern across knit rows as follows: *for the smaller size, repeat sts 1–24 three times; for the larger size, work sts 19–24 once, and then repeat sts 1–24 three times.* Work purl rows in reverse. Continue in pattern until you have worked row 24 (28) of the second working of the pattern chart and the front measures approximately 12¼ (13)in from cast-on edge.

Shape armhole and neck: Continuing in pattern, bind off 10 (12) sts at the beginning of the next row, then work pattern across to the last 2 sts; k2 tog. Continuing in pattern, decrease one st at the armhole edge on the next 18 (19) rows; then work armhole edge straight. *At the same time,* continue to decrease one st at neck edge on every following 4th row after the first decrease, 15 (16) times – 28 (30) sts remain. Then work neck edge straight until you have completed row 36 (42) of the third working of pattern chart and front measures approximately 21¼ (22)in from cast-on edge.

Shape shoulder: Bind off 10 sts at the beginning of the next row. Then bind off 9 (10) sts at the beginning of the following 2 alternate rows.

Right front

Work in the same way as left front, but reverse armhole, neck and shoulder shapings.

BACK

With no 1 needles and yarn B, cast on 140 (152) sts. Work 2in in k1, p1 twisted rib, increasing 4 sts across the last (wrong-side) row by working twice into every 35th (38th) st, 4 times in all – 144 (156) sts. Change to no 2 needles and continue to work entire back in twisted rib in the following three-color stripe sequence:

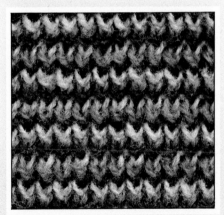

back of vest

Row 1: Yarn E
Row 2: Yarn A
Row 3: Yarn B
Carry yarns not in use up the sides of the work until required. Work straight until back measures approximately 12¼ (13)in from cast-on edge to start of armhole shaping.

Shape armholes: With right side facing, bind off 3 (4) sts at the beginning of the next 2 rows. Then k2 tog at each end of every row until 104 (110) sts remain. Work armhole edges straight until back measures approximately 21¼ (22)in and matches fronts from cast-on edge to start of shoulder shaping.

Shape shoulders: With right side of work facing, bind off 10 sts at the beginning of the next 2 rows; then bind off 9 (10) sts at the beginning of the following 4 rows. Divide the remaining 48 (50) sts equally in half and transfer each half to a spare needle or stitch holder.

Join fronts to back at shoulders.

FRONT BANDS

Right front

Using no 1 needles and yarn B and with the right side of the work facing, beginning at lower edge, pick up and knit 101 (105) sts up right front opening edge as far as start of neck shaping. Then continue to pick up and knit 84 (88) sts around neck edge as far as center-back, including the 24 (25) sts on the first spare needle – 185 (193) sts in all. Work 3 rows of k1, p1 twisted rib in yarn B.

Buttonholes: Make 5 buttonholes in the 4th row of ribbing as follows: rib 4 sts, bind off 3 sts, rib 20 (21) sts; repeat from * 3 more times, bind off 3 sts and then rib to end of row. Rib back across the next row (row 5) as before, but cast on 3 sts directly over those bound off in the previous row. Then work 4 more rows in rib in yarn B. Join in yarn E and work one row in rib in yarn E. Bind off in yarn E.

Left front

Beginning at the center-back with yarn B, rib the 24 (25) sts on the remaining spare needle; then pick up and knit 60 (63) sts around neck edge to start of neck shaping and a further 101 (105) sts down front to lower edge. Work to correspond with right front band, but omit buttonholes.

ARMHOLE BANDS

With no 1 needles and yarn B and with the right side of the work facing, pick up and knit 155 (163) sts around one armhole. Work to correspond with left front band. Repeat for other armhole.

FINISHING

Join fronts to back at either side as for shoulders. Press Fair Isle parts and seams carefully from wrong side, avoiding all ribbing. Join ribbing at back of neck. Sew on the 5 buttons to left front band to correspond with buttonholes.

SEAGULLS

Seagulls sweeping against a blue sky lend this boat neck sweater
a nautical flavor. It is an ideal sailing sweater for men or women.

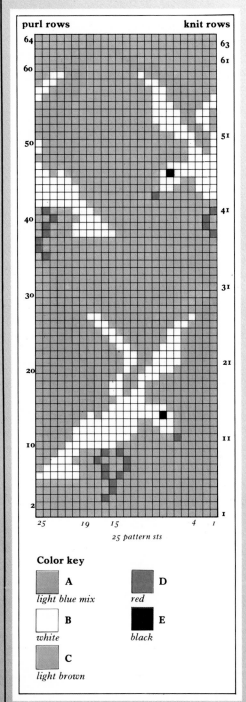

purl rows   **knit rows**

64   63
  61
60
  51
50
  41
40
  31
30
  21
20
  11
10
  1
2

25   19   15   4   1

25 pattern sts

Color key

A — *light blue mix*

D — *red*

B — *white*

E — *black*

C — *light brown*

MATERIALS

Yarn
Use wool fingering yarn.
Yarn A 6¼ (6¼, 7)oz (175, 175, 200g) *(light blue mix)*
Yarn B 3½oz (100g) *(white)*
Yarn C 3½ (3½, 4½)oz (100, 100, 125g) *(light brown)*
Yarn D 1oz (25g) *(red)*
Yarn E 1oz (25g) *(black)*
Needles
1 pair no 3
1 pair no 0

MEASUREMENTS

To fit chest 34 (36, 42)in (86, 91, 107cm). *(See also chart on p. 122.)*
Stitch gauge
32 sts and 32 rows measure 4in over Seagull pattern on no 3 needles.

BACK and FRONT

Work the back and front in the same way. With no 0 needles and yarn C, cast on 130 (136, 149) sts. Work 3¼in in k1, p1 twisted rib, increasing across the last wrong-side row as follows: rib 2 (5, 10) sts, *rib twice into the next st, rib 8 (6, 4) sts; repeat from * 13 (17, 25) more times, rib 2 (5, 9) sts – 144 (154, 175) sts. Change to no 3 needles and st st and work Seagull pattern from chart, reading odd (knit) rows from right to left and even (purl) rows from left to right. Work the pattern across knit rows as follows: *for the small size (34in),* repeat sts *1–25* five times across the row and then work sts *1–19* once to complete row; *for the medium size (36in),* repeat sts *1–25* six times and then work sts *1–4* once; *for the large size (42in),* repeat sts *1–25* seven times. Work purl rows in reverse. Continue thus in pattern until you have worked row 26 (26, 46) of the second working of the pattern chart and the work measures approximately 14¼ (14¼, 16½)in from cast-on edge.
Shape armholes: Continuing in pattern, bind off 10 (12, 16) sts at the beginning of the next 2 rows – 124 (130, 141) sts. Then work straight in pattern until you have worked row 64 (2, 34) of the second (third, third) working of the pattern chart and the work measures approximately 19 (19, 22¾)in from cast-on edge. Join in yarn C and work top yoke in yarn C as follows: knit one row, then work 4¼in in k1, p1 twisted rib, ending with a wrong-side row. Join in yarn B, and work the next (right-side) row in rib in yarn B. Bind off in rib in yarn B.

SLEEVES

With no 0 needles and yarn B, cast on 60 (62, 71) sts. Work one row in k1, p1 twisted rib in yarn B. Join in yarn C and work a further 4 (4¼, 4¼)in in twisted rib in yarn C, increasing across the last wrong-side row as follows: rib 2 (2, 7) sts, *rib 2 sts, rib twice into the next st; repeat from * eighteen more times, rib 1 (1, 7) sts – 79 (79, 90) sts. Change to no 3 needles and st st and work Seagull pattern from chart. Work the pattern across knit rows as follows: *for the small and medium sizes,* repeat sts *1–25* three times, then work sts *1–4* once; *for the large size,* work sts *1–25* three times, then work sts *1–15* once. Work purl rows in reverse. Continue thus in pattern, *at the same time,* shaping the sides by increasing one st at each end of the 3rd and every following 4th row until there are 135 (139, 148) sts on the needle. Take the extra sts into the pattern as they are made. Then work straight in pattern until you have completed the second working of the pattern chart. *For the large size only,* work an extra 2 rows in st st and yarn A only. The sleeve should now measure approximately 19¾ (19¾, 20)in from the cast-on edge. Bind off right across row, fairly loosely; this bound-off edge should measure approximately 17 (18, 19¼)in to fit into armhole.

FINISHING

Press all pieces lightly from wrong side, avoiding ribbing. Join front to back at side seams. Overlap the edge of the front neck welt and the back neck welt by ¾in and hold each side with a pin. Lift the front welt slightly and sew the underneath of the front welt to the back welt for about 2in from outside shoulder edge, so that stitches do not show on right side. Repeat for other shoulder. Join sleeve seams, leaving 1¼ (1½, 2)in of sleeve seam unstitched at top of seam. Pin top of sleeve into top of armhole and pin either side of the unstitched section of sleeve seam across the straight bound-off edge at the bottom of armhole. Sew in position and repeat for other sleeve. Press seams lightly from wrong side.

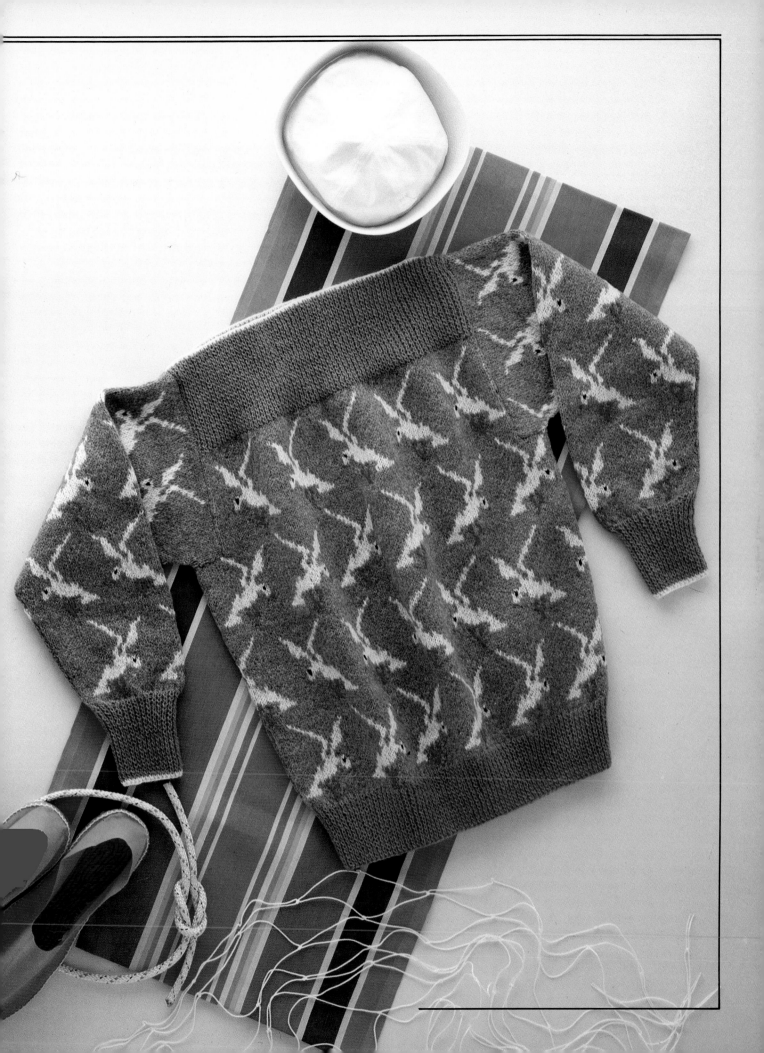

STARING CATS

*Black Cats with eager yellow eyes on a ground of pink and blue
form the pattern for this men's or women's
loose-fitting crew neck sweater.*

MEASUREMENTS

To fit chest 34 (36, 38, 40)in (86, 91,
97, 101cm).
(See also chart on p. 122.)
Stitch gauge
32 sts and 30 rows measure 4in over Cats
pattern on no 3 needles.

MATERIALS

Yarn
Use wool fingering yarn.
Yarn A 7 (7, 8, 8¾)oz (200, 200, 225, 250g)
(red/blue mix)
Yarn B 3½ (3½, 3½, 4½)oz (100, 100, 100,
125g) *(mid-blue mix)*
Yarn C 1¾ (1¾, 2¾, 2¾)oz (50, 50, 75, 75g)
(ivory)
Yarn D 1¾ (1¾, 2¾, 2¾)oz (50, 50, 75, 75g)
(black)
Yarn E 1oz (25g) *(rust)*
Yarn F 1oz (25g) *(yellow)*
Needles
1 pair no 3
1 pair no 1

BACK

**With no 1 needles and yarn A, cast on
120 (128, 138, 148) sts. Work 2 (2, 2¼,
2¼)in in k1, p1 twisted rib in yarn A,
increasing across the last (wrong-side) row
as follows: rib 0 (9, 3, 8) sts, *rib 5 (4, 5,
5) sts, rib twice into the next st; repeat
from * 19 (21, 21, 21) more times, rib 0 (9,
3, 8) sts – 140 (150, 160, 170) sts in all.
Change to no 3 needles and st st and
work Cats pattern from chart, reading
odd (knit) rows from right to left and even
(purl) rows from left to right. Work the
pattern across knit rows as follows: *for
size 34in*, repeat the basic 20 pattern sts
seven times across the row; *for size 36in,*

repeat sts *1–20*, seven times across the row and then work sts *1–10* once; *for size 38in*, work sts *1–20*, eight times across the row; *for size 40in*, work sts *1–20*, eight times across the row and then work sts *1–10* once. Work purl rows in reverse. Continue to work pattern thus, until you have worked row 20 (24, 24, 28) of the third working of the pattern chart and back measures approximately 16½ (17, 17¼, 18)in.

Shape armholes: Bind off 12 (13, 14, 15) sts at the beginning of the next 2 rows.** Then work straight in pattern until you have worked row 38 (46, 46, 46) of the fourth working of the pattern chart and back measures approximately 24¾ (26, 26½, 26½)in. *For the larger size* (size 40in), continue in st st and yarn A only (to avoid having a broken pattern at shoulder edge) until back measures 26¾in from cast-on edge, ending on a wrong-side row. Then continue as follows for all sizes.

Shape shoulders: Bind off 13 (14, 15, 15) sts at the beginning of the next 2 rows. Then bind off 11 (12, 13, 14) sts at the beginning of the next 4 rows. Leave the remaining 46 (48, 50, 54) sts on a spare needle or stitch holder.

FRONT

Work as for back from ** to ** – 116 (124, 132, 140) sts. Continuing in pattern work straight until you have worked row 14 (18, 18, 22) of the fourth working of the pattern chart, and front measures approximately 21¾ (22, 22½, 23¼)in from the cast-on edge.

Shape neck: On the next row, work the first 43 (46, 49, 52) sts of the row in the pattern and then turn, leaving the remaining 73 (78, 83, 88) sts on a spare needle. Continue to work pattern on these 43 (46, 49, 52) sts and decrease one st at the neck edge on the next 8 (8, 8, 9) rows – 35 (38, 41, 43) sts remain. Then work neck edge straight, continuing in pattern for the two smaller sizes and working a few rows in yarn A for the two larger sizes, until the front measures the same as the back from the cast-on edge to the start of the shoulder shaping, ending on a wrong-side row – approximately 24¾ (26, 26½, 26¾)in.

Shape shoulder: Bind off 13 (14, 15, 15) sts at the beginning of the next row. Then bind off 11 (12, 13, 14) sts at the beginning of the following two alternate rows, so completing left shoulder edge. Rejoin yarn to remaining sts on spare

needle. Bind off the first 30 (32, 34, 36) sts to form neck edge and then work the pattern to the end of the row. Finish right shoulder to correspond with left shoulder, reversing neck and shoulder shapings.

SLEEVES

With no 1 needles and yarn A, cast on 58 (60, 62, 64) sts. Work 4in in k1, p1 twisted rib in yarn A. Increase across the next wrong-side row as follows: rib 10 sts, rib twice into each of the next 38 (40, 42, 44) sts, rib 10 sts – 96 (100, 104, 108) sts in all.
Change to no 3 needles and st st and work the next 8 rows in the following stripe sequence:
Row 1: (Yarn D) knit.
Row 2: (Yarn F) purl.
Row 3: (Yarn E) knit.
Row 4: (Yarn D) purl.
Row 5: (Yarn F) knit.
Row 6: (Yarn E) purl.
Row 7: (Yarn D) knit.
Row 8: (Yarn A) purl.
Then continue to work sleeve in st st in yarn A only. Shape sides by increasing one st at each end of the next and every following 8th row until there are 116 (124, 132, 140) sts on the needle. Then work straight until sleeve measures 20½ (20½, 21¼, 21¼)in from the cast-on edge. Bind off right across this edge, taking into account that this edge should measure approximately 15¾ (17, 18, 19)in to fit armhole. Make another sleeve in the same way.

NECKBAND

Join right shoulder seam.
With no 1 needles and yarn A, beginning at left shoulder, pick up and knit 27 (29, 31, 33) sts down left side of neck, 28 (30, 32, 34) sts across center-front bound-off edge, 27 (29, 31, 33) sts up right side of neck to right shoulder seam, and then the 46 (48, 50, 54) sts on the spare needle at the back of the neck – 128 (136, 144, 154) sts in all. Work 12 rows in k1, p1 twisted rib in yarn A. Bind off in rib in yarn A.

FINISHING

Press all pieces lightly from the wrong side, avoiding ribbing. Join left shoulder seam and neckband. Join side seams and sleeve seams, leaving 1½ (1½, 1½, 2)in unstitched at the top of the sleeve seam. (This unstitched section will then fit straight bound-off edge at the bottom of the armhole.) Pin bound-off edge of sleeve top into top of armhole easing edges if necessary, and pin the unstitched sides of the sleeve seam across the straight edge at the bottom of the armhole. Sew in position and repeat for other sleeve. Press seams from wrong side.

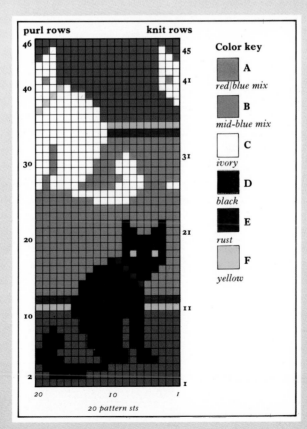

purl rows	knit rows
46	45
40	41
30	31
20	21
10	11
2	1

20   10   1

20 pattern sts

Color key

A
red/blue mix

B
mid-blue mix

C
ivory

D
black

E
rust

F
yellow

95

BOYS ON BLACK

*This crew neck sweater uses the running boys motif,
set here against a black background which emphasises the pattern.
The neck and cuff ribbing are edged with contrasting yarn.*

MATERIALS

Yarn
Use wool fingering yarn.
Yarn A 8¾ (9¾)oz (250, 275g) *(black)*
Yarn B 1¾oz (50g) *(bluebell)*
Yarn C 1oz (25g) *(rust)*
Yarn D 1oz (25g) *(yellow)*
Yarn E 1¾oz (50g) *(red)*
Yarn F 1oz (25g) *(leaf green)*
Yarn G 1oz (25g) *(sand)*

Needles
1 pair no 3
1 pair no 2
1 pair no 1
1 set of four no 1 double-pointed needles
or no 1 circular needle.

MEASUREMENTS

To fit chest 34–36 (38–40)in (86–91, 97–102cm).
(See also chart on p. 122.)

Stitch gauge
30 sts and 28 rows measure 4in over Fair Isle pattern on no 3 needles.

BACK

**With no 1 needles and yarn A, cast on 135 (150) sts. Work 2in in k1, p1 twisted rib in yarn A, increasing across the last (wrong-side) row as follows: *p8 (5), purl twice into the next st; repeat from * to end of row – 150 (175) sts.
Change to no 3 needles and st st and work Fair Isle pattern from chart, reading odd (knit) rows from right to left and even (purl) rows from left to right. Repeat the 25 pattern sts six (seven) times across the rows. Continue straight in pattern until you have worked row 38 (42) of the second working of the pattern chart, and the back measures approximately 17 (17¾)in from cast-on edge.
Shape armholes: Continuing in pattern, bind off 10 (15) sts at the beginning of the next 2 rows** – 130 (145) sts. Then work straight until you have worked row 28 (36) of the third working of the pattern chart and work measures approximately 25¼ (26½)in from cast-on edge.
Shape shoulders: Continuing in pattern, bind off 15 sts at the beginning of the next 2 rows. Then bind off 13 (15) sts at the beginning of the next 4 rows. Transfer the remaining 48 (55) sts to a spare needle or stitch holder.

FRONT

Work as for back from ** to ** – 130 (145) sts. Then work straight in pattern until you have worked row 68 of the second working of the pattern chart (row 8 of the third working of the pattern chart) and front measures approximately 21¼ (22½)in from cast-on edge.
Shape neck: On the next (right-side) row, work the first 47 (53) sts of the pattern, and transfer them to a spare needle or stitch holder; then bind off the next 36 (39) sts; continue in pattern across remaining 47 (53) sts of row. Con-

tinue to shape neck on these last 47 (53) sts, decreasing one st at the neck edge on the next 6 rows. Then work straight in pattern on these remaining sts until the right front measures the same as the back from the cast-on edge to start of shoulder shaping – approximately 25¼ (26½)in.
Shape shoulders: With wrong side facing, bind off 15 (17) sts at beginning of next row, then bind off 13 (15) sts at beginning of the following 2 alternate rows. With wrong side facing, rejoin yarn to the 47 (53) sts of the left front on the remaining spare needle at neck edge. Work left front to correspond with right front, reversing the neck and shoulder shapings.

SLEEVES

With no 1 needles and yarn C, cast on 60 (66) sts and work one row in k1, p1 twisted rib in yarn C. Join in yarn A and continue in twisted rib until the work measures 3½in.
Change to no 3 needles and work the entire sleeve in st st and yarn A. Shape sides of sleeve by increasing one st at the end of the first and every following 4th row, until there are 130 (136) sts on the needle. Then work a few rows straight until the sleeve measures 20¾in from the cast-on edge. Bind off fairly loosely across the row. (This bound-off edge across top of sleeve joins with the straight edge around the top of the armhole. The last 1½ (2)in of underarm sleeve seam will join with the 10 (15) bound-off sts at the bottom of the armhole.)
Make another sleeve in the same way.

NECKBAND

Join front to back at the shoulders. Using the four no 1 double-pointed needles or circular needle, beginning at the left shoulder seam and using yarn A, pick up and knit 33 sts down left side of the neck, 34 (37) sts across the bound-off edge at center-front, 33 sts up the right side of the neck and finally the 48 (55) sts from the spare needle at the back of the neck – 148 (158) sts in all. Then work 10 rounds in k1, p1 twisted rib in yarn A. Join in yarn C and work one further round of twisted rib in yarn C. Bind off in rib in yarn C.

FINISHING

Press all pieces carefully from the wrong side, avoiding ribbing. Join front to back at the side seams. Join sleeve seams in the same way, leaving the last 1½ (2)in at the top of the seam unstitched. Pin the straight bound-off edge at the top of the sleeve into the top of the armhole, easing sleeve head if necessary; pin either side of the unstitched 1½ (2)in of sleeve seam across straight bound-off edge at the bottom of armhole. Sew in position and repeat for other sleeve. Press seams.

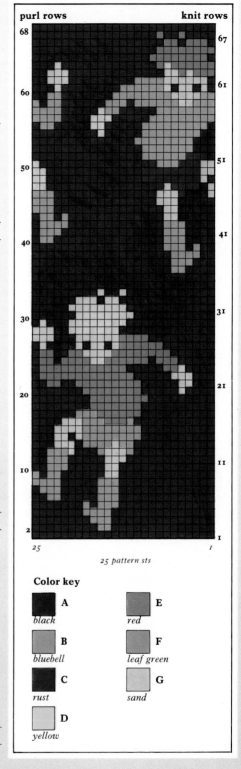

purl rows   **knit rows**

25 pattern sts

Color key

■ A *black*		■ E *red*	
■ B *bluebell*		■ F *leaf green*	
■ C *rust*		☐ G *sand*	
☐ D *yellow*			

BUTTERFLIES

*Blue and yellow Butterflies against meadow shades of green and beige
form the pattern of this one-size vest. The vest is worked in one piece
as far as the armholes and bordered with cable pattern.*

MATERIALS

Yarn
Use wool fingering yarn.
Yarn A 3½oz (100g) *(olive mix)*
Yarn B 1oz (25g) *(light brown)*
Yarn C 1oz (25g) *(mustard)*
Yarn D 1oz (25g) *(light blue)*
Yarn E 1oz (25g) *(bright blue)*
Yarn F 1oz (25g) *(orange mix)*
Yarn G 1¾oz (50g) *(chocolate)*
Yarn H 2¾oz (75g) *(oat)*

Needles
1 pair no 4
1 pair no 3
1 circular needle no 3
1 circular needle no 1
1 cable needle

Notions
5 × ⅝ buttons

MEASUREMENTS

One-size: to fit chest 34–36in (86–91cm).
(See also chart on p. 122.)

Stitch gauge
32 sts and 32 rows measure 4in over Fair
Isle pattern on no 3 needles.
Note: The front and back of the vest are
knitted in one piece using a circular
needle, until the start of the armhole
shaping; knit as usual in rows.

BACK and FRONTS

With the no 1 circular needle and yarn
A, cast on 284 sts. Work 4in in k1, p1
twisted rib in yarn A. On the last (wrong-
side) row, increase as follows: *p9, purl
twice into the next st, p4; repeat from *
across row until last 4 sts; p4 – 304 sts in all.
Change to the no 3 circular needle and
st st and work pattern from chart. Read
odd (knit) rows from right to left and even
(purl) rows from left to right. Work the
extra 2 sts indicated (sts *1–2*) at the beginning of knit rows; then work the basic 30
sts (sts *3–32*) indicated, ten times across
the row and finish the row with sts *33* and
34. Work purl rows in reverse, starting
with sts *34–33* and finishing with sts *2–1*.
Continue thus in pattern until you have
completed row 64 of first working of
pattern chart, and the work measures
approximately 11¾in from cast-on edge.

Shape neck and armhole: To shape
neck edge k2 tog at each of the next and
every following 3rd row. *At the same time,*
when you have completed row 16 of the
second working of the pattern chart and
the work measures approximately 14½in
from cast-on edge, divide work for armholes as follows: on the next row, change
to the pair of no 3 needles and work the
first 65 sts of the row, then turn, leaving
the remaining sts in the row on a spare
needle.

Row 9: Knit
Row 10: K3, p6, k3
These 10 rows form the cable pattern.
Work rows 1–4 again.
Buttonholes: Make 4 buttonholes in the next row as follows:
Row 5: *K5, bind off 2, k5
Row 6: K3, p2, cast on 2, p2, k3
Then work 28 rows straight in cable pattern*. Repeat from * to * twice more, then make one more buttonhole in the next 2 rows as before.
Continue straight in cable pattern (repeating rows 1–10 and omitting buttonholes), until strip is long enough to fit from lower edge, up right front, around back of neck and down left front, slightly stretching the strip as you measure. Then bind off.

Armholes

With no 4 needles and yarn A, cast on 12 sts. Work rows 1–10 of the cable pattern as before, repeating them until the strip measures 20in. Then bind off. Make another strip in the same way.

FINISHING

Press the vest lightly from the back avoiding all ribbing.
Front borders: Pin cable strip around front opening edges and neck, so that the top buttonhole is just below the start of the neck shaping on the right front. Attach to main body of vest with a flat seam sewn from the wrong side. Sew five buttons to left front border, to match buttonholes.
Armhole borders: Overlap the short ends of one armhole border piece, so right sides of both ends face uppermost, to form a 'V' (see p. 140). Hold a pin and then neatly sew around the sides of the over-lapping ends to hold them together. Pin the complete cable strip around one armhole, with right sides together, fitting the point of the 'V' where the ends join into the base of the armhole. Oversew borders to main work sewing from the wrong side with matching yarn. Repeat for other armhole, and press seams lightly from wrong side.

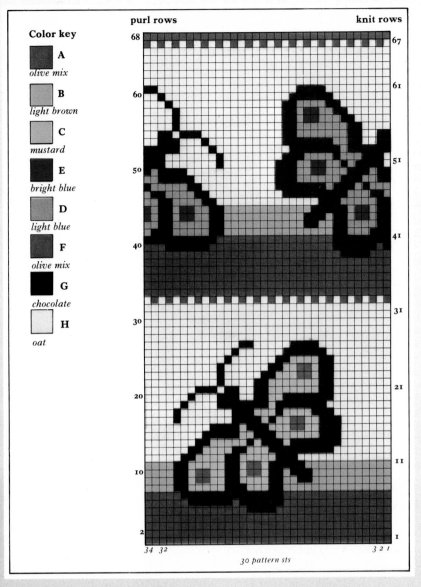

Color key

■	**A**	*olive mix*
■	**B**	*light brown*
□	**C**	*mustard*
■	**E**	*bright blue*
■	**D**	*light blue*
■	**F**	*olive mix*
■	**G**	*chocolate*
□	**H**	*oat*

purl rows   knit rows

30 pattern sts

Right front

Continuing in pattern on these first 65 sts, decrease one st at the front edge on the next and every following 3rd row, as before, until 40 sts remain. Then work straight until you have completed row 27 of the third working of pattern chart, and the front measures approximately 24in from the cast-on edge. With the wrong side facing, bind off right across the row. Now turn to the remaining sts on the spare needle. Work the next 160 sts in the row (row 17). Then turn, leaving the remaining 65 sts on a spare needle. Work the pattern across the 160 sts to form back. Continue in pattern until you have worked row 28 of the third working of the pattern chart, and back measures approximately 24in from the cast-on edge. Then bind off.

Left front

With right side of work facing join the yarn to remaining 65 sts on spare needle. Work across row (row 17 of pattern chart) from armhole edge to neck edge, shaping neck edge in the same way as for right

front. Work to correspond with right front, ending with row 27 of the third working of the pattern chart and reversing neck shaping. Bind off across row.

CABLE BORDERS

Note: To work the instruction 'cable 6' (see row 7 below), slip the next 3 sts in the row on to a cable needle and hold to the front of the work; knit the next 3 sts, then knit the 3 sts from the cable needle.

Join fronts to back at shoulder seams.

Fronts

With no 4 needles and yarn A, cast on 12 sts. Then work border as follows:
Row 1: Knit
Row 2: K3, p6, k3
Row 3: Knit
Row 4: K3, p6, k3
Row 5: Knit
Row 6: K3, p6, k3
Row 7: K3, cable 6, k3
Row 8: K3, p6, k3

DACHSHUND

Busy Dachshunds trot across the fronts of this dashing vest,
which has two front pockets and a striped rib back. The background color
could be lightened to give a more distinctive pattern.

MATERIALS

Yarn
Use wool fingering yarn.
Yarn A 3½oz (100g) *(sand)*
Yarn B 2¾oz (75g) *(rust/blue mix)*
Yarn C 1oz (25g) *(chocolate)*
Yarn D 1oz (25g) *(mid-brown mix)*
Yarn E 1oz (25g) *(rust)*

Needles
1 pair no 3
1 pair no 2
1 pair no 1

Notions
5 buttons

MEASUREMENTS
To fit chest 32 (34, 36)in (81, 86, 96cm).
(See also chart on p. 122.)

Stitch gauge
32 sts and 30 rows measure 4in over
Dachshund pattern on no 3 needles.

FRONTS

Left front
With no 1 needles and yarn B, cast on
66 (72, 78) sts. Work 2in in k1, p1
twisted rib in yarn B.
Change to no 3 needles and st st and
work the Dachshund pattern from the
chart, reading odd (knit) rows from right
to left and even (purl) rows from left to
right. Work the pattern across knit rows
as follows: *for the small size* (32in), work
sts 1–36 once and then work sts 1–30 once
to finish the row; *for the medium size*
(34in), repeat sts 1–36 twice; *for the
large size* (36in), repeat sts 1–36 twice
and then work sts 1–6 once to finish
the row. Work purl rows in reverse.
Continue thus in pattern until you have
completed row 16 of the pattern chart.
Pocket: Introduce pocket in the next row
(row 17) as follows: work the first 19 (20,
21) sts of the row, bind off the next 28
(32, 36) sts and then work the pattern to
the end of the row. On the next row (row
18), work the pattern across the first 19
(20, 21) sts in the row, cast on 28 (32, 36)
sts over those bound off in the previous
row and then work the pattern to the end
of the row.
Work straight in pattern until you have
worked row 10 (14, 18) of the third working of the pattern chart and the front
measures approximately 11¾ (12¼, 12½)in.
Shape armhole and neck: Bind off 12
(13, 14) sts at the beginning of the next
row (row 11, 15, 19 of chart); then work
pattern to the last 2 sts; k2 tog. Continuing in pattern, decrease one st at the armhole edge on the next 15 (16, 17) rows.
Then work armhole edge straight. *At the
same time,* continue to decrease one st at
the neck edge on every following 4th row

after the first decrease row until 24 (27,
30) sts remain on the needle. Then work
straight in pattern until you have worked
row 8 (16, 24) of the fifth working of the
pattern chart and the front measures
approximately 19¾ (20¾, 21¾)in from the
cast-on edge.
Shape shoulder: Continuing in pattern,
bind off 12 (13, 14) sts at the beginning of
the next (right-side) row, then work
pattern to end of row. On the next row,
slip one st, then work pattern to end. Bind
off remaining sts.

Right front
Work as for left front, but reverse pocket,
armhole, neck and shoulder shapings.

BACK
With no 1 needles and yarn B, cast on
132 (144, 156) sts. Work 2in in k1, p1
twisted rib in yarn B. Change to no 2
needles and continue to work entire back
in twisted rib in the following three-color
stripe sequence:
Row 1: Yarn B
Row 2: Yarn C
Row 3: Yarn A
Carry wools not in use up the sides of the
work until required. Continue repeating
rows 1–3 of stripe pattern until the back
measures the same as the fronts from cast-
on edge to start of armhole shaping,
ending on a wrong-side row – approximately 11¾ (12¼, 12½)in.
Shape armholes: Bind off 3 (4, 6) sts at
the beginning of the next and following
row. Then k2 tog at each end of every
row until 100 (104, 108) sts remain on the
needle. Continuing in stripes, work

straight until back measures the same as
the fronts from cast-on edge to start of
shoulder shaping, ending on a wrong-side
row – approximately 19¾ (20¾, 21¾)in.
Shape shoulders: Continuing in pattern,
bind off 9 (10, 10) sts at the beginning of
the next 2 rows. Then bind off 9 (9, 10)
sts at the beginning of the next 4 rows.
Divide the remaining 44 (48, 50) sts in
half and transfer each half to a spare
needle or stitch holder.

Join fronts to back at shoulders.

FRONT BANDS

Right front
With right side of work facing, and using
no 1 needles and yarn B, beginning at
lower edge, pick up and knit 97 (101, 105)
sts up front opening edge to start of neck
shaping. Then pick up and knit a further
82 (88, 93) sts around neck to center-back,
including the 22 (24, 25) sts on the first
spare needle – 179 (189, 198) sts in all.
Work 3 rows in k1, p1 twisted rib in
yarn B.
Buttonholes: Make 5 buttonholes in the
4th row of ribbing as follows: rib 4 sts,
bind off 3 sts, rib 19 (20, 21) sts; repeat
from * 3 more times, bind off 3 sts and rib
to end of row. On the next row, work back
in rib but cast on 3 sts directly over those
bound off in previous row. Work 4 more
rows in rib in yarn B. Join in yarn C and
work one row in rib in yarn C. Bind off in
rib in yarn C.

Left front
Beginning at the center-back of neck, rib
the 22 (24, 25) sts on the remaining spare

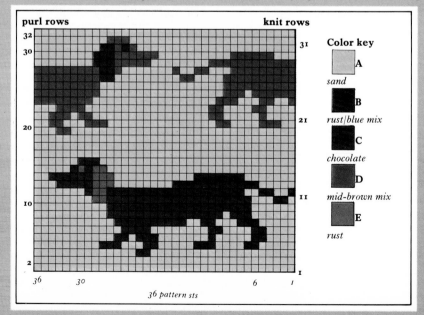

purl rows | knit rows

32
30
20
10
2
31
21
11
1
36 30 6 1
36 pattern sts

Color key
A *sand*
B *rust/blue mix*
C *chocolate*
D *mid-brown mix*
E *rust*

needle and then pick up and knit 60 (64, 68) sts as far as start of neck shaping; then pick up and knit 97 (101, 105) sts down left front to lower edge – 179 (189, 198) sts in all. Work to correspond with right front band but omit buttonholes.

ARMHOLE BANDS

With right side of work facing, and using no 1 needles and yarn B, pick up and knit 145 (153, 161) sts around one arm-hole. Work band to correspond with left front border. Repeat for other armhole.

POCKETS

Pocket tops

With right side facing, using no 1 needles and yarn B, pick up and knit 28 (32, 36) sts across the lower bound-off edge of one pocket slit. Work to correspond with left border. Repeat for other pocket.

Pocket linings

Holding work upside down and with right side facing, using no 1 needles and yarn B, pick up and knit 28 (32, 36) sts across the upper bound-off edge of one pocket slit, behind pocket top. Work 2¾in in st st in yarn B, starting with a purl row. Bind off. Repeat for other pocket.

FINISHING

Press all pieces lightly from the wrong side, avoiding ribbing. Join fronts to back at side seams. Join ribbing at center-back of neck and underarm points with flat seams. Catch down pocket linings to wrong side of vest fronts and sew down sides of each pocket top. Sew on the five buttons to left front band to correspond with buttonholes.

PROWLING CATS

Stealthy Ginger Toms and Black Alley Cats
tip-toe across this one-size crew neck baggy sweater.
The neckband, welt and cuffs are all worked in striped rib.

MATERIALS

Yarn
Use wool fingering yarn.
Yarn A 9¾oz (275g) *(oat)*
Yarn B 2¾oz (75g) *(black)*
Yarn C 2¾oz (75g) *(rust mix)*
Yarn D 1oz (25g) *(deep pink mix)*
Yarn E 1oz (25g) *(jade mix)*

Needles
1 pair no 3
1 pair no 1
1 set of four no 1 double-pointed *or* circular no 1 needle

BACK

**With no 1 needles and yarn B, cast on 135 sts. Work in k1, p1 twisted rib in the following two-color stripe sequence:
Row 1: Yarn B
Row 2: Yarn C
Row 3: Yarn C
Row 4: Yarn B
Repeat rows 1–4 until work measures approximately 2in, ending with row 4 of stripe sequence. On the next row increase as follows: (yarn B) *p8; purl twice into the next st; repeat from * to end of row – 150 sts.
Change to no 3 needles and st st and work Fair Isle pattern from chart, reading odd (knit) rows from right to left, and even (purl) rows from left to right. Repeat the 30 pattern sts five times across the row in all. (You may prefer to darn in the cat's eyes instead of carrying yarns across.)
Continuing in pattern, work straight until you have worked row 60 of the second working of the pattern chart, and the back measures approximately 17¾in from cast-on edge.
Shape armhole: Bind off 10 sts at the beginning of the next 2 rows – 130 sts.** Then work armhole edges straight until you have worked row 62 of the third working of the pattern chart, and the back measures approximately 26in from cast-on edge.
Shape shoulders: With right side facing, continue to work back in st st and yarn A only. Bind off 15 sts at the beginning of the next 2 rows. Then bind off 13 sts at the beginning of the next 4 rows; transfer the remaining 48 sts to a spare needle or stitch holder.

FRONT

Work the same as for back from ** to ** (130 sts) so that ribbing, pattern and start of armhole shaping all match. Then continue to work armhole edges straight until you have worked row 30 of third working of pattern chart, and the front measures approximately 22in from cast-on edge.
Shape neck: On the next row, work the

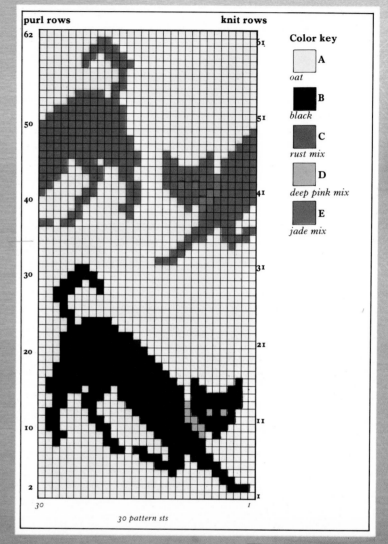

purl rows | knit rows

Color key

A *oat*

B *black*

C *rust mix*

D *deep pink mix*

E *jade mix*

30 pattern sts

first 47 sts in the pattern, then slip these 47 sts on to a spare needle or stitch holder. Bind off the next 36 sts in the row and then continue to work the last 47 sts of row in the pattern. Continuing in pattern on these last 47 sts, decrease one st at the neck edge on the next 6 rows. Then work the remaining 41 sts straight, until the right front measures the same as the back from cast-on edge to start of shoulder shaping – approximately 26in – ending on row 61 of third working of pattern chart.
Shape shoulder: (Right shoulder) Bind off 15 sts at the beginning of the next row using yarn A, then bind off 13 sts at the beginning of the following 2 alternate rows. With the wrong side facing, rejoin the yarn to the remaining 47 sts on the spare needle at the left front. Finish left neck edge and shoulder to correspond with right neck edge, reversing all shapings.

SLEEVES

With no 1 needles and yarn B, cast on 60 sts. Work 3½in in k1, p1 twisted rib, following same two-color sequence as for back welt.
Change to no 3 needles and work Fair Isle pattern from chart as before, repeating the 30 pattern sts twice across rows and increasing one st at each end of the 3rd and every following 4th row until there are 130 sts on the needle. Take the extra sts into the pattern as they are made. When there are 130 sts on the needle, work straight in pattern until you have worked row 6 of the third working of the pattern chart, and the sleeve measures approximately 20½in. Bind off right across. (This bound-off edge across top of sleeve fits around top of armhole. The last 1½in of sleeve seam fits across straight bound-off edge at bottom of armhole.)
Make another sleeve in the same way.

NECKBAND

Join front to back at shoulders.
With right side facing, using the four
no 1 double-pointed needles or the
circular needle and yarn B, beginning at
the left shoulder, pick up and knit 34 sts
down the left side of the neck, 34 sts
across the bound-off edge at the center-
front, 34 sts up the right side of the neck
as far as shoulder seam, and finally the 48
sts on the spare needle around the back of
the neck – 150 sts in all. Work 12 rounds
in twisted rib, following the same two-
color sequence as for back welt. Bind off
in rib in yarn B.

MEASUREMENTS

One-size; to fit chest 36–39in (91–99cm).
(See also chart on p. 122.)
Stitch gauge
30 sts and 30 rows measure 4in over Cats
pattern on no 3 needles.

FINISHING

Press all pieces carefully from the wrong
side, avoiding ribbing. Join front to back
at sides. Join sleeve seams in the same
way, leaving the last 1½in at the top of the
seam unstitched. With wrong sides
together, pin straight bound-off edge of
sleeve head around top of armhole; pin
each side of the unstitched section of the
sleeve seam across the straight bound-off
edge at the bottom of the armhole. Stitch
sleeve into armhole. Repeat for other
sleeve. Press seams.

ALEXANDER BEETLE

*A buttonless vest worked in Beetle pattern
against a plain background. The front bands, hem, armbands and pocket tops
are all worked from a separate border pattern.*

MATERIALS

Yarn

Use wool fingering yarn.

Yarn A 6¼oz (175g) *(oat)*
Yarn B 1¾oz (50g) *(peat)*
Yarn C 1oz (25g) *(crimson)*
Yarn D 1oz (25g) *(royal blue)*
Yarn E 1oz (25g) *(emèrald green)*
Yarn F 1oz (25g) *(rust/blue mix)*
Yarn G 1oz (25g) *(purple)*

Needles

1 pair no 3
1 pair no 2
1 pair no 1

MEASUREMENTS

To fit chest 32 (34)in (81, 86cm).
(See also chart on p. 123.)

Stitch gauge

30 sts and 30 rows measure 4in over
Beetle pattern on no 3 needles.

BACK

Hem: With no 1 needles and yarn A,
cast on 132 (144) sts. Work 12 rows in
st st in yarn A, ending with a purl row.

Hem border: Change to no 3 needles,
and still in st st, work the 12 rows of the
border pattern from chart A, reading odd
(knit) rows from right to left and even
(purl) rows from left to right. *For the
smaller size (34in), repeat sts 1–10,
thirteen times across a knit row and then
work sts 1–2 to finish the row; for the
larger size (36in), work sts 1–10, fourteen
times across the row and then work sts
1–4 to finish the row.* Work purl rows in
reverse. Continue in border pattern until
the 12 rows have been completed.

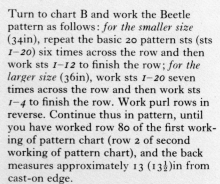

Turn to chart B and work the Beetle
pattern as follows: *for the smaller size
(34in),* repeat the basic 20 pattern sts (sts
1–20) six times across the row and then
work sts 1–12 to finish the row; *for the
larger size (36in),* work sts 1–20 seven
times across the row and then work sts
1–4 to finish the row. Work purl rows in
reverse. Continue thus in pattern, until
you have worked row 80 of the first working of pattern chart (row 2 of second
working of pattern chart), and the back
measures approximately 13 (13½)in from
cast-on edge.

Shape armholes: Continuing in pattern,
bind off 3 (4) sts at the beginning of the
next 2 rows. Then k2 tog, at each end of
every row until 96 (104) sts remain. Continuing in pattern work armhole edge
straight until you have worked row 64 (68)
of the second working of the pattern
chart, and the back measures approximately 22 (22½)in from cast-on edge.

Shape shoulders: Bind off 9 (10) sts at
the beginning of the next 6 rows. Divide
the remaining 42 (44) sts equally in half
and transfer each half to a spare needle or
stitch holder.

FRONTS

Left front

Hem: With no 1 needles and yarn A,
cast on 66 (72) sts and work 12 rows in st
st in yarn A, ending with a purl row.

Hem border: Change to no 3 needles
and work border pattern from chart A in
st st, as before, but *for the smaller size
(34in),* on knit rows, work sts 1–10, six
times, and then work sts 1–6 to finish
row, and *for the larger size (36in),*
work sts 1–10, seven times and then
work sts 1–2 once. Work purl
rows in reverse. Continue to
work pattern until the 12 rows
of the border are complete.

Turn to chart B and work Beetle
pattern from chart as follows:
on knit rows, *for the smaller size,*
repeat sts 1–20, three times across the
row and then work sts 1–6 once; *for the
larger size,* work sts 1–20, three times
across the row and then work sts 1–12
once. Work purl rows in reverse. Continue
to work pattern until you have worked
row 20 of the chart.

Pockets: Introduce pockets in the next
row (row 21) as follows: work the first 20
(22) sts of the row in pattern, bind off the
next 26 (28) sts, then continue pattern
across the last 20 (22) sts of row. On row
22, work pattern across the 20 (22) sts at
beginning of row, cast on 26 (28) sts over
those bound off in previous row, then continue in pattern across last 20 (22) sts in
the row.

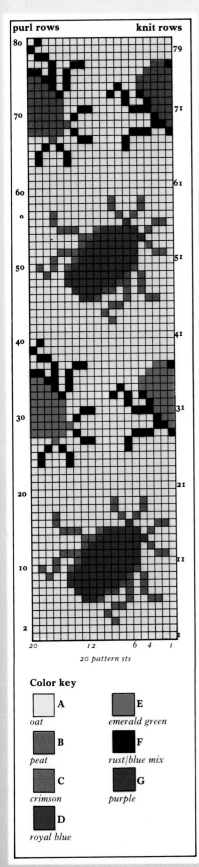

purl rows   **knit rows**

80   79

70   71

60   61

50   51

40   41

30   31

20   21

10   11

2   1

20   12   6   4   1

20 pattern sts

Color key

☐ **A**		◩ **E**	
oat		*emerald green*	
◪ **B**		■ **F**	
peat		*rust/blue mix*	
◪ **C**		◪ **G**	
crimson		*purple*	
◪ **D**			
royal blue			

Chart B

Continuing in pattern, work front straight until you have worked row 80 of first working of pattern chart (row 2 of second working of pattern chart), and front measures same as back from cast-on edge to start of armhole shaping – approximately 13 (13½)in.

Shape armhole and neck edge: Bind off 11 (13) sts at the beginning of the next row, then work pattern to the last 2 sts of row; k2 tog. Continuing in pattern, decrease one st at the armhole edge on the next 15 rows, then work armhole edge straight. *At the same time,* continue to decrease one st on the neck edge on every following 4th row after the first decrease at neck edge, until 26 (27) sts remain on the needle. Then work a few rows straight in pattern, until you have worked row 64 (68) of second working of pattern chart and front measures approximately 22 (22½)in from cast-on edge.

Shape shoulder: Bind off 11 (12) sts at the beginning of the next row – row 65 (69). Slip one st at the beginning of the next row, then continue in pattern to end of row. Bind off.

Right front

Work as for left front, but reverse pocket, armhole, neck and shoulder shapings.

Join fronts to back at shoulders.

BORDERS

Right front

Leave the first 12 rows of plain st st in yarn A free for hem.

With right side facing, using no 2 needles and yarn A, beginning at start of border pattern (row 13), pick up and knit 94 sts up front opening edge as far as start of neck shaping; then continue to pick up and knit 82 (88) sts around neck as far as center-back, including the 21 (22) sts on the first spare needle – 176 (182) sts in all. Work the next row in purl, using yarn A only. Then work the 12 rows of border pattern from chart A, repeating the 10 pattern sts across the rows, as follows: *for the smaller size* (34in), work sts *1–10,* seventeen times and then work sts *1–6* once; *for the larger size* (36in), work sts *1–10,* eighteen times and then work sts *1–2* once. Work purl rows in reverse. When the 12 rows of the pattern are complete, work 12 more rows in st st and yarn A only, starting with a knit row; then bind off in A.

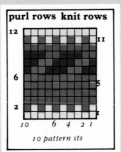

purl rows   knit rows

12   11

6   5

2   1

10   6   4   2   1

10 pattern sts

Left front

Beginning at center-back of neck, in the same way as for right front, knit the 21 (22) sts on the remaining spare needle, then pick up and knit 61 (66) sts around neck to start of neck shaping and then a further 94 sts down front opening edge as far as start of hem border, leaving the 12 rows of st st in yarn A free. Work to correspond with right front border.

Armhole borders

With right side of vest facing, using no 2 needles and yarn A, pick up and knit 134 (140) sts round one armhole. Work the next row in purl in yarn A. Then work border pattern from chart A as follows: *for the smaller size,* on knit rows, repeat sts *1–10,* thirteen times and then work sts *1–4* once; *for the larger size,* work sts *1–10,* fourteen times. Work purl rows in reverse. Continue thus in pattern until the 12 rows are complete. Then change to no 1 needles and yarn A and work 12 rows of plain st st in yarn A. Bind off in yarn A. Repeat for other armhole.

POCKETS

Pocket tops

With no 1 needles and yarn A, pick up and knit the 24 (26) sts across the lower bound-off edge of one pocket slit. Purl one row in yarn A. Then change to no 2 needles and work border pattern from chart A as follows: *for the smaller size,* work sts *1–10* twice and then *1–4* once; *for the larger size,* work sts *1–10* twice and then *1–6* once. Work purl rows in reverse. Continue in pattern until you have worked row 10 of chart A.

Then change to no 1 needles and yarn A and work 8 rows in st st in yarn A only. Bind off. Repeat for other pocket.

Pocket linings

Holding the work upside down and with right side facing, using no 1 needles and yarn A, pick up and knit the 26 (28) sts of cast-on edge of one pocket slit behind pocket top. Work 2¾in in st st, in yarn A, starting with a purl row. Bind off. Repeat for other pocket.

FINISHING

Press Fair Isle parts lightly from wrong side. Then turn up the 12 rows of plain st st around hem to wrong side. Pin, and slip stitch in position. Join front borders together at center-back with a flat seam and then turn under plain half of front border in the same way as hem. Pin and slip stitch in position, catching down front border neatly at hem. Join armhole borders at underarm points with flat seams and turn in and slip stitch plain half in the same way. Sew the three free sides of each pocket lining to the back of the vest fronts. Turn in plain half of pocket tops and slip-stitch in position. Then sew down the sides of each pocket top. Press borders lightly.

RAINGIRLS

Rain-girls with umbrellas and boots rush hither and thither across this short cardie which has three-quarter length sleeves, pleated into the armhole.

MATERIALS

Yarn

Use wool fingering yarn.

Yarn A 5¼oz (150g) *(oat)*
Yarn B 1¾oz (50g) *(red)*
Yarn C 1¾oz (50g) *(yellow)*
Yarn D 2¾oz (75g) *(black)*
Yarn E 1oz (25g) *(orange mix)*
Yarn F 1oz (25g) *(leaf green)*
Yarn G 1oz (25g) *(bright blue)*

Needles

1 pair no 3
1 pair no 0

Notions

5 buttons

MEASUREMENTS

To fit chest 34 (36)in (86, 91cm).
(See also chart on p. 123.)

Stitch gauge

31 sts and 32 rows measure 4in over
Raingirls pattern on no 3 needles.

BACK

With no 0 needles and yarn D, cast on
124 (128) sts. Work 2in in k1, p1 twisted
rib in yarn D, increasing across the last
(wrong-side) row as follows: rib 2 sts,
*rib 9 (8) sts, rib twice into the next st;
repeat from * 11 (13) more times, rib 2 sts
– 136 (144) sts.
Change to no 3 needles and st st and
work pattern from chart, reading odd
(knit) rows from right to left and even
(purl) rows from left to right. Work the

pattern across knit rows as follows: *for the
smaller size (34in), repeat sts 1–28 four
times and then work sts 1–24 once; for the
larger size (36in), repeat sts 1–28 five
times and then work sts 1–4 once.* Work
purl rows in reverse. Join in separate
lengths of yarns B, C, G and F when
working dolls. Continue thus in pattern,
until you have completed row 72 of chart
and back measures approximately 11in.
Shape armholes: Continuing in pattern,
bind off 8 sts at the beginning of the next
2 rows. Then k2 tog at each end of every
row, 10 times – 100 (108) sts. Work
straight in pattern until end of row 62 (66)
of the second working of chart and back
measures approximately 18½ (19)in.
Shape shoulders: Continuing in pattern,
bind off 6 sts at the beginning of the next
4 rows. Then bind off 6 (7) sts at the
beginning of the following 6 rows. Divide
the remaining 40 (42) sts in half and leave
each half on a spare needle or stitch holder.

FRONTS

Left front

With no 0 needles and yarn D, cast on 56 (58) sts. Work 2in in k1, p1 twisted rib, increasing across last (wrong-side) row as follows: rib one st, *rib 8 (6) sts, rib twice into the next st; repeat from * 5 (7) times more, rib one st – 62 (66) sts. Change to no 3 needles and st st and work pattern from chart. Work pattern across knit rows as follows: *for the smaller size*, repeat sts *1–28* twice and then work sts *1–6* once; *for the larger size*, repeat sts *1–28* twice and then work sts *1–10* once. Work purl rows in reverse. Continue in pattern until you have completed row 64 of the pattern chart and front measures approximately 9¾in.

Shape neck and armhole: Continuing in pattern, *work pattern across the next (right-side) row to last 2 sts; k2 tog. Work 3 rows straight*. Repeat from * to * once more – 60 (64) sts. Continue to shape neck, decreasing one st at the neck edge on every following 5th row after first de-crease and *at the same time,* shape armhole by binding off 8 sts at the beginning of the next row (row 1 of second working of chart). Then k2 tog at armhole edge on the following 10 rows. Then work armhole edge straight but continue to decrease at front edge on every 5th row, as before, until 30 (33) sts remain. Now work straight in pattern until you have completed row 62 (66) of the second working of chart and front measures approximately 18½ (19)in.

Shape shoulders: Bind off 6 sts at the beginning of the next and following alternate row; then bind off 6 (7) sts at the beginning of the following 3 alternate rows.

Right front

Work as for left front, but reverse neck, armhole and shoulder shapings.

SLEEVES

With no 0 needles and yarn D, cast on 64 sts. Work 2¾in in k1, p1 twisted rib, increasing across the last (wrong-side) row as follows: rib 10 sts, rib twice into each of the next 44 sts, rib 10 sts – 108 sts. Change to no 3 needles and st st and work pattern from chart. Work pattern across knit rows as follows: *for both sizes,* repeat sts *1–28* three times and then work sts *1–24* once to complete row. Work purl rows in reverse. Continue in pattern until you have completed row 72 of the first working of chart and sleeve measures approximately 11½in from cast-on edge.

Shape top of sleeve: Continuing in pattern, bind off 8 sts at the beginning of the next 2 rows. Then k2 tog at each end of the next and every following alternate

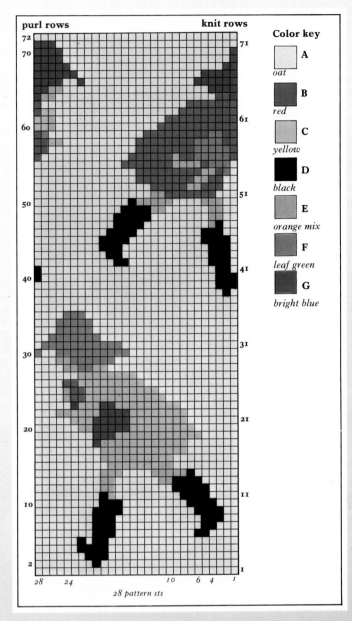

purl rows / knit rows / 28 pattern sts

Color key

A
oat

B
red

C
yellow

D
black

E
orange mix

F
leaf green

G
bright blue

row, 10 times – 72 sts. Now work 20 (24) rows straight in pattern, then k2 tog at each end of the next and every following alternate row, 6·times in all – 60 sts. Then k2 tog at end of the following 10 rows – 40 sts. Bind off – this wide sleeve top will be pleated into the armhole later.

Join both shoulder seams.

FRONT BANDS

Right front

With no 0 needles and yarn D, begin-ning at the lower edge and with right side facing, pick up and knit 93 sts up front opening edge to start of neck shaping; then pick up and knit a further 99 (103) sts around neck to center-back including the 20 (21) sts on the first spare needle at the back of neck – 192 (196) sts. Work 3 rows in k1, p1 twisted rib.

Buttonholes: Make 5 buttonholes in 4th row as follows: rib 4 sts, *bind off 3 sts, rib 18 sts; repeat from * three more times, bind off 3 sts, rib to end. Rib back along 5th row, casting on 3 sts over those bound off in the previous row. Work a further 3 rows in rib. Bind off.

Left front

Work in the same way as right front, but begin picking up sts at the center-back of neck with the 20 (21) sts on remaining spare needle and work to lower edge, and omit buttonholes.

FINISHING

Press all pieces lightly from wrong side, avoiding ribbing. Join ribbing, side seams and sleeve seams. Pin sleeve into armhole, pleating the fullness around the top of the sleeve into 3 pleats to fit armhole either side of shoulder seam. Sew in position and repeat for other sleeve. Press seams from wrong side. Sew buttons on to left front band to correspond with buttonholes.

COTTON CATS

*Cats gazing out of windows on summer days set against a background
of pale gray and yellow stripes form the pattern for this cotton vest.
The back of the vest is worked in striped rib.*

MATERIALS

Yarn
Use No. 8 cotton yarn.
Yarn A 7oz (200g) *(pale gray)*
Yarn B 3½oz (100g) *(écru)*
Yarn C 1¾oz (50g) *(deep pink)*
Yarn D 1¾oz (50g) *(bluebell)*
Yarn E 1¾oz (50g) *(brown)*
Yarn F 1¾oz (50g) *(black)*

Needles
1 pair no 3
1 pair no 2
1 pair no 1

Notions
5 × ⅝in buttons

MEASUREMENTS

To fit chest 32 (34, 38)in (81, 86, 96cm).
(See also chart on p. 123.)

Stitch gauge
32 sts and 32 rows measure 4in over
Cotton Cats pattern on no 3 needles.

FRONTS

Left front
With no 1 needles and yarn A, cast on
64 (70, 76) sts. Work 2in in k1, p1
twisted rib in yarn A, increasing one st at
each end of the final (wrong-side) row – 66
(72, 78) sts.
Change to no 3 needles and st st and
work pattern from chart reading odd
(knit) rows from right to left and even
(purl) rows from left to right. Work the
pattern across knit rows as follows: *for the
small size (32in)*, work sts *15–20* at the
beginning of row and then repeat sts *1–20*
three times; *for the medium size (34in)*,
work sts *9–20* once, and then repeat sts
1–20 three times; *for the large size (38in)*,
work sts *3–20* once and then repeat sts
1–20 three times. Work purl rows in
reverse. Continue in pattern until you have
completed row 22 of chart.
Pocket: Introduce pocket in row 23 of
pattern chart as follows: work the first 19
(20, 21) sts of the row, then bind off the
next 28 (32, 36) sts, and continue in
pattern across the last 19 (20, 21) sts in the
row. On the next row (row 24), work the
first 19 (20, 21) sts in the row, then cast
on 28 (32, 36) sts directly over those
bound off in previous row, and continue in
pattern across the last 19 (20, 21) sts in the
row. Continuing in pattern, work straight
until you have completed row 26 (30, 34)
of the second working of the pattern chart
and front measures
approximately
11½ (11¾, 12¼)in
from cast-on edge.

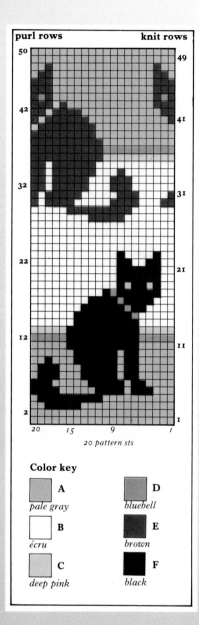

purl rows   **knit rows**

20 pattern sts

Color key

▦	**A**	▦	**D**
pale gray		*bluebell*	
☐	**B**	■	**E**
écru		*brown*	
▨	**C**	■	**F**
deep pink		*black*	

Shape armhole and neck:
Bind off 8
(10, 12) sts at the beginning of the next
row, then work pattern to the last 2 sts,
k2 tog. Continuing in pattern, decrease
one st at the armhole edge on the next 17
rows; then work armhole edge straight. *At
the same time*, continue to decrease one st
at the neck edge on every following 4th
row after the first decrease on row 27 of
chart, until 26 (28, 30) sts remain. Then
work neck edge straight until front
measures approximately 20½ (21¼, 22½)in.

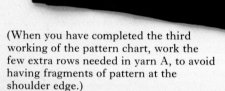

(When you have completed the third
working of the pattern chart, work the
few extra rows needed in yarn A, to avoid
having fragments of pattern at the
shoulder edge.)
Shape shoulder: Using yarn A, bind off
10 sts at the beginning of the next (right-
side) row. Then bind off 8 (9, 10) sts at
the beginning of the following 2 alternate
rows.

Right front
Work as for left front, but reverse pocket,
armhole, neck and shoulder shapings.

BACK

With no 1 needles and yarn A,
cast on 128 (140, 152) sts. Work
2in in k1, p1 twisted rib in yarn A,
increasing 4 sts across the last
(wrong-side) row by working
twice into every 32nd
(35th, 38th) st, four
times in all –
132 (144, 152)
sts.

Change to no 2 needles
and continue to work entire
back in k1, p1 twisted rib in the
following three-color stripe sequence:
Row 1: Yarn B
Row 2: Yarn D
Row 3: Yarn A
Work straight, repeating rows 1–3 until
the back measures the same as the fronts

from cast-on edge to start of armhole shaping – approximately $11\frac{1}{2}$ ($11\frac{3}{4}$, $12\frac{1}{4}$)in.
Shape armholes: Bind off 3 (4, 6) sts at the beginning of the next 2 rows. Then k2 tog at each end of every row until 100 (104, 110) sts remain. Work straight until the back measures the same as the fronts from cast-on edge to start of shoulder shaping – approximately $20\frac{1}{2}$ ($21\frac{3}{4}$, $22\frac{1}{2}$)in.
Shape shoulders: On the next right-side row, bind off 9 (10, 10) sts at the beginning of this and the following row. Then bind off 9 (9, 10) sts at the beginning of the following 4 rows. Divide the remaining 46 (48, 50) sts equally in half and transfer each half to a spare needle or stitch holder.

Join fronts to back at shoulders.

FRONT BANDS
Right front
With no 1 needles and yarn A and beginning at the lower edge, pick up and knit 97 (101, 105) sts up right front opening edge as far as start of neck shaping; then continue to pick up and knit a further 80 (84, 88) sts around the neck edge as far as the center-back, including the 23 (24, 25) sts on the first spare needle. Work 3 rows of k1, p1 twisted rib in yarn A.
Buttonholes: Make 5 buttonholes in 4th row of ribbing as follows: rib 4 sts, *bind off 3 sts, rib 19 (20, 21) sts; repeat from * three more times, then bind off 3 sts and rib to end of row. On the next row (row 5) work back in rib, but cast on 3 sts directly over those bound off in previous row. Work 4 more rows in rib in yarn A. Join in yarn D and work one row in twisted rib in yarn D. Bind off in rib in yarn D.

Left front
Beginning at center-back, with yarn A and no 1 needles, rib the first 23 (24, 25) sts from the spare needle, then pick up and knit the remaining 57 (60, 63) sts as far as the start of the neck shaping; then continue to pick up and knit 97 (101, 105) sts down front to lower edge. Work to correspond with right front band, but omit buttonholes.

ARMHOLE BANDS
With the right side facing, using no 1 needles and yarn A, pick up and knit 145 (153, 161) sts around one armhole. Then work 10 rows in k1, p1 twisted rib in yarn A. Join in yarn D and work a further row of rib. Bind off in rib in yarn D. Repeat for other armhole.

POCKETS
Pocket tops
With the right side of vest front facing, using no 1 needles and yarn A, pick up and knit the 28 (32, 36) sts across the lower bound-off edge of one pocket slit. Work 11 rows of k1, p1 twisted rib to correspond with left front border. Repeat for other pocket opening.

Pocket linings
Holding vest upside down, and with the right side facing, using no 2 needles and yarn A, pick up and knit the 28 (32, 36) sts across the cast-on edge of one pocket slit, behind pocket top. Starting with a purl row, work $2\frac{3}{4}$in in st st in yarn A; then bind off. Repeat for other pocket.

FINISHING
Press fronts and back lightly from wrong side, avoiding all ribbing. Join front to back at side seams. Join ribbing at center-back and underarm points with flat seams. Sew the three free sides of each pocket lining to the wrong side of the vest fronts. Sew down each side of the pocket tops. Sew the 5 buttons to the left front border to correspond with buttonholes.

WINTER SCOTTIES

*Black and white Scotty dogs worked in Shetland yarn
in a variety of garments for men and women.*

WINTER SCOTTIES

Chart A

knit rows

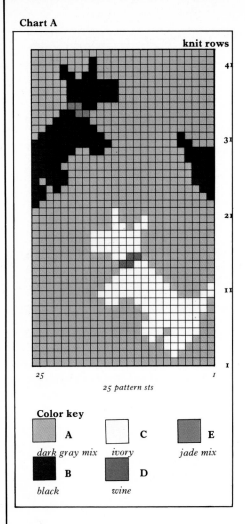

25 pattern sts

Color key

A *dark gray mix*

C *ivory*

E *jade mix*

B *black*

D *wine*

MATERIALS Hat

Yarn

Use wool fingering yarn.

Yarn A 1¾oz (50g) *(dark gray mix)*

Yarn B 1oz (25g) *(black)*

Yarn C 1oz (25g) *(ivory)*

Yarn D 1oz (25g) *(wine)*

Yarn E 1oz (25g) *(jade mix)*

Needles

Set of four no 3 *or*

circular no 3

Set of four no 1 *or*

circular no 1

MEASUREMENTS

One-size: to fit an average head.

(See also chart on p. 123.)

Stitch gauge

32 sts and 32 rows measure 4in over

Scotty pattern on no 3 needles.

Headband

Work in the round. With no 1 needles

and yarn B, cast on 160 sts (53 sts on each

of two needles and 54 on the third needle

if using four needles). Work 4¼in in k1,

p1 twisted rib in the following three-

color stripe sequence:

Round 1: Yarn A

Round 2: Yarn D

Round 3: Yarn B

Repeat rounds 1–3, ending with a round

in yarn B. Join in yarn A and increase

across the next row as follows: knit 35 sts,

knit twice into each of the next 90 sts,

knit 35 sts – 250 sts.

Change to no 3 needles and work Scotty

pattern from chart, working in rounds,

reading *every* row knit on chart A

from right to left. Repeat sts 1–25 ten

times across one round. Work in pattern

until you have completed row 21 of the

second working of the pattern chart.

Shape crown: Change from pattern back

to the three-color stripe sequence as

before (yarn A, yarn D, yarn B) and

decrease as follows:

Round 1: (Yarn A) *k8, slip 1, k1, psso;

repeat from * all round.

Work 2 rounds straight (yarns D and B).

Round 4: (Yarn A) *k7, slip 1, k1, psso,

repeat from * all round (200 sts).

Work 2 rounds straight (yarns D and B).

Round 7: (Yarn A) *k6, slip 1, k1, psso,

repeat from * all round (175 sts).

Continue to decrease in this way on every

third round until you have worked the

round *k2, slip 1, k1, psso; repeat from *

to end (50 sts). On the next round, k2 tog

all round – 25 sts. Work 2 rounds straight.

Repeat these last 3 rounds twice more.

Break yarn, leaving about a 6in end.

Thread the end through the remaining

sts, draw up and secure.

FINISHING

Press lightly from wrong side, avoiding

ribbing. Fold ribbed headband in half to

inside and pin in position. Slip stitch this

inner edge loosely to inside of hat so that

stitches will stretch when the hat is put on.

MATERIALS Legwarmers

Yarn

Use wool fingering yarn.

Yarn A 3½oz (100g) *(dark gray mix)*

Yarn B 2¾oz (75g) *(black)*

Yarn C 1¾oz (50g) *(ivory)*

Yarn D 1oz (25g) *(wine)*

Yarn E 1oz (25g) *(jade mix)*

Needles

1 pair no 3

1 pair no 1

Notions

1½yd of fine hat elastic.

MEASUREMENTS

One-size: to fit an average leg.

(See also chart on p. 123.)

Stitch gauge

32 sts and 32 rows measure 4in over

Scotty pattern on no 3 needles.

Lower welt

With no 1 needles and yarn B, cast on

125 sts. Work 4in in k1, p1 twisted rib.

Join in yarn D and work 2 rows in yarn D

in rib.

Change to no 3 needles and st st and

work Scotty pattern from chart, reading

odd (knit) rows from right to left and even

(purl) rows from left to right. Repeat the

25 pattern sts (1–25) five times across the

rows. Work straight in pattern until you

have completed row 42 of the second

working of the pattern chart. (For longer

legwarmers, work the 42 rows of the

pattern again.) Join in yarn D and work 2

rows in twisted rib in yarn D. Then join

in yarn B and work 4in in twisted rib.

Bind off in rib in yarn D. Make another

legwarmer in the same way.

FINISHING

Press both pieces lightly from the wrong

side, avoiding ribbing. Join back seam of

each legwarmer. Cut lengths of elastic to

fit around lower and upper edges of leg-

warmers and thread through the cast-on

and bound-off edges of the welts from the

wrong side, securing ends. For wider

legwarmers, do not apply the elastic to

the lower edge.

Chart B

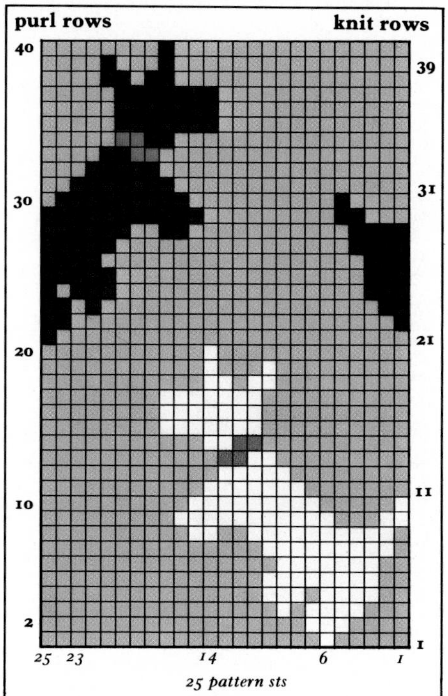

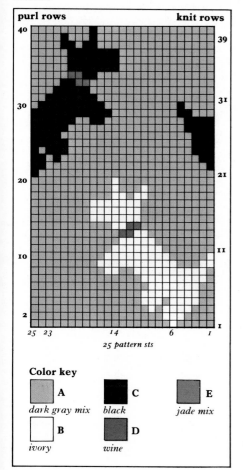

purl rows
knit rows
40
39
31
30
21
20
11
10
2
1
25 23
14
6
1
25 pattern sts

Color key

A *dark gray mix*
C *black*
E *jade mix*
B *ivory*
D *wine*

MATERIALS V-neck sweater

Yarn

Use wool fingering yarn.

Yarn A 8 ($8\frac{3}{4}$, $8\frac{3}{4}$, $8\frac{3}{4}$)oz (225, 250, 250, 250g) *(dark gray mix)*

Yarn B $3\frac{1}{2}$oz (100g) *(black)*

Yarn C $2\frac{3}{4}$oz (75g) *(ivory)*

Yarn D 1oz (25g) *(wine)*

Yarn E 1oz (25g) *(jade mix)*

Needles

1 pair no 3

1 pair no 1

1 pair no 0

1 set of four double-pointed no 1

MEASUREMENTS

To fit chest 36 (38, 40, 42)in (91, 96, 102, 106cm).

(See also chart on p. 123.)

Stitch gauge

32 sts and 32 rows measure 4in over Scotty pattern on no 3 needles.

BACK

**With no 0 (0, 1, 1) needles and yarn B, cast on 132 (136, 144, 152) sts. Work 2in in k1, p1 twisted rib increasing across the last (wrong-side) row as follows: rib 2 (8, 2, 6) sts, *rib 7 (5, 6, 6) sts, rib twice into the next st; repeat from * 15 (19, 19, 19) times more, rib 2 (8, 2, 6) sts – 148 (156, 164, 172) sts.

Change to no 3 needles and st st and work Scotty pattern from chart B, reading odd (knit) rows from right to left and even (purl) rows from left to right. Work the pattern across knit rows as follows: *for size 36in,* repeat sts *1–25* five times and work sts *1–23* once to complete row; *for size 38in,* repeat sts *1–25* six times and then work sts *1–6* once; *for size 40in,* work sts *1–25* six times and then work sts *1–14* once; *for size 42in,* work sts *1–25* six times, and then work sts *1–22* once. Work purl rows in reverse. Continue thus in pattern until you have worked row 2 (6, 10, 14) of the second working of the pattern chart and back measures approx. 17 ($17\frac{1}{4}$, $17\frac{3}{4}$, 19)in from cast-on edge.

Shape armholes: Continuing in pattern, bind off 12 (12, 14, 16) sts at the beginning of the next 2 rows.** Then work straight in pattern until you have completed row 28 (36, 4, 12) of the fifth (fifth, sixth, sixth) working of the pattern chart and back measures approximately $24\frac{3}{4}$ (26, $27\frac{1}{2}$, 28)in from cast-on edge.

Shape shoulder: Continuing in pattern, bind off 14 (16, 17, 16) sts at the beginning of the next 2 rows. Then bind off 13 (13, 13, 14) sts at the beginning of the next 4 rows. Leave the remaining 44 (48, 50, 52) sts on a spare needle or stitch holder.

FRONT

Work in the same way as back from ** to ** – 124 (132, 136, 140) sts.

Shape neck: Divide for 'V' neck as follows: on the next row, with right side facing, work the pattern across the first 60 (64, 66, 68) sts of the row, k2 tog and turn; leave remaining sts on a spare needle. Continue in pattern on these first sts, decreasing one st at the neck edge on the next and every following 3rd row at the neck edge, until 40 (42, 43, 44) sts remain. Then work a few rows straight in pattern until you have completed row 28 (36, 4, 12) of the fifth (fifth, sixth, sixth) working of the pattern chart and front measures approximately $24\frac{3}{4}$ (26, $27\frac{1}{2}$, 28)in from cast-on edge.

Shape shoulder: Continuing in pattern, bind off 14 (16, 17, 16) sts at the beginning of the next row, then bind off 13 (13, 13, 14) sts at the beginning of the following 2 alternate rows. Rejoin yarn to remaining 64 (66, 68, 70) sts at the neck edge; k2 tog and work pattern to end of row. Finish left side of neck and shoulder to correspond with right side, reversing shapings.

SLEEVES

With no 1 needles and yarn B, cast on 56 (60, 64, 70) sts. Work $3\frac{1}{2}$in in k1, p1 twisted rib, increasing across the last (wrong-side) row as follows: *rib 6 (4, 7, 13) sts, rib twice into the next st; repeat from* 7 (11, 7, 4) more times – 64 (72, 72, 75) sts in all.

Change to no 3 needles and st st and work pattern from chart. Work the pattern across knit rows as follows: *for size 36in,* repeat sts *1–25* twice and then work sts *1–14* once; *for sizes 38 and 40in,* repeat sts *1–25* twice and then work sts *1–22* once; *for size 42in,* work sts *1–25* three times. Work purl rows in reverse.

Continue in pattern, *at the same time* shaping the side edges by increasing one st at each end of the 5th (7th, 5th, 3rd) row and every following fourth row until there are 132 (136, 140, 147) sts on the needle. Take the extra sts into the pattern as they are made. Now work a few rows straight in pattern until you have completed row 24 (28, 32, 32) of the fourth working of the pattern chart and sleeve measures approximately $21\frac{1}{4}$ ($21\frac{3}{4}$, 22, 22)in from cast-on edge. Bind off right across row – this bound-off edge should measure approximately $16\frac{1}{4}$ (17, 18, 19)in to fit armhole.

NECKBAND

Join both shoulder seams. With the set of four double-pointed no 1 needles and yarn B, beginning at the left shoulder seam, pick up and knit 60 (64, 68, 72) sts down left side of neck edge, knit one st from the center, pick up and knit 59 (63, 67, 71) sts up right side of neck, and then knit the 44 (48, 50, 52) sts from the back of the neck on spare needle – 164 (176, 186, 196) sts in all. Work 11 rounds of k1, p1 twisted rib, decreasing one st at each side of the center-front st on every round. Join in yarn D and rib one round, decreasing as before. Bind off in rib in yarn D, taking 2 sts together each side of center-front as before.

FINISHING

Press all pieces lightly from wrong side, avoiding ribbing. Join side seams. Join underarm sleeve seams, leaving $1\frac{1}{2}$ ($1\frac{1}{2}$, 2, 2)in unstitched at the top of the seam. Pin straight bound-off edge of top of sleeve into top of armhole and pin either side of the unstitched section of the sleeve seam across the straight bound-off edge at base of armhole. Sew sleeve in place and repeat for other sleeve. Press seams lightly from wrong side.

WINTER SCOTTIES

MATERIALS Vest

Yarn
Use wool fingering yarn.
Yarn A 4½oz (125g) (*pale gray mix*)
Yarn B 3½oz (100g) (*white*)
Yarn C 1¾oz (50g) (*black*)
Yarn D 1oz (25g) (*wine*)
Yarn E 1oz (25g) (*jade mix*)

Needles
1 pair no 4
1 pair no 3
1 pair no 1
1 cable needle

Notions
4 buttons

MEASUREMENTS

One-size: to fit chest 36–38in (91–97cm).
(*See also chart on p. 123.*)

Stitch gauge
32 sts and 32 rows measure 4in over
Scotties pattern on no 3 needles.

BACK

With no 1 needles and yarn B, cast on
140 sts. Work 4in in k1, p1 twisted rib
in yarn B. Change to yarn A and increase
across the next row as follows: *p6, purl
twice into the next st; repeat from * to end
of row – 160 sts.
Change to no 3 needles and st st and
work Scotty pattern from chart, reading
odd (knit) rows from right to left and even
(purl) rows from left to right. Work knit
rows as follows: work sts *1–3* once, then
work sts *4–28,* six times and finally work
sts *4–10* once to complete row. Work purl
rows in reverse. Continue thus, repeating
the 40 rows of the pattern, until you have
worked row 40 of the fourth working of
the pattern chart and back measures
approximately 23½in from the cast-on
edge. Then bind off right across the row.

FRONTS

Left front
**With no 1 needles and yarn B, cast on
60 sts. Work 4in in k1, p1 twisted rib.
Change to yarn A and increase across next
(wrong-side) row as follows: *p4, purl
twice into the next st; repeat from * to
end of row – 72 sts.**
Change to no 3 needles and st st and
work pattern from chart, working knit
rows as follows: work sts *11–28* once, then
sts *4–28* twice and finally sts *29–32* once.
Work purl rows in reverse. Continue thus,
repeating the 40 rows of the pattern chart
until you have worked row 22 of the
second working of the pattern chart and
front measures approx. 11½in from cast-on
edge. There are no armhole shapings.
Shape neck: Decrease one st at the neck
edge on the next row (row 23) and every
following 3rd row, 32 times in all – 40 sts.
Then work straight in pattern until you
have worked row 40 of the fourth working
of the pattern chart and front measures
approximately 23½in from cast-on edge.
Bind off right across the row.

Right front
Work right front in the same way as left
front from ** to ** – 72 sts.
Change to no 3 needles and st st and
work pattern from chart as for left front,
but reversing all shapings.

CABLE BORDERS

Fronts
Note: To work the instruction 'cable 6'
(see below) work as follows: slip the next
3 sts on to a cable needle and hold to front
of work, knit 3 sts, then knit 3 sts from
cable needle (see also p. 133).
Sew fronts to back at shoulder seams.
With no 4 needles and yarn B, cast on
12 sts, then work cable borders as follows:
Row 1: Knit
Row 2: K3, p6, k3
Row 3: Knit
Row 4: K3, p6, k3
Row 5: Knit
Row 6: K3, p6, k3
Row 7: K3, cable 6, k3
Row 8: K3, p6, k3
Row 9: Knit
Row 10: K3, p6, k3
These 10 rows form the cable pattern.
Repeat the first 4 rows (rows 1–4) again.
Buttonholes: Make the first buttonhole in
rows 5 and 6 as follows: *(row 5) k5 sts,
bind off 2 sts, k5 sts. On the next row (row
6), k3 sts, p2 sts, cast on 2 sts, p2 sts, k3
sts. Then work the next 28 rows in cable
pattern (rows 7–10, 1–10, 1–10, 1–4).*
Repeat from * to * twice more. Then
make the fourth buttonhole in the next 2
rows (rows 5 and 6 of the 11th working of
the cable pattern). Then continue straight
in cable pattern from row 7 until strip is
long enough to fit up right front opening
edge, around back of neck and back down

left front opening edge, when slightly
stretched. Bind off.

Armholes
With no 4 needles and yarn B, cast on
12 sts. Work rows 1–10 of cable pattern as
for front border, repeating them until
strip measures 20in. Bind off. Repeat for
other armhole.

FINISHING

Press all pieces lightly from wrong side,
including cable borders, but avoiding
ribbing. Join side seams starting at a point
9¾in down from shoulder edge to allow
for armhole, and sewing down to lower
edge, so forming the armholes. Pin front
cable border in position around front
opening edges – the top buttonhole should
come just below the start of the neck
shaping on the right front opening edge.
Sew cable border to main work with a flat
seam sewn from the wrong side.
Armhole borders: Join the short ends of
one armhole border by placing one end
over the other so that the wrong side of
the top end is against the right side of the
underneath end and the two ends form a
'V' (see p. 140). Pin into armhole so that
the point of the 'V' fits into the bottom of
the armhole. Sew into armhole as before.
Repeat for other armhole. Sew on buttons
to left front border to match buttonholes.

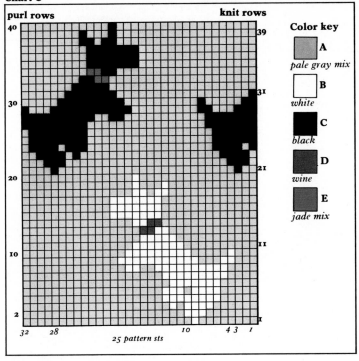

Chart C

purl rows / knit rows

Color key
A *pale gray mix*
B *white*
C *black*
D *wine*
E *jade mix*

25 pattern sts

MEASUREMENTS AND YARNS

GEOMETRIC

Alongside the measurements charts on the following pages are samples of the yarns used in each of the individual sweaters. Whereas the colored boxes given with the pattern charts are representative of the shades used, the yarns given below are the exact colors found in each sweater. Different yarns such as cotton or mohair are not distinguished here – see the patterns for these details.

HARRIET p. 20
A 20½ (21¼)in bust
B 33¾ (34¼)in length
C 21¼ (21¼)in sleeve

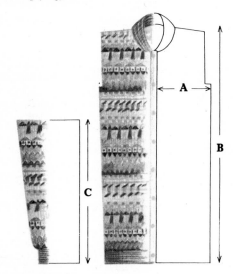

dark fawn

blue/wine mix

peat

pale lilac mix

rust

pale green mix

lilac/green mix

rust brown mix

pale pink mix

rust mix

PAINTBOX p. 22
A 16½ (18, 20)in chest
B 22¾ (24, 24¾)in length

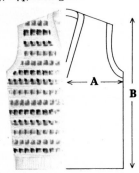

white

yellow

brown

pale green

pink

rust

mid-blue

bottle green

lilac

DESERT RIBBONS p. 24
A 19in bust
B 20in length
C 12¼in sleeve

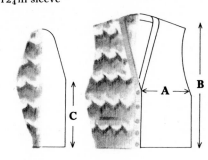

sand

ivory

pale lilac mix

mid-brown mix

pearl

sage green

OPTICAL COPPER p. 26
A 16¼ (17¾, 19¼)in chest
B 20½ (21¼, 22)in length

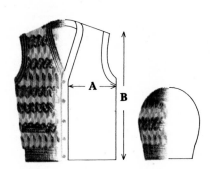

black

copper

rust

peat

wine

Hat 13in from crown to edge of headband

RIBS p. 28
A 13in bust
B 21¼in length
C 19¾in sleeve

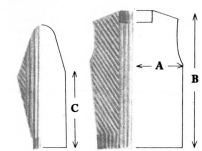

deep pink mix

BRAMBLE p. 28

A $15\frac{3}{4}$in bust
B $21\frac{1}{4}$in length
C 18in sleeve

petrol blue

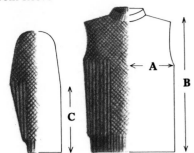

SQUARES ON BLACK p. 36

A $23\frac{1}{2}$ ($24\frac{1}{2}$, $26\frac{1}{2}$)in length
B 17 (18, $19\frac{1}{4}$)in bust
C $15\frac{1}{4}$ (17, $17\frac{1}{4}$)in sleeve

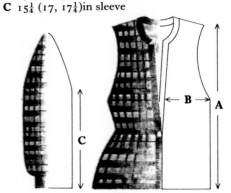

black
yellow
peat
sage green
pink
rust
ivory
green
lilac/green mix
bluebell

RIBBONS p. 32

A 18 ($19\frac{1}{4}$)in chest
B 24 ($24\frac{1}{2}$)in length
C $19\frac{1}{4}$ (20)in sleeve

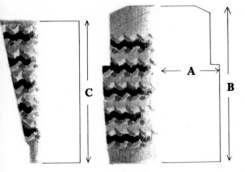

peat
black
red
green
bright blue
mustard

Hat $34\frac{1}{2}$in from bobble to edge of headband

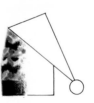

COPPER DIAMONDS p. 38

A $17\frac{1}{4}$ (19, $20\frac{1}{2}$, 22)in chest
B $24\frac{1}{2}$ ($25\frac{1}{2}$, $26\frac{3}{4}$, 27)in length
C $19\frac{1}{4}$in sleeve

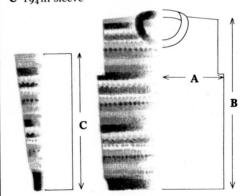

blue/orange mix
blue/fawn mix
mid-blue mix
copper
mid-brown mix
oat
bright blue
rust/blue mix
tan

CHEQUER-BOARD p. 34

A 19 ($21\frac{1}{4}$)in chest
B $27\frac{1}{2}$ ($28\frac{1}{2}$)in length
C 20 ($20\frac{3}{4}$)in sleeve

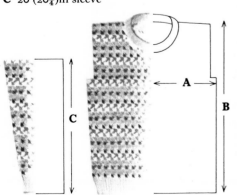

oat
ivory
dark fawn
rust
lilac/green mix
clan green
bottle green
purple
peat

MAURICE p. 40

A $17\frac{3}{4}$ ($19\frac{3}{4}$, $20\frac{3}{4}$)in chest
B $20\frac{3}{4}$ ($22\frac{1}{2}$, $23\frac{1}{4}$)in length

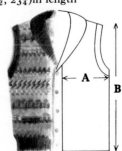

blue/wine mix
peat
lilac/green mix
pale green mix
rust mix
rust/blue mix
pale lilac mix
rust
dark fawn
pale pink mix

FLOWERS

WALLFLOWERS p. 44

A 18 ($19\frac{1}{4}$)in bust
B $22\frac{1}{2}$ ($23\frac{1}{4}$)in length
C $17\frac{3}{4}$ ($17\frac{3}{4}$)in sleeve

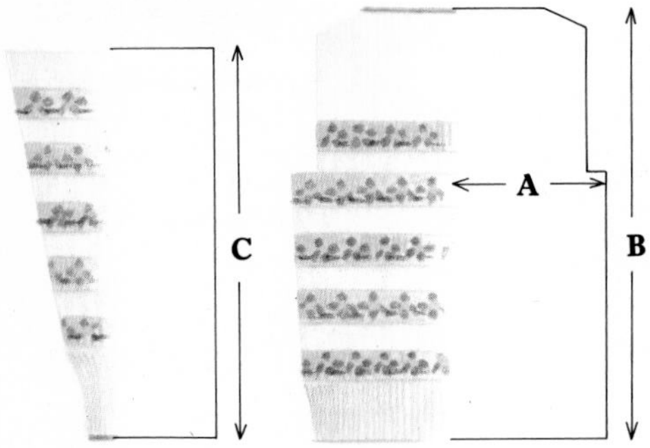

écru
beige
orange
crimson
olive
yellow

PURPLE PANSY p. 50

A $19\frac{3}{4}$in chest
B $28\frac{1}{4}$in length
C $21\frac{1}{4}$in sleeve

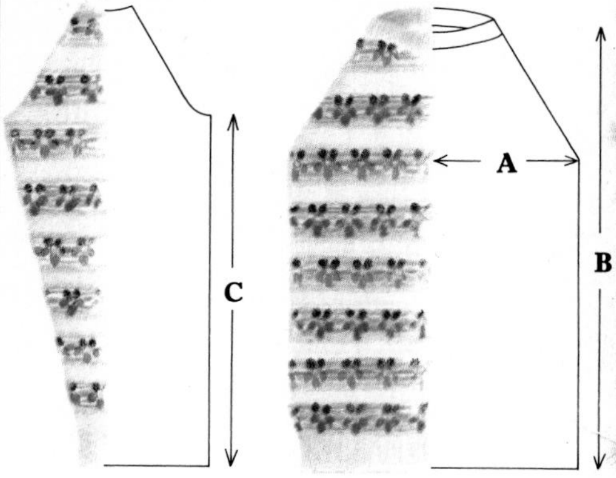

ivory
purple
oat
yellow
clan green
pale lilac mix
wine
violet
bluebell
navy
wine mix
silver

IRIS p. 46

A $17\frac{3}{4}$ (19)in bust
B $21\frac{1}{4}$ ($21\frac{3}{4}$)in length
C $17\frac{3}{4}$ (18)in sleeve

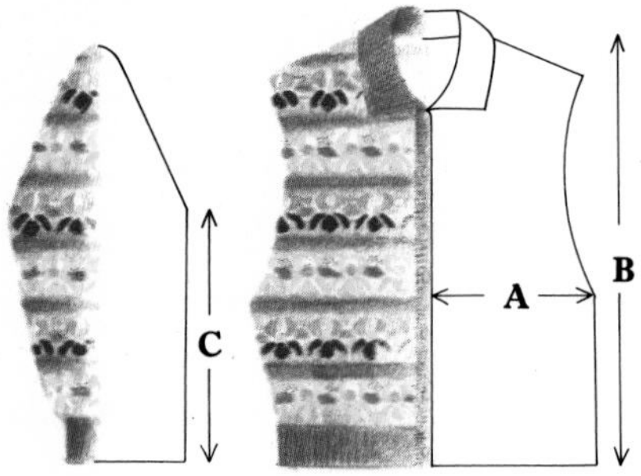

pale lilac mix
lilac/green mix
violet
purple
sage green
wine
pale yellow
yellow
gold
wine mix

ROSES p. 52

A $17\frac{3}{4}$ ($18\frac{1}{2}$)in bust
B $23\frac{1}{4}$ (24)in length
C $19\frac{1}{4}$ ($19\frac{1}{4}$)in sleeve

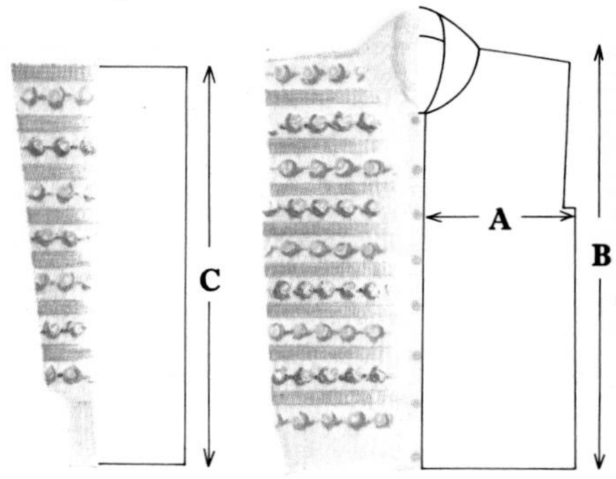

écru
pale gray
pale blue
mid-blue
brown
pink
deep pink

MARIGOLD p. 48

A $16\frac{1}{4}$ ($17\frac{3}{4}$, $19\frac{1}{4}$)in bust
B $21\frac{1}{4}$ (22, $23\frac{1}{4}$)in length

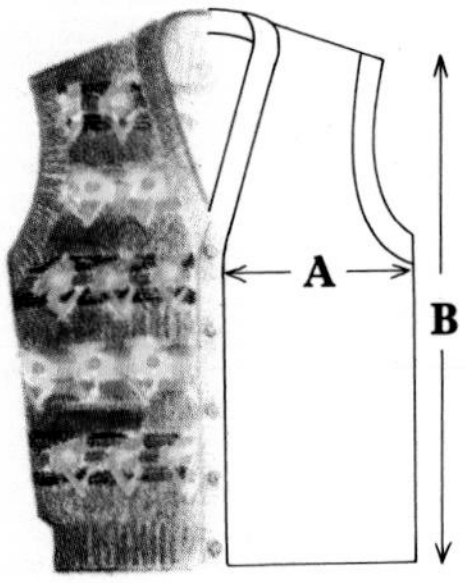

brown/green mix
rust
yellow
dark orange mix
copper
chocolate
clan green
brown mix

DAISY p. 54

A $16\frac{1}{4}$ ($17\frac{3}{4}$, $19\frac{1}{4}$)in chest
B $20\frac{1}{2}$ ($21\frac{1}{4}$, $21\frac{3}{4}$)in length

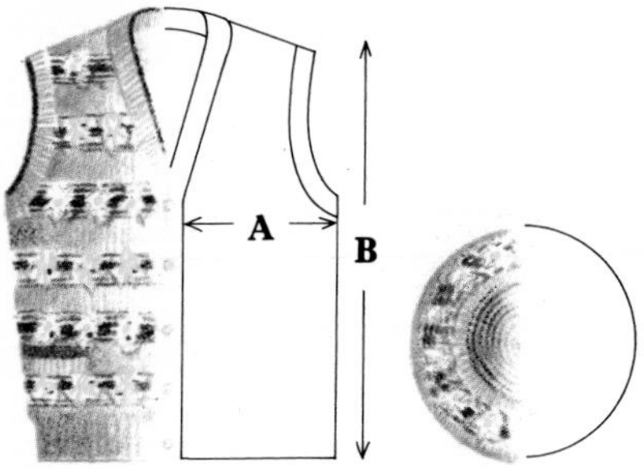

Hat $11\frac{3}{4}$in from crown to edge of headband

pale gray mix
ivory
yellow
dark gray mix
peat
sage green
silver
pale gray

ETHNIC

SWEET PEAS p. 56
A 15 (15¼)in bust
B 14½ (15)in length

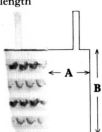

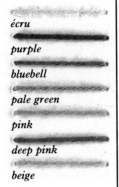

écru

purple

bluebell

pale green

pink

deep pink

beige

CACTUS p. 62
A 17¾ (19¼, 20¾, 22)in chest
B 22¾ (24, 24¾, 26)in length

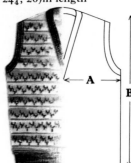

clan green

bottle green

peat

pale green mix

dark fawn

oat

pale gray mix

mustard

blue/wine mix

red/blue mix

PRETTY PANSIES p. 58
A 19in bust
B 20¼in length
C 12¼in sleeve

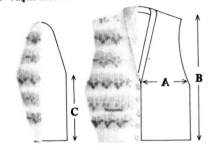

ivory

pale yellow

pale lilac mix

powder blue

wine mix

lilac/green mix

clan green

pale pink mix

white

silver

DOUBLE DUTCH p. 64
A 20½in chest
B 26½in length
C 20½in sleeve

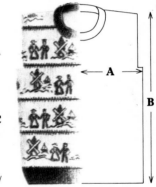

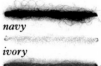

navy

ivory

crimson

NAVAJO p. 66
A 16¼ (17¾, 19¼)in chest
B 22½ (23¼, 24½)in length

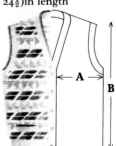

oat

rust

black

mustard

lilac/green mix

olive mix

PIERROT p. 68
A 17¾ (18½)in chest
B 20½ (21¼)in length
C 17¼ (18)in sleeve

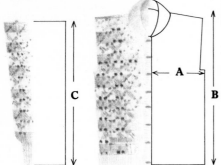

écru

pale blue

lilac

bluebell

deep pink

yellow

purple

CHITIMACHA p. 74
A 18 (20¾)in chest
B 19¼ (22¾)in length

rust

mustard

jade mix

oat

black

STERLING ZIG-ZAG p. 70
A 17¼ (18, 19)in bust
B 24½ (26, 27)in length
C 17 (17¼, 17¾)in sleeve

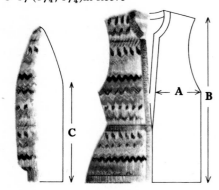

wine

olive

mustard

copper

pale lilac mix

fawn

peat

chocolate

dark wine mix

WILLOW p. 76
A 18 (19¼)in chest
B 20¾ (21¾)in length

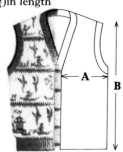

mid-blue mix

ivory

navy

CAMISOLE p. 71
A 13in bust
B 11½in length of back

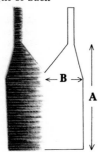

peat

wine

copper

ISLAMIC p. 78
A 16¼ (17¾, 19¼)in chest
B 20¾ (21¾, 22¾)in length

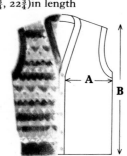

chocolate

peat

wine

powder blue

ivory

orange mix

blue/orange mix

lilac/green mix

royal blue

NURSERY

LEAVES p. 80

A 17 (18½)in bust
B 21¾ (22¾)in length
C 18 (18½)in sleeve

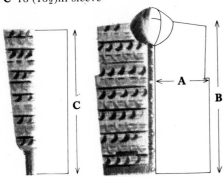

bottle green

dark fawn

chocolate

rust

peat

brown/green mix

wine

oat

deep pink mix

rust mix

flax

pale green mix

SUMMER SCOTTY p. 86

A 17¾ (19)in bust
B 19¾ (20)in length
C 11¾ (11¾)in sleeve

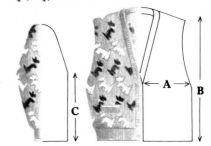

gray

black

white

yellow

lilac

MOSAIC p. 82

A 18 (20½, 22½)in chest
B 23½ (24¾, 26)in length

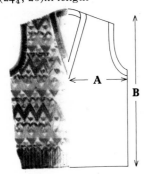

navy

rust

olive

bottle green

ivory

mustard mix

dark fawn

sage green

rust mix

BOYS ON BLUE p. 88

A 17¾ (19)in chest
B 22¾ (23½)in length
C 20 (20)in sleeve

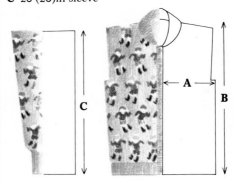

pale blue mix

oat

black

red

green

mid-blue

yellow

rust

royal blue

TEDDY-BEAR p. 90

A 17¾ (19¼)in chest
B 22 (22¾)in length

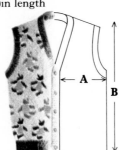

dark fawn

chocolate

red

violet

mid-brown

jade mix

mid-blue

SEAGULLS p. 92

A $17\frac{3}{4}$ (19, $21\frac{3}{4}$)in chest
B $23\frac{1}{4}$ ($23\frac{1}{4}$, 27)in length
C $18\frac{1}{2}$ ($18\frac{1}{2}$, $18\frac{1}{2}$)in sleeve

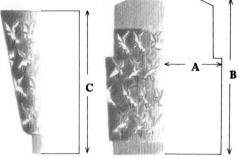

light blue mix
white
light brown
red
black

STARING CATS p. 94

A $17\frac{1}{4}$ ($18\frac{1}{2}$, $19\frac{3}{4}$, $20\frac{3}{4}$)in chest
B $25\frac{1}{2}$ ($26\frac{3}{4}$, 27, $27\frac{1}{2}$)in length
C 19 (19, $19\frac{3}{4}$, $19\frac{3}{4}$)in sleeve

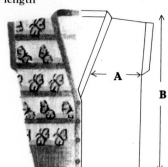

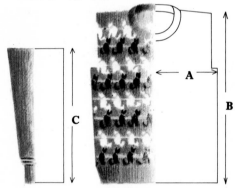

red/blue mix
mid-blue mix
ivory
black
rust
yellow

BOYS ON BLACK p. 96

A $19\frac{3}{4}$ ($22\frac{3}{4}$)in chest
B 26 (27)in length
C 19 ($19\frac{1}{4}$)in sleeve

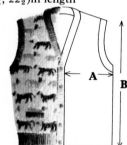

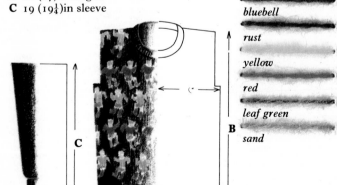

black
bluebell
rust
yellow
red
leaf green
sand

BUTTERFLIES p. 98

A 19in chest
B 24in length

olive mix
light brown
mustard
light blue
bright blue
orange mix
chocolate
oat

DACHSHUND p. 100

A $16\frac{1}{4}$ ($17\frac{3}{4}$, $19\frac{1}{4}$)in chest
B $20\frac{1}{2}$ ($21\frac{3}{4}$, $22\frac{1}{2}$)in length

sand
mid-brown mix
chocolate
rust/blue mix
rust

PROWLING CATS p. 102

A $19\frac{3}{4}$in chest
B $26\frac{3}{4}$in length
C 19in sleeve

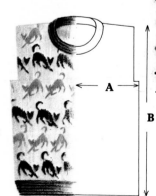

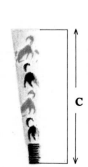

oat
black
rust mix
deep pink mix
jade mix

ALEXANDER BEETLE p. 104
A $16\frac{1}{4}$ ($17\frac{3}{4}$)in chest
B $22\frac{3}{4}$ ($23\frac{1}{4}$)in length

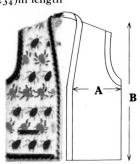

oat

peat

crimson

royal blue

emerald green

rust/blue mix

purple

WINTER SCOTTIES p. 110
LEGWARMERS AND HAT
A $14\frac{1}{2}$in length

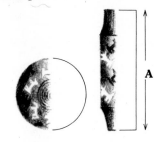

$13\frac{3}{4}$in crown to edge of headband

dark gray mix

black

ivory

wine

jade mix

RAINGIRLS p. 106
A $17\frac{1}{4}$ (18)in bust
B $19\frac{3}{4}$ (20)in length
C $11\frac{1}{2}$in sleeve

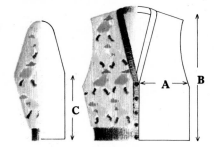

oat

red

yellow

black

orange mix

leaf green

bright blue

V-NECK SWEATER
A 18 ($19\frac{1}{4}$, 20, $21\frac{1}{4}$)in chest
B $25\frac{1}{2}$ ($26\frac{3}{4}$, $28\frac{1}{4}$, $28\frac{3}{4}$)in length
C $19\frac{3}{4}$ (20, 20, 20)in sleeve

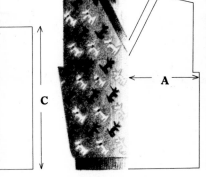

dark gray mix

ivory

black

wine

jade mix

COTTON CATS p. 108
A $16\frac{1}{4}$ ($17\frac{3}{4}$, $18\frac{1}{2}$)in chest
B $21\frac{1}{4}$ ($22\frac{1}{2}$, $23\frac{1}{4}$)in length

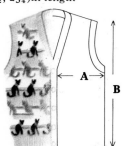

pale gray

écru

deep pink

bluebell

brown

black

VEST
A $19\frac{3}{4}$in chest
B $23\frac{1}{2}$in length

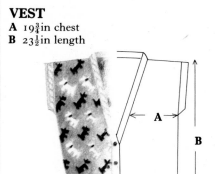

pale gray mix

white

black

wine

jade mix

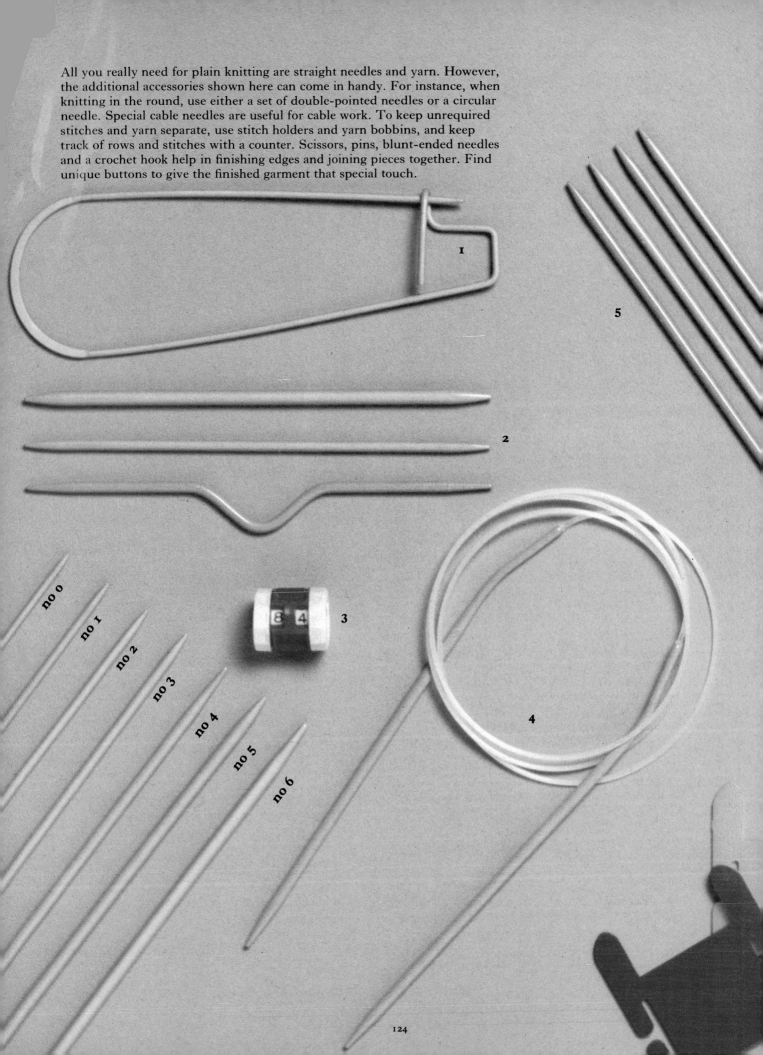

All you really need for plain knitting are straight needles and yarn. However, the additional accessories shown here can come in handy. For instance, when knitting in the round, use either a set of double-pointed needles or a circular needle. Special cable needles are useful for cable work. To keep unrequired stitches and yarn separate, use stitch holders and yarn bobbins, and keep track of rows and stitches with a counter. Scissors, pins, blunt-ended needles and a crochet hook help in finishing edges and joining pieces together. Find unique buttons to give the finished garment that special touch.

1

5

2

no 0

no 1

no 2

no 3

no 4

no 5

no 6

8 4

3

4

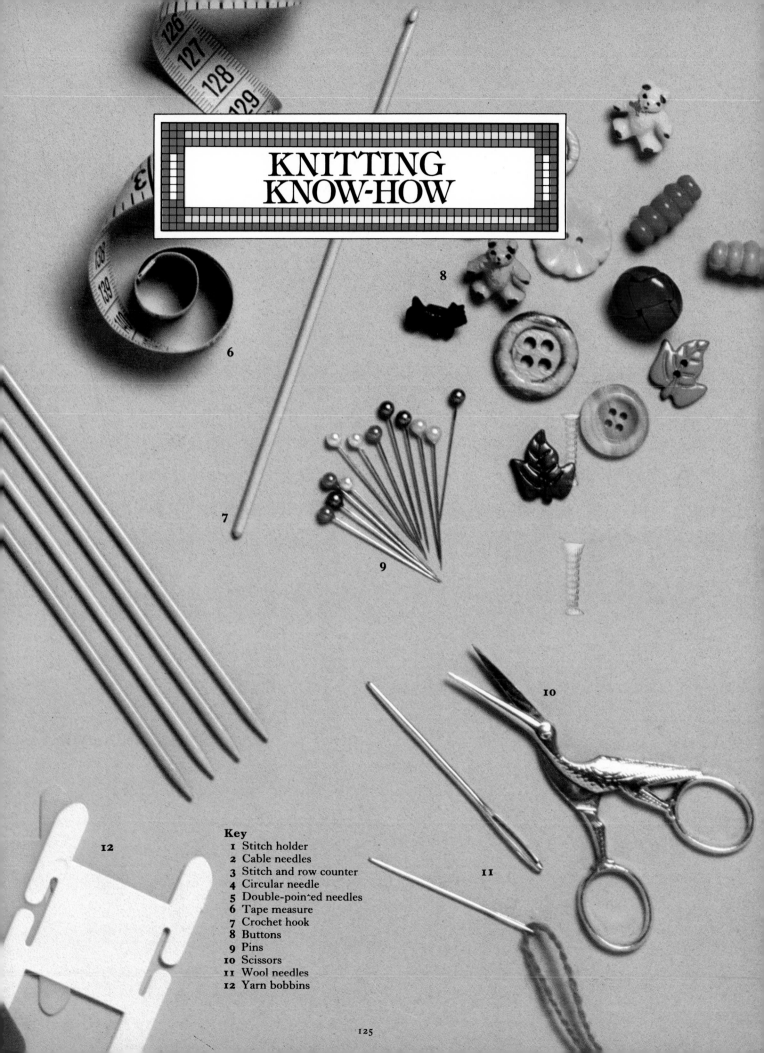

KNITTING KNOW-HOW

Key
1 Stitch holder
2 Cable needles
3 Stitch and row counter
4 Circular needle
5 Double-pointed needles
6 Tape measure
7 Crochet hook
8 Buttons
9 Pins
10 Scissors
11 Wool needles
12 Yarn bobbins

6
8
7
9
10
11
12

BASIC TECHNIQUES

The information on the following pages will tell you all you need to know to make the sweaters in the book as well as helping you to design your own patterns.

The instructions are written and illustrated for right-handed knitters. If you are left-handed, reverse any instructions for left and right, or prop the book up in front of a mirror and follow the diagrams in reverse.

CASTING ON

When you begin to work on a pattern, placing the first row of stitches on the needles is known as "casting on". All further rows are worked into these initial loops. Casting on can be done in a number of ways, but when you are casting on to work a welt in twisted rib, it is best to cast on into the back of the stitch.

A slip loop is the first stitch to be made and is the foundation for all the subsequent stitches.

MAKING A SLIP LOOP

1 Wrap the yarn twice around two fingers.

2 With the knitting needle, pull a loop through the twisted yarn on the fingers.

3 Pull both ends of yarn to tighten the slip loop.

CASTING ON WITH TWO NEEDLES

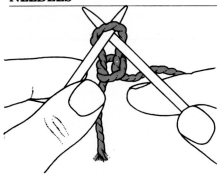

1 With the slip loop on your left-hand needle, insert your right-hand needle through the loop from front to back.

2 Bring the yarn under and over your right-hand needle.

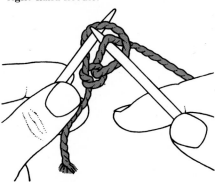

3 Draw up the yarn through the slip loop to make a stitch.

4 Place the stitch on the left-hand needle*. Continue to make more stitches in the same way, drawing the yarn through the last stitch on your left-hand needle.

CASTING ON WITH ONE NEEDLE

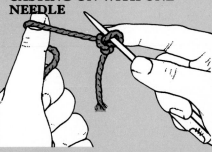

1 Hold the needle with the slip loop in the right hand. Wrap the working end of the yarn around the left thumb and hold it in the left palm, ready to begin casting on.

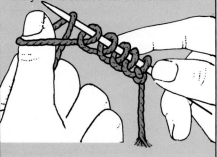

2 Put the needle through the yarn behind the thumb. Slip the thumb out of the yarn and pull the working end of the yarn to secure the new stitch.

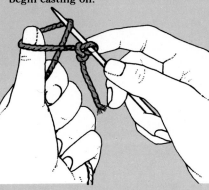

3 Repeat these steps until the required number of stitches has been cast on.

WINDING WOOL

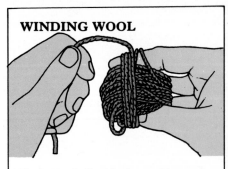

To form a ball with the working end on top, unwrap yarn from a hank and wind tightly over three fingers. Remove the coils, change the position and continue winding to form a ball.

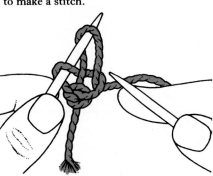

CASTING ON INTO THE BACK OF THE STITCH

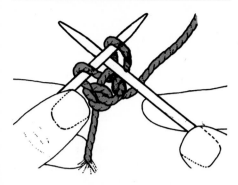

1 Begin by following steps 1 to 4 of casting on with two needles as far as the asterisk. Put the right-hand needle between the slip loop and the first stitch.

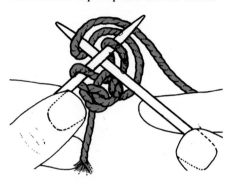

2 Wrap the working yarn under and over the right-hand needle.

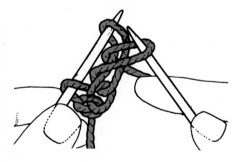

3 Draw the right-hand needle through to form a new stitch.

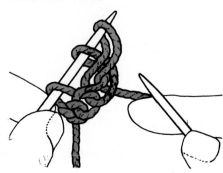

4 Place the new stitch on the left-hand needle. Continue until the required number of stitches has been cast on.

HOLDING NEEDLES AND YARN

The way in which you hold your knitting will affect the tension and evenness of the fabric. Threading the working end of the yarn through the fingers not only makes knitting faster, but also produces a firm, even result.

Holding yarn in the right hand
With the working yarn in your right hand, use the right forefinger to wrap the yarn over the needles.

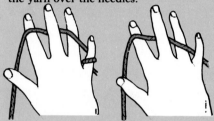

Threading the yarn
Place the working yarn through the fingers of your left hand in either of the ways shown above.

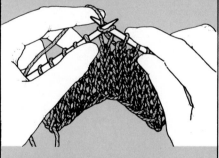

Holding yarn in the left hand
With the working yarn in your left hand, use the left forefinger to position the yarn while you move the right needle to encircle the yarn to form a new loop.

Threading the yarn
Place the working yarn through the fingers of your right hand in either of the ways shown above.

BINDING OFF

When you end a piece of knitting, such as a sleeve, or part of a piece of knitting, such as up to the neck, you must secure all the stitches by "binding off". This is preferably done on a knit row but you can employ the same technique on a purl row. The stitches, whether knit or purl, should be made loosely. With ribbing, you must follow the pattern, and bind off in both knit and purl.

In knit stitch

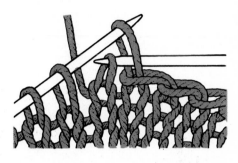

1 Knit the first two stitches and insert the tip of your left-hand needle through the first stitch.

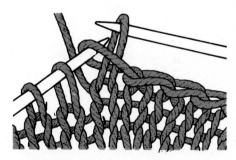

2 Lift the first stitch over the second stitch and discard it. Knit the next stitch and continue to lift the first stitch over the second stitch to the end of the row. Be careful not to knit too tightly. For the last stitch, cut your yarn, slip the end through the stitch and pull the yarn tight to fasten off securely.

In purl stitch

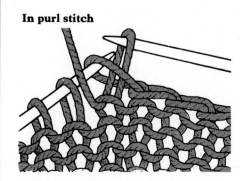

Purl the first two (and all subsequent) stitches and continue as for knit stitch above.

BASIC STITCHES

Knit stitch and purl stitch are the two basic knitting stitches. When every row is knitted back and forth on two needles, garter stitch is formed. When one row is knitted and the next purled, stockinette stitch is formed (*see overleaf*).

KNIT STITCH (k)

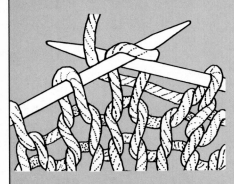

1 With the yarn at the back, insert your right-hand needle from front to back into the first stitch on your left-hand needle.

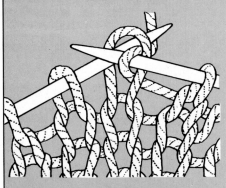

2 Bring your working yarn under and over the point of your right-hand needle.

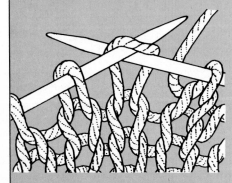

3 Draw a loop through and slide the first stitch off your left-hand needle while the new stitch is retained on your right-hand needle. Continue in this way to the end of the row.

4 To knit the next row, turn the work around so that the back is facing you and the worked stitches are held on the needle in your left hand. Proceed to make stitches as above, with the initially empty needle held in your right hand.

PURL STITCH (p)

1 With the yarn at the front, insert your right-hand needle from back to front into the first stitch on your left-hand needle.

2 Bring your working yarn over and around the point of your right-hand needle.

3 Draw a loop through and slide the first stitch off your left-hand needle while the new stitch is retained on your right-hand needle. Continue in this way to the end of the row.

4 To purl the next row, turn the work around so that the back is facing you and the worked stitches are held on the needle in your left hand. Proceed to make stitches as above, with the initially empty needle held in your right hand.

TENSION

Before starting to make any garment you must make a tension sample in order to measure stitch gauge. You should do this in order to check your individual control of the yarn against the pattern you are following, so that the desired measurements are the same as in the pattern. It is also imperative to do this when you are planning a design of your own, or adapting one.

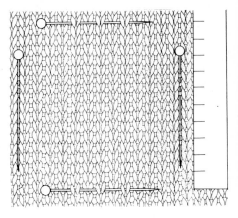

The stitch gauge, or tension, is always given at the beginning of a pattern. It is written as the number of stitches, and the number of rows in a particular pattern, e.g. stockinette stitch, to a specified size, such as 4in, using the yarn and needles called for in the pattern. An example is 32 sts and 32 rows to 4in over Fair Isle pattern on no 2 needles.

A variation in tension within a garment will result in an uneven appearance. By knitting the required number of stitches and rows, your sample will reveal whether the yarn and needles you are using will make up into the size and shape you require. When working your tension sample, you must take into account the pattern and the method of carrying yarns across the back of the work (see p. 137).

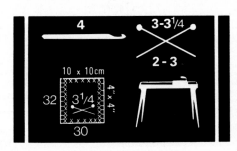

The paper band around your ball of wool provides important information regarding stitch gauge. The one shown above gives metric and US crochet hook and needle sizes and the ideal tension sample. It is advisable to consult the ball band if the yarn you are using is different from that specified in the pattern.

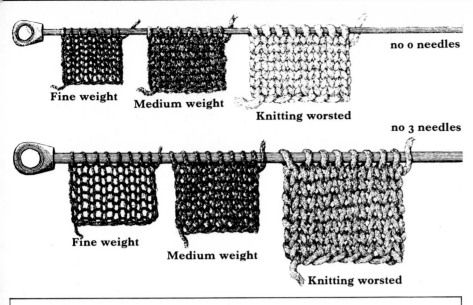

Fine weight Medium weight Knitting worsted no 0 needles

Fine weight Medium weight Knitting worsted no 3 needles

MAKING A TENSION SAMPLE

Using the same yarn, needles and stitch pattern called for in the pattern, knit a sample slightly larger than 4in square, incorporating the pattern from the chart if there is one. Smooth out the finished sample on a flat surface being careful not to stretch it. Using pins, mark out the tension measurement given in the chosen pattern.

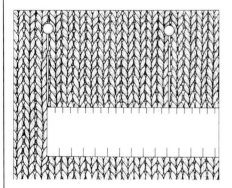

Measuring the number of stitches
To determine the width of the knitting, place a steel ruler or tape measure across the sample and count the number of stitches between the pins. Remember to include any half stitches over the width of a garment, a half stitch which is not taken into account may amount to several inches in the final width.

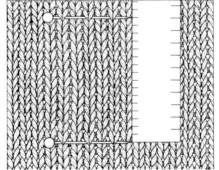

Measuring the number of rows
To determine the length of the knitting, place a steel ruler or tape measure vertically along the fabric and count the number of rows to the inch.

ADJUSTING THE TENSION

If the number of stitches given in the pattern knit up to too wide a measure your knitting is too loose and you should change your knitting needles to a smaller size. If they knit up to too small a measure, then your knitting is too tight and you should change your knitting needles to a larger size.

Changing the needles one size larger or one size smaller makes a difference of one stitch usually every two inches. Changing your needle size will normally be sufficient to adjust the dimensions. Sometimes, however, the width will match but not the length. If there are more vertical rows than indicated in the pattern, you must calculate the length of the garment from your tension sample and adjust the increasing and decreasing rows accordingly. However, in the majority of patterns in this book, the shaping is dependent on a specific number of vertical rows. If your vertical tension matches but not your horizontal then in this case it is better to lose some stitches across the width. This is particularly so in the Fair Isle patterns, which rely on a definite number of vertical pattern repeats.

MEASUREMENTS

Before you knit up any garment make sure the measurements given in the pattern are suitable for you. The sizes of the sweaters in this book are all given on pp. 116–123. The measurements included are: length of sweater, length of underarm seams and chest/bust width. The chest/bust sizes given in the patterns are the sizes the sweaters are designed to fit, not the actual size of the sweaters.

Taking measurements

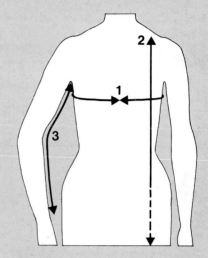

1 **Chest/bust** Measure around the fullest part.

2 **Length** Measure from the nape of the neck to the bottom of the sweater.

3 **Sleeve** Measure from the armpit to the wrist.

An easy way of checking whether the length of the sleeve and length of sweater are suitable for you, is to measure an existing sweater and compare the given measurements with that.

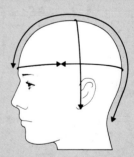

Hats
To calculate the minimum size needed for a hat or cap, measure around the head at the widest part to obtain the circumference. Measure across the top of the head from ear tip to ear tip and divide by two to obtain the minimum length necessary from the crown to the headband edge.

GARTER STITCH

Knitting or purling every row back and forth on two needles produces garter stitch. This stitch is used to separate bands of pattern in the sweaters.

STOCKINETTE STITCH (st st)

Knitting the first and every odd row and purling the second and every even row produces stockinette stitch when using two needles. Knitting every row produces stockinette stitch when working in the round (see p. 133).

TURKISH STITCH

Turkish stitch is a decorative stitch used to break up rows of pattern horizontally. It features on the Rose cardigan, the Wallflower boat neck sweater and the Sweetpea camisole. It is a much more open stitch than stockinette stitch and forms a mesh pattern which is the same on both sides of the garment. Knit the first stitch in the row and then continue as follows:

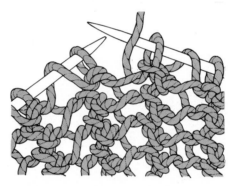

1 Bring the wool forward.

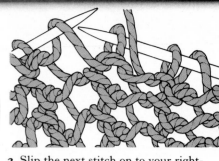

2 Slip the next stitch on to your right-hand needle.

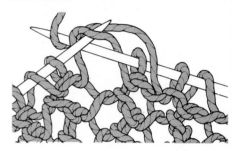

3 Knit the next stitch.

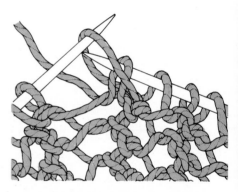

4 Pass the slipped stitch over the knit stitch. Repeat this sequence to the last stitch in the row. Knit the last stitch.

RIBBING

A combination of knit and purl stitches in the same row is known as ribbing. Ribbing is used on sleeve and body edges to form a neat stretchable finish. It is usually worked on smaller needles than the body of the garment. In this book twisted rib is used as this gives a tighter, neater finish. It is worked in almost the same way as ordinary rib, except that the right-hand needle is put into the *back* of the knit stitch instead of the front.

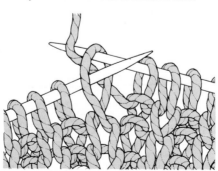

1 Knit into the back of the first and every knit stitch.

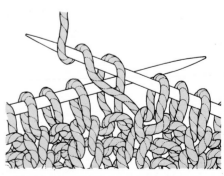

2 Purl in the ordinary way. Work back across the following rows in the same way, beginning every row with a knit stitch.

DROPPED STITCHES

Occasionally, a stitch may fall off your needle. This is especially likely if you leave off working in the middle of a row.

LADDERS

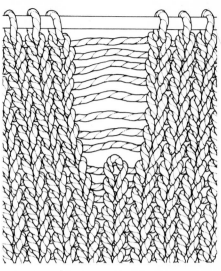

Picking up a dropped knit stitch

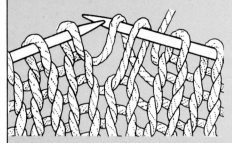

1 Pick up both the stitch and strand on your right-hand needle, inserting the needle from front to back.

Picking up a dropped purl stitch

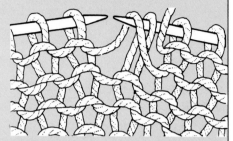

1 Pick up both the stitch and strand on your right-hand needle, inserting the needle from back to front.

If a dropped stitch is left, it can unravel downwards and form a "ladder". In such a case it is easiest to use a crochet hook to pick up the stitches in pattern although you can try it with your needles. If you make a mistake in your knitting, you may have to "unpick" a stitch, in which case a ladder may result. Pick up one dropped stitch at a time, securing any others with a safety pin to prevent further unraveling.

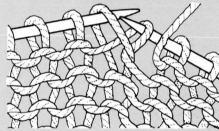

2 Insert your left-hand needle through the stitch only, from back to front. With your right-hand needle only, pull the strand through the stitch to make the extra stitch. (Drop the stitch from your left-hand needle.)

2 Insert your left-hand needle through the stitch only, from front to back. With your right-hand needle only, pull the strand through the stitch to make the extra stitch. (Drop the stitch from your left-hand needle.)

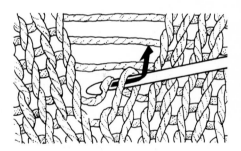

Correcting a knit ladder
Insert a crochet hook through the front of the dropped stitch. Hook up one strand and pull it through the stitch to form a new stitch one row up. Continue in this way to the top of the ladder then continue in pattern.

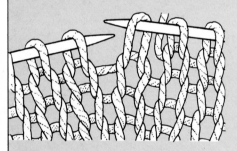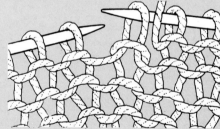

3 Transfer the re-formed stitch back to your left-hand needle, so that it untwists and faces the correct way. It is now ready for knitting again.

3 Transfer the re-formed stitch back to your left-hand needle, so that it untwists and faces the correct way. It is now ready for purling again.

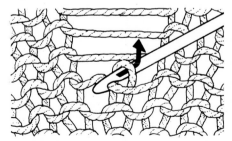

Correcting a purl ladder
Insert a crochet hook through the back of the dropped stitch. Hook up one strand and pull it through the stitch to form a new stitch one row up. Continue to re-insert hook to make stitches until you reach the top of the ladder.

UNPICKING MISTAKES

Holding the stitch on your right-hand needle insert your left-hand needle into the row below and undo the stitch. Transfer the stitch back to your right-hand needle and repeat undoing until the error has been reached. Correct stitch as if it had been a ladder, see right.

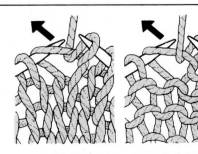

INCREASING

When shaping garments it is usually necessary to add additional stitches. Stitches can be added at the outer edges of the piece you are knitting, such as sleeve edges, or they can be added evenly across the row to give slight fullness, such as across a front or back in the last row of ribbing. There are several ways of increasing, but the method shown below is most suitable for these sweaters. If stitches are made "invisibly", there will be no hole or gap left in the fabric. The "invisible" method shown below uses part of an existing stitch to create a new one.

In a knit row

Knit into the front of the stitch in the usual way. Without discarding the stitch on your left-hand needle, knit into the back of it, making two stitches.

In a purl row

Purl into the front of the stitch in the usual way. Without discarding the stitch on your left-hand needle, purl into the back of it, making two stitches.

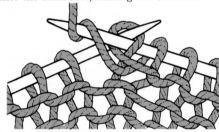

At the beginning or end of knit or purl rows

Use the same technique illustrated above, but work twice into the first or last stitch in the row.

DECREASING

There are two ways to lose stitches for shaping and these are to knit or purl two stitches together (k2 tog or p2 tog) at the beginning, end or at any given point in a row, or to use the slip stitch method (sl 1). Knitting stitches together is the simpler method, and the one used in most of the patterns, but slipping stitches produces a more decorative effect on a garment. Decreases are always visible and have a definite angled slant. It is important to pair decreases so that the direction of slant for the decreases is balanced.

SLIP STITCH DECREASE

Abbreviated as sl 1, k1, psso (slip one, knit one, pass slip stitch over), the decrease forms a slant to the left on the front of the knitting. A slant to the right is formed on the front if it is made on the purl row – sl 1, p1, psso (slip one, purl one, pass slip stitch over).

In a knit row

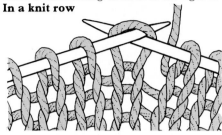

1 Insert your right-hand needle "knit-wise" and lift off the first stitch from your left-hand needle.

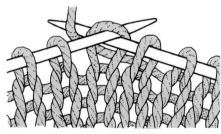

2 Leave the stitch on the needle and knit the next stitch on your left-hand needle in the usual way.

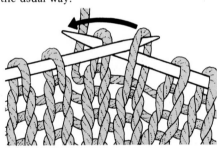

3 Using the point of your left-hand needle, bring the slipped stitch off your right-hand needle, over the knitted stitch.

In a purl row

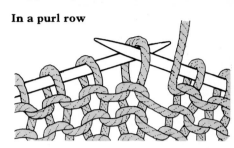

1 Insert your right-hand needle "purl-wise" and lift off the first stitch from your left-hand needle.

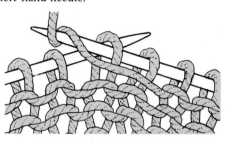

2 Leave the stitch on the needle and purl into the next stitch on your left-hand needle in the usual way.

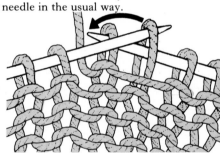

3 Using the point of your left-hand needle, bring the slipped stitch off your right-hand needle, over the purled stitch.

KNITTING TWO STITCHES TOGETHER

Abbreviated as k2 tog or p2 tog, the decrease forms a slant to the right if the stitches are knitted together through the front, and a slant to the left if knitted together through the back.

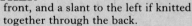

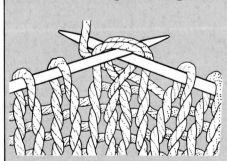

In a knit row

Insert your right-hand needle through the front of the first two stitches on your left-hand needle. Knit them together as a single stitch.

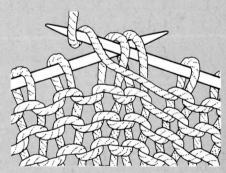

In a purl row

Insert your right-hand needle through the front of the first two stitches on your left-hand needle. Purl them together as a single stitch.

KNITTING IN THE ROUND

It is sometimes easier to make garments working with circular or double-pointed needles. Such needles produce a seamless garment, and the front of the work always faces you, making patterns somewhat easier to follow. Circular needles are used from the beginning when knitting a garment, but a set of double-pointed needles are more useful when picking up stitches, such as when knitting necklines and fingers for gloves. Two circular needles can also be used for flat knitting on very large-sized items.

USING A CIRCULAR NEEDLE

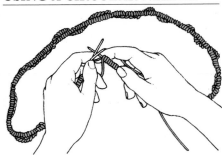

This is a flexible nylon tube which has two pointed metal ends which are traditionally sized. To knit in the round, cast on stitches in the usual way and then knit into the first stitch to make a continuous round. You should always mark the beginning of a new row with a piece of contrasting yarn. Remember, the outside of the work will always face you, so that when knitting stockinette stitch, you simply knit every row. If you wish to knit straight, and not in the round, simply use the two ends of the needle in the same way as ordinary needles.

USING THREE OR MORE NEEDLES

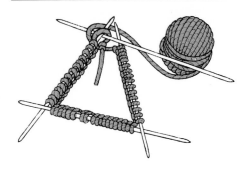

Sets of double-pointed needles are sold in the traditional sizes. As many as six needles can be used if the area is large. When knitting with double-pointed needles, the stitches are divided among all but one of the needles. This needle is used to knit off, so that each needle in turn holds stitches and then is used to knit off.

To knit, divide your stitches among the needles and knit a round. To close the circle, knit the first stitch with the working yarn from the last stitch. Keep your last and first needle as close together as possible. Make sure your first knitted stitch (you should mark this) is close to the last needle so that no gap forms in the knitting.

Continue to work around in this way, using your empty needles to knit off and keeping the stitches evenly divided. Hold the two working needles as usual, and drop the others to the back of the work when not in use.

CABLES

Special, small, double-pointed needles of varying shapes are used to produce the individual patterns called "cables". These are created when stitches are moved out of position so that plaited rope-like twists form in the knitting. Such a needle is necessary to hold stitches to the front or back of the work as required in a pattern.

Use the cable needle to form twists in the knitting. Stitches held at the front will twist the cable from right to left when knitted off; stitches held at the back will twist the cable from left to right when knitted off.

Cabling

In the illustration of a six stitch cable, the first three stitches are slipped onto a cable needle and held at the front of the work. The next three stitches are knitted from the left-hand needle, followed by knitting the three stitches from the cable needle. This produces a cable twist from right to left.

Rows 1, 3, 5 and 9 Knit to end.
Rows 2, 4, 6, 8 and 10 K3, p6, k3.
Row 7 K3, slip the next 3 sts onto a cable needle and hold to front of work, k3, then k3 from cable needle, k3.

READING THE CHARTS

Nearly all the designs in this book are based on Fair Isle or figurative patterns, so reading the charts correctly is essential to the successful working of the patterns. As you will see, different designs stretch over a different number of stitches in a row, but overall the number of stitches and the number of rows in the basic block of the design must relate to the proportions of the finished garment. However, although the pattern might fit perfectly with a garment in a certain size, when the size is increased or decreased, a few extra stitches may need to be worked in the pattern at the beginning and end of rows to achieve the correct number of stitches required by that particular size. Since many of the patterns carry instructions for working the pattern charts in a number of sizes, it is necessary to pick up the design in different places on the chart to accommodate the individual sizes.

The pattern charts are read from right to left on knit rows and from left to right on purl rows. This means that for your first row you start with the stitch at the bottom right-hand corner and work across to the bottom left-hand corner. The chart is always read upwards from bottom to top. The rows are numbered on the left and right-hand sides of the charts; odd (knit) rows are marked on the right and even (purl) rows are marked on the left. The stitches are numbered in italics across the bottom of the chart and are numbered as for working knit rows.

WORKING A SIMPLE CHART

Given right is an example of a chart for a sweater based on a pattern which is made up of a certain number of stitches which, when multiplied, fit exactly into the width of the sweater for both sizes given. This is the simplest way of working a pattern across the rows. The instructions for this chart would read as follows (instructions in brackets are for the larger size):

Repeat the 25 pattern stitches 6 (7) times across the row.

This means that you start at stitch *1* on row 1, and knit across from right to left until you have worked stitch *25*. It is then necessary to repeat the pattern chart another five (six) times across to complete the row. Having worked stitch *25*, you therefore start at *1* again and work across to *25*, five (six) times in all. You will then have completed your first knit row. (Weave the different colored yarns in, or strand them as you introduce new colors, see p. 137.) Your next row, row 2, will be a purl row. Purl rows are worked in *reverse,* which means that you start with stitch *25* and work back across to stitch *1*. You will then repeat stitches *25–1,* five (six) more times to complete the row. Continue working the pattern in this way until you have completed the number of rows in the chart (68 in this case). You have now completed the first working of the pattern chart. To achieve the required length you will probably need to repeat the pattern chart once, twice or several times. This means that when you have worked row 68, you go back to row 1 at the bottom of the chart, and work up the chart again in the same way.

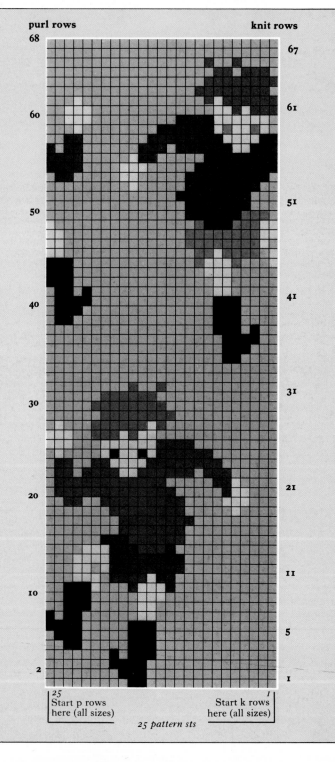

purl rows   knit rows

25
Start p rows here (all sizes)

1
Start k rows here (all sizes)

25 pattern sts

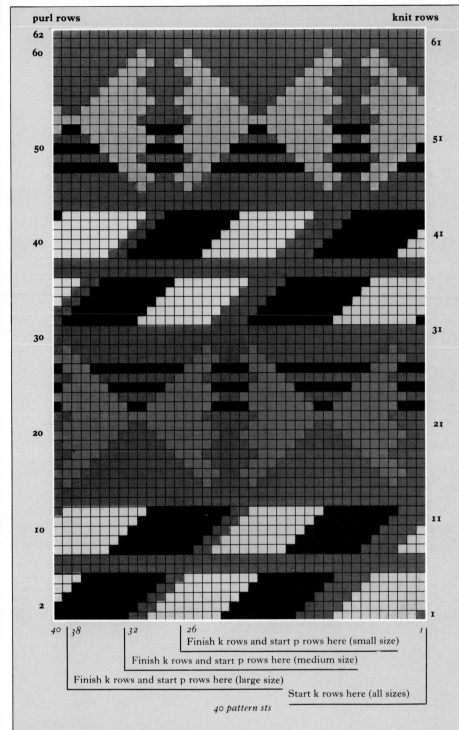

purl rows   knit rows

40   38   32   26   1

Finish k rows and start p rows here (small size)

Finish k rows and start p rows here (medium size)

Finish k rows and start p rows here (large size)

Start k rows here (all sizes)

40 pattern sts

MORE COMPLEX CHARTS

Sometimes a pattern chart will not fit exactly into the width of a sweater, or, when sized up or down, the proportions of the sweater no longer correspond exactly with the proportions of the chart. To repeat the pattern across the rows in this instance it is necessary to work an extra part of the chart to complete the row. This may also happen when working other parts of the sweater, such as the sleeves so, although a front or back might start with the basic number of pattern stitches, the sleeves might need to start

in a different place on the chart. For example, a pattern which contains three sizes is written and worked like this: Work the pattern across knit rows as follows: *for the small size,* work sts *1–40* once, then work sts *1–26* once; *for the medium size,* work sts *1–40* once, then work sts *1–32* once; *for the large size,* work sts *1–40* once, then work sts *1–38* once. Work purl rows in reverse (i.e. work *26–1* once, then *40–1* once for the small size and so on).

TAKING EXTRA STITCHES INTO THE PATTERN

When you are working a shaped piece such as a sleeve, the side edges are shaped as you progress. Normally the stitches are increased at the side edge, but the extra stitches so made must be taken into the pattern. To do this you treat the new stitch in the same way as you would work the next stitch in the row. So if, for example, your row finished with stitch *16* of a pattern comprising *16* basic pattern stitches, and you increased on stitch *16,* you would work the new stitch in the same way as stitch *1.*

REPEATING THE PATTERN CHART UP THE GARMENT

The number of times the pattern chart is repeated as you work up the garment is referred to as so many workings of the pattern chart. When you work through the pattern you will see that the number of rows worked is related to the approximate length of the work at that point, and this measurement is dependent on the tension of your knitting. If you are not working at the required tension you will find that the measurements and the number of rows do not tally.

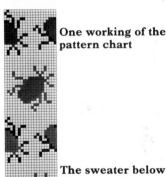

One working of the pattern chart

The sweater below illustrates how a pattern chart is repeated horizontally and vertically over a sweater.

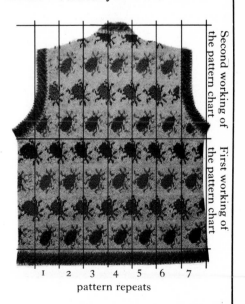

Second working of the pattern chart

First working of the pattern chart

1   2   3   4   5   6   7

pattern repeats

WORKING WITH MORE THAN ONE COLOR

Since most of my designs are multi-colored, there are several techniques you need to know about in order to successfully complete one of these sweaters. When more than one color is being used in a row, the yarn that is not being used has to be carried across the back of the knitting ready to be used when called for by the chart. The way in which this is done can greatly influence the tension of the knitting and so it must be done correctly. There are various ways of joining in yarns and carrying yarns across, and different patterns and different parts of a sweater will require different methods, these different methods are all explained below. Yarn bobbins can be used to help keep the different yarns separate, or when working a block of color.

Make the back of your work as neat as possible, darning in ends of yarn

ADDING NEW YARN AT THE BEGINNING OF A ROW

This is the way in which you should join in the yarn if you are working striped rib, either for the welts and cuffs or when working an entire back in striped rib. When you work with the additional colors it is best to carry the yarns not in use up the sides of the work until they are required again. When you have finished using a particular color of yarn, darn the end of the yarn neatly into the edge or the back of the work.

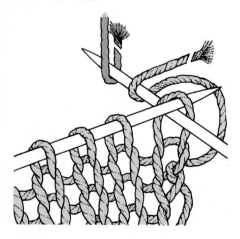

1 Insert right-hand needle through first stitch on left-hand needle and wrap the old, and then the new yarn over it. Knit (or purl) the stitch using both yarns.

2 Leaving the old yarn at the back, knit (or purl) the next two stitches using the double length of the new yarn.

3 Discard the short end of the new yarn and continue to knit as usual. On the following row treat the three double stitches as single stitches.

ADDING NEW YARN IN THE MIDDLE OF A ROW

This method is not recommended when a color is repeated right across the row and up several rows. It is only suitable for working a small area of stitches in one color. If you join in the yarn for each block of color in a figurative pattern you will find that your tension is completely thrown and a much larger garment results, with small holes where each of the yarns has been added.

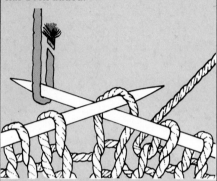

1 Insert your right-hand needle through the first stitch on your left-hand needle. Wrap the new yarn over, and knit (or purl) the stitch with the new yarn. Leave the old yarn at the back of the work.

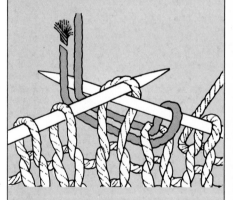

2 Knit (or purl) the next two stitches using the double length of new yarn.

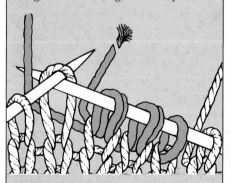

3 Discard the short end of the new yarn and continue to knit as usual. On the following row, treat the two double stitches as single stitches.

CARRYING YARN ACROSS THE BACK OF THE WORK

The two following methods – stranding and weaving – are the most suitable for carrying the different colors across the rows, and both avoid holes appearing as you introduce a new color. Choose the method which you feel most comfortable with. Weaving is the most effective, as it leaves the back of the work neat and hard-wearing, whereas stranding leaves loose yarns at the back which are easily pulled. Whether stranding or weaving, try to keep your tension as close as you can to the tension given in the pattern. You may find you prefer to mix the two techniques, stranding those yarns which appear infrequently and weaving those which recur often. As a general guide, strand yarn over two to five stitches, weave yarn when it has to be carried over more than five stitches.

STRANDING YARN

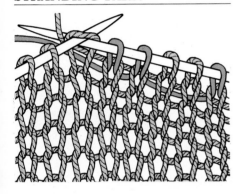

In a knit row

With both yarns at the back of the work, knit the required number of stitches with yarn A (in this case two), and then drop it to the back. Pick up yarn B and knit the required number of stitches and then drop it to the back. Both yarns should be stranded loosely along the back of the work.

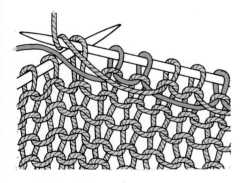

In a purl row

With both yarns at the front of the work, purl the required number of stitches with yarn A (in this case two), and then drop it. Pick up yarn B and purl the required number of stitches and then drop it. Both yarns should be stranded loosely along the front (side facing you).

WEAVING YARN

In a knit row

1 Hold yarn A in your right hand and yarn B in your left hand to the back of the work.

2 Knit one stitch with yarn A and, at the same time, bring yarn B below yarn A. When yarn B is being used weave yarn A as above.

In a purl row

1 Hold yarn A in your right hand and yarn B in your left hand to the front of the work.

2 Purl one stitch with yarn A but this time bring yarn B below yarn A. When yarn B is being used, weave yarn A as above.

CHECKING YOUR TECHNIQUE

To prevent the different yarns getting tangled, the strands must be caught up in the back of the work, but not so as they interfere with the pattern or produce undesired effects.

If you have worked weaving correctly, the yarns will cross evenly and remain at the same depth. A "smocking" effect means that you have pulled the yarns too tightly. It is better for the yarns to be woven too loosely than too tightly.

If you have worked stranding correctly, the yarns will be running evenly across the back of the work at the same tension as the knitting. Puckering indicates that you have pulled the yarns too tightly.

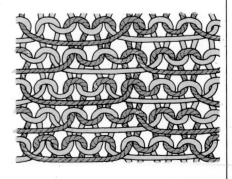

PICKING UP STITCHES AND RIBBING

After working the fronts, back and sleeves, the ribbing for the front bands, armhole bands, pocket tops and neckband should be worked. When a garment has a collar, this is usually knitted after the main body of the sweater has been completed, and sewn on afterwards. K1, p1 twisted rib is used for all these features (see p. 130), and usually it is worked on to a bound-off edge or side selvedge. To do this, stitches have to be picked up from these edges, and the ribbing then worked on these newly picked up stitches.

Sometimes the shoulder seams have to be joined before picking up and ribbing stitches. For instructions on seams see right.

PICKING UP STITCHES

Always pick up stitches with the right side of the work facing you. Where you start on a garment will depend on which piece of the garment you are working on, because you always work from right to left. If, for example, you are picking up stitches along the right front opening edge of a vest, start at the hem edge for the right front opening edge and at the center-back of the neck for the left front opening edge. The number of stitches you pick up does not necessarily correspond with the number of rows in the edge along which you are picking up the stitches. The number of buttonholes needed and the appropriate number of stitches between them will dictate the number of stitches down a front opening edge. For a stronger, neater finish, pick up stitches from the last line of knitting before the bound-off edge or side selvage.

Use this method of picking up stitches for buttonhole and button bands, armhole bands, pocket tops and linings, and neck-bands. Once you have picked up the stitches, work the bands in k1, p1 twisted rib in the same way as the welts. Sometimes a contrasting colored yarn is joined in for the last row of rib. In this case, bind off in rib in this color yarn.

When you encounter stitches which have been left on a spare needle or stitch holder, merely knit these in as you put them on the needle. Then work in rib along with all other picked up stitches.

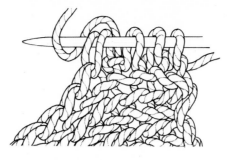

1 Place your needle through the work and bring the yarn around as if knitting the stitch.

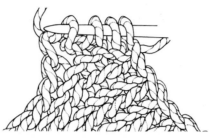

2 Pull the yarn through the stitch from the main work, to make a stitch on the needle.

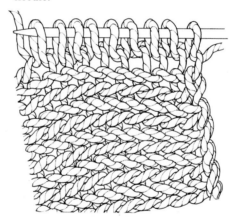

3 Continue making stitches in this way, always placing the needle into a firm stitch on the main piece of work, until you have the correct amount on the needle. Sew the ends of the yarn in when the band is complete.

SELVAGES

The sides of a piece of knitting are also known as selvages. Special care must be taken to ensure that these are kept straight. There are various ways of working edges, but for the purposes of this book a stockinette stitch is best. The first and last stitches must be firmly made, particularly on front opening edges and armhole edges, since stitches will be picked up from these later. All knit row stitches are knitted and all purl row stitches are purled.

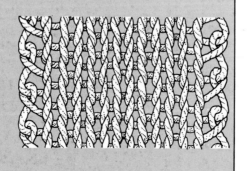

BUTTONHOLE BANDS

Join the front to the back at the shoulder seams. Work the required number of rows of twisted rib as given in the pattern, after picking up the stitches. The first edge of the button-hole is usually made in a right-side row. Normally the buttonhole occupies 3 stitches, so if you need to calculate the number of stitches required between buttonholes, take this into account. In these patterns the positions of the buttonholes are already worked out. Rib the required number of stitches in the row in the usual way, then bind off three stitches, then rib the number of stitches required between this and the next buttonhole edge, and so on, until you have bound off the correct number of edges for the buttonholes. On the next row, rib back in the same way as before, but each time you reach the bound-off edge in the previous row, cast on 3 stitches directly over this bound-off edge. Continue in rib for the required number of rows, then bind off.

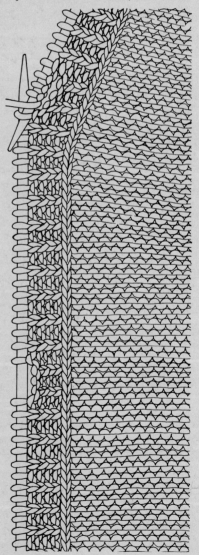

Wrong side of buttonhole band

NECKBANDS

Stitches around the neck can be picked up and worked either in the round, using four double pointed needles, or a circular needle, or they can be picked up in the same way as buttonhole bands using two needles, and the two ends of ribbing can then be joined together with a flat seam. If using two needles you will have to join the front to the back at one shoulder. If working in the round, join both shoulder seams. (See p. 133 for working in the round.) Complete the band in the same way as all other bands.

POCKETS

Pockets are worked in either of two ways in this book. Either the lower edge of the pocket opening is bound off, or these stitches are transferred to a spare needle or stitch holder. Where they have been bound off the appropriate number of stitches must be picked up across this edge. The pocket top is then worked in rib as before. Where the stitches are left on a spare needle, merely rib them from the spare needle.

Similarly, pocket linings are either worked on a cast-on edge directly over the bound-off edge, or they are incorporated in the main working of the fronts. If the stitches are picked up from a cast-on edge, pick up in the usual way, but work the lining in stockinette stitch, not rib.

FINISHING

Many of the sweaters in this book are based on six basic shapes, and therefore share many of the same methods of finishing. Given overleaf are the basic ways of finishing vests, a crew neck sweater, a boat neck sweater, a V-neck cardigan and a round neck cardigan. Full instructions are given with each pattern for camisoles, peplum jackets, hats and legwarmers. Before finishing, you may wish to block the individual pieces of knitting, see right.

SEAMS

There are several different methods for joining pieces of knitting together. The following techniques are suitable for use with the sweaters in this book. Use yarn to match the main or background color of the sweater.

RIDGED EDGE-TO-EDGE SEAM

Use this seam for sleeve seams, shoulder seams and side seams. Since it is worked from the right side it is easy to match patterns. It forms a visible seam ridge on the inside, but gives a neater finish on the right side than the flat edge-to-edge seam.

Place the pieces to be joined, edge-to-edge, right side up. Match the pieces carefully, row for row and stitch for stitch. Using the main yarn, make the seam from the right side in the same way

as the flat edge-to-edge seam, but do not sew into the edge stitches, instead make the seam one stitch in from the edge, so that a ridge forms on the inside of the garment.

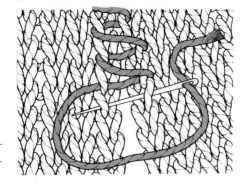

FLAT EDGE-TO-EDGE SEAM

The ends of front bands, neckbands and armhole bands should be joined with this seam since it gives a flat finish. It is worked from the right side.

Place the pieces to be joined edge-to-edge, right side up. Match the pieces carefully, row for row and stitch for stitch. Using the main yarn, sew the edge stitches of both pieces together so that the edges meet.

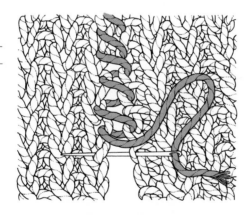

BACKSTITCH SEAM

Backstitched seams are made from the wrong side, so carefully pin the seams first to make sure the patterns match on the right side.

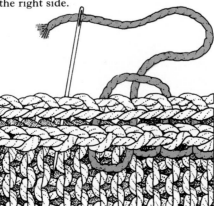

BLOCKING AND PRESSING

Before pattern pieces are joined, they are usually blocked and pressed to ensure a good fit. It's always a good idea to check the yarn band for any special instructions. The pieces are blocked when dry and are pressed with a damp cloth.

Garment pieces may need blocking, or putting into shape, before they can be joined. Cover a table with a folded blanket and a sheet. Lay the knitting the wrong side up on the sheet. Using rustless pins pin the knitting by its edges to the blanket, gently pulling it into shape and to the correct measurements, making sure that the rows run in straight lines. Be careful not to stretch or distort the fabric since if you do so, during use it will resume its original size and shape.

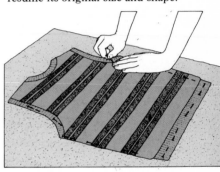

Blocking

After blocking, the garment pieces are usually pressed in position. Use a warm iron and a clean, absorbent, damp cloth on wool. Lay the iron on the fabric and lift up, do not move it over the surface. Do not press too heavily as this will flatten the knitting. Do not remove any of the pins until the piece has cooled and dried completely.

Raised and embossed patterns should be pressed under a damp cloth, but remove the pins and adjust the fabric while it is still hot to avoid the patterns being flattened.

Avoid pressing ribbing and fancy stitches, such as Turkish stitch, as they will lose their elasticity.

Pressing

BUTTON-DOWN VEST

Before working the front bands and arm-hole bands it is necessary to join each vest front to the back at the shoulder seams. When you have worked the front bands and the armhole bands and the pockets, sew the vest fronts to the back at the side seams. Start at the hem edge and join the welts, taking care not to make a bulky seam at the bottom edge. Work up to the armhole band. Join the two ends of the armhole band together at the underarm point with a flat edge-to-edge seam, to avoid bulk. Repeat for the other armhole. Join the front bands together with a flat edge-to-edge seam at the center-back of the neck. Sew the pockets as instructed right.

Cable borders
Where there is a cable border around the armholes and front edges (Butterfly and Scotty vests), the borders are knitted separately and then sewn to the vest. The shoulder and side seams must be sewn before the armhole borders are attached. The borders should be fitted into the bottom of the armhole so that they lie flat. Overlap the two short ends of one cabled border so that the wrong side of the upper one is against the right side of the underneath one. Hold with a pin and check that the band fits the armhole. Then sew around the overlapped ends. Fit this "V" shape into the base of the armhole and sew the band in place around the armhole. Repeat for the other armhole border.

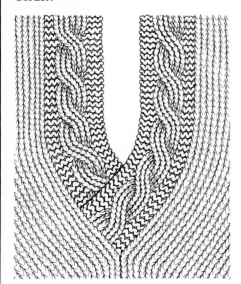

Pockets
Turn the vest inside out and position the pocket lining against the back of the vest front. Sew all around the three free sides of the lining with small stitches which should be invisible on the right side. Repeat for the other pocket. Turn the vest back to the right side and stitch each side of the pocket top to the vest front with tiny invisible stitches. Repeat for the other pocket.

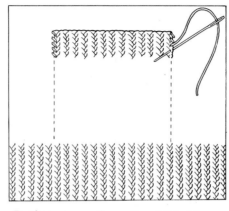

Pocket as seen from the right side

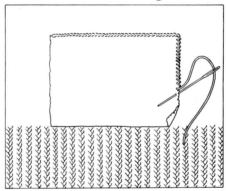

Pocket as seen from the wrong side

V-NECK VEST

Join one shoulder seam and work the neckband in rib as instructed in the pattern. Sew the remaining shoulder seam and then work the armhole bands. Join the ends of the neckband with a flat edge-to-edge seam. Sew the front to the back at the side seams, starting at the hem edge. Work up to the armhole band and join the two ends of the armhole band together at the underarm point with a flat edge-to-edge seam.

BOAT NECK SWEATER

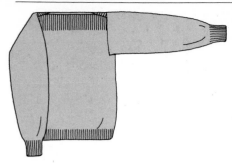

Sew the front to the back at the side seams. Overlap the front of the boat neck ribbing and the back of the boat neck ribbing by $1\frac{1}{2}$in along each shoulder. Hold with a pin and then sew neatly in position, starting at the outside shoulder edge and stitching along for about 2in. Do not make the seam on the very edge of the ribbing, make it about $\frac{1}{2}$in in from the edge. Repeat for the other shoulder.

Sleeves
Join each sleeve seam, starting at the welt edge, taking care not to make the welt seam bulky. Then continue to sew the seam together until you reach a point $1\frac{1}{2}$in from the end of the seam. Stop the seam here and leave the rest of the seam open. Set the sleeve into the armhole, so that each side of the $1\frac{1}{2}$in of unstitched seam at the top of the sleeve seam is pinned across the straight bound-off edge at the bottom of the armhole. Ease around the top of the sleeve if the sleeve is slightly full. Pin, then sew the sleeve into the armhole. Repeat for the other sleeve.

CREW NECK SWEATER

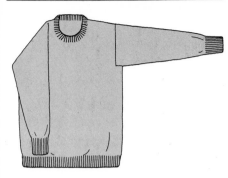

To make the neckband you will already have sewn together at least one of the shoulder seams. Join the remaining one if necessary, and join the neckband with a flat seam if you have not worked the neckband in the round. Join the front to the back at the side seams. Set the sleeves into the armholes in the same way as for a boat neck sweater.

V-NECK CARDIGAN

Before working the front bands join the fronts to the back at the shoulders. Join the front bands together with a flat edge-to-edge seam at the center-back of the neck. Sew the fronts to the back at the side seams. Start at the hem edge and join the welts, taking care not to make a bulky seam at the bottom edge. Sew the pockets as for a vest.

Sleeves

The tops of the sleeves are made larger than the armhole, and should be pleated to fit. Join the sleeve seam, then pin the sleeve into the armhole, pinning about four small pleats into the top of the sleeve, so that the sleeve fits the armhole. Sew in position and repeat for the other sleeve.

ROUND NECK CARDIGAN

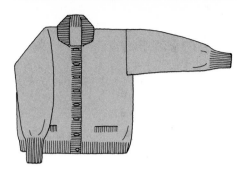

Work the front bands along only the front opening edge. Sew the shoulder seams and side seams. Sew the pockets as for a vest. Join the sleeve seams and set the sleeves in as for a boat neck sweater.

Collar

The collar is worked as a separate piece, and then attached to the cardigan. Pin the cast-on and shaped edge of the collar around the neck from the inner edge of the left front band to inner edge of the right front band. Sew in position. Then fold the collar in half so that the bound-off edge aligns with the cast-on edge which you have just sewn. Pin this bound-off edge so that it just covers the neck seam and then slip stitch it in place around the neck.

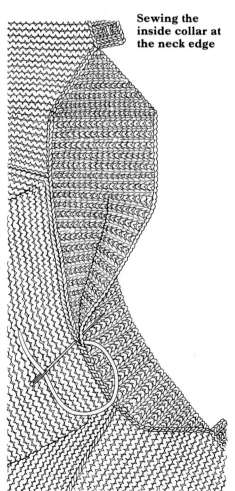

Sewing the inside collar at the neck edge

MAKING A CHAIN LOOP BUTTONHOLE

The peplum jackets (Sterling and Squares on black) fasten at the waist with a loop buttonhole so that an edge-to-edge fastening is made. A loop buttonhole may be made from a length of crochet chain stitches using the main color yarn.

1 Make a slip loop (see p. 126). Thread your yarn in your left hand and hold the crochet hook with the slip loop in the right hand. Twist the hook first under and then over the yarn to make a loop.

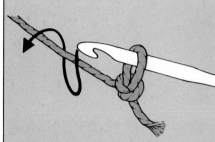

2 Draw the hook with the yarn on it through the slip loop to form a chain.

3 Repeat step 2 until the chain is the required length. Sew the chain on to the garment at the waist, using matching yarn.

ABBREVIATIONS

beg	beginning
dec	decrease
foll	following
garter st	knit or purl every row
g	gram
in	inch
inc	increase
k	knit
k2 tog	knit two stitches together
moss st	k1, p1 to end; next row p1, k1 to end
()	repeat all the instructions between brackets as many times as indicated
psso	pass slip stitch over
p	purl
rep from *	repeat all the instructions that follow asterisk
sl	slip
st	stitch
st st	stockinette stitch
tog	together
Turkish st	k1, *yfwd, sl 1, k1, psso; repeat from *
turn	turn the work around at the point indicated, before the end of a row
up 1 k	insert needle from front to back into loop of st below next one to be knitted, knit loop, then knit next st on left hand needle
up 1 p	insert needle from back to front into top of st below next one to be knitted, purl this loop, then purl next st on left hand needle
up 1 p k	insert needle from back to front into top of st below next st to be knitted, purl this loop, then knit next st on left hand needle
yfwd	yarn forward

CENTIMETERS/INCHES CONVERSION CHART

cm	in	cm	in
1	$\frac{1}{2}$	21	$8\frac{1}{4}$
2	$\frac{3}{4}$	22	$8\frac{3}{4}$
3	$1\frac{1}{4}$	23	9
4	$1\frac{1}{2}$	24	$9\frac{1}{2}$
5	2	25	$9\frac{3}{4}$
6	$2\frac{1}{4}$	26	$10\frac{1}{4}$
7	$2\frac{3}{4}$	27	$10\frac{3}{4}$
8	$3\frac{1}{4}$	28	11
9	$3\frac{1}{2}$	29	$11\frac{1}{2}$
10	4	30	$11\frac{3}{4}$
11	$4\frac{1}{4}$	31	$12\frac{1}{4}$
12	$4\frac{3}{4}$	32	$12\frac{1}{2}$
13	5	33	13
14	$5\frac{1}{2}$	34	$13\frac{1}{2}$
15	6	35	$13\frac{3}{4}$
16	$6\frac{1}{4}$	36	$14\frac{1}{4}$
17	$6\frac{3}{4}$	37	$14\frac{1}{2}$
18	7	38	15
19	$7\frac{1}{2}$	39	$15\frac{1}{4}$
20	$7\frac{3}{4}$	40	$15\frac{3}{4}$

◀ Please note that these conversions are approximate to the nearest $\frac{1}{4}$ inch.

GRAMS/OUNCES CONVERSION CHART

grams	ounces
25	1
50	$1\frac{3}{4}$
75	$2\frac{3}{4}$
100	$3\frac{1}{2}$
125	$4\frac{1}{2}$
150	$5\frac{1}{4}$
175	$6\frac{1}{4}$
200	7
225	8
250	$8\frac{3}{4}$
275	$9\frac{3}{4}$
300	$10\frac{1}{2}$
325	$11\frac{1}{2}$
350	$12\frac{1}{4}$
375	$13\frac{1}{4}$
400	14
425	15
450	$15\frac{3}{4}$

◀ Please note that these conversions are approximate. One ounce = approximately 28.35 grams.

KNITTING NEEDLES CONVERSION CHART

U.S.	0	1	2	3	4	5
Metric (mm)	$2\frac{1}{4}$	$2\frac{3}{4}$	3	$3\frac{1}{4}$	$3\frac{3}{4}$	4
English	13	12	11	10	9	8

WASHING KNITWEAR

Always use a mild soap, preferably one especially designed for knitwear, and warm water. Before washing a brightly-colored garment, check that it is color-fast by dipping a small piece of it into the soapy water. Press it out in a white cloth. If it leaves a stain, wash in cold water.

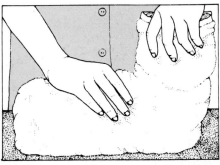

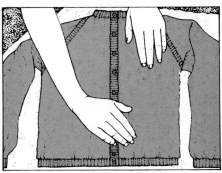

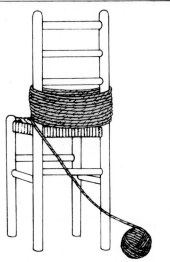

1 Always squeeze the suds into the garment gently and do not rub or felting will occur. Don't leave the garment to soak, but rinse and remove quickly. Make certain the rinse water is clear before removing the garment. You can add fabric softener to the last rinse if you wish.

2 Place the garment in a thick towel, white if possible, and roll both up. You can place extra towels on top of the garment for extra absorption if you like before rolling up. Press the roll with your hands or "hammer" it with your fists to remove as much water as possible. You can repeat this with another towel if the garment is still very wet, or to facilitate drying.

3 Finish drying the garment by laying it out flat on another clean towel, away from direct heat. Make sure the knitting is correctly shaped. Store the garment in a drawer; never hang it up as it can be easily pulled out of shape.

RE-USING YARN

If you are unpicking a finished garment, undo the seams first and then locate the last bound-off stitch. Start here to unravel the knitting, winding it around the back of a chair to keep the yarn from getting tangled or stretched, and to facilitate washing. Fasten the hank at two ends; catch the end of the yarn in one of the ties. Hand wash then rewind yarn into loose balls when dry.

YARN INFORMATION

Packs of the same yarn in sufficient amounts for knitting each of the sweaters in this book are available from:
Fireside Yarns Inc.
P.O. Box 357
Whitehouse, New Jersey
08888

100 % wool fingering yarn is available from Brunswick Yarns. For the name of your nearest stockist, write to:
Brunswick Yarns
P.O. Box 276
Pickens, South Carolina
29671

The 2-ply jumper weight Shetland yarn that I use can be ordered directly from:
Jamieson & Smith
(Shetland Wool Brokers) Ltd.
90 North Road
Lerwick
Shetland Isles, ZE1 0PQ

The cotton yarn used for these sweaters is distributed by Scheepjeswol (US) Inc. For a list of stockists write to:
Scheepjeswol (US) Inc.
155 Lafayette Avenue
White Plains, New York
10603

SASHA KAGAN SWEATERS

I can supply many of the sweaters in this book knitted up as special orders. Send for details to:
Sasha Kagan Knitwear
Sweater Service
Llanidloes
Powys
Wales SY18 6AD

Note: While the patterns are long-standing, individual yarn shades may go out of stock in time. I am willing to suggest and/or supply alternative yarns and colorways.

ACKNOWLEDGEMENTS

The author and publishers would like to thank the following people
for their help in producing this book:

Illustrators
Elaine Anderson
Lindsay Blow
John Hutchinson
Edwina Keene
Coral Mula

Photographers
Paul Fletcher
Colin Molyneux
Ian O'Leary
Colin Thomas

Reproduction
Reprocolor International

Typesetters
Chambers Wallace

Melanie Miller, Debra Grayson and Grail Dorling for
their editorial help; Workshop Clothing Ltd for lending
many of the shirts and skirts used in the photographs;
Neal Street East shop for Oriental goods; Monsoon for
accessories. We are also extremely grateful to the following
for kindly lending us props for the photographs: Bayat van
Dunk, Jubilee Market; Boosey & Hawkes Ltd; Dutch
Dairy Bureau; Freed of London; Lucy Goffin; Clare
Hart; The Hat Shop; London Graphic Centre; David
Mellor; Stuart Mooney, Jubilee Market; Moss Bros Ltd;
Mulberry Co. (Design) Ltd; Naturally British, British
Handmade Crafts; Oasis Trading Ltd; Geraldine
St. Aubin Hubbard; The Scotch House; Scotts of Camden
Town; Souleiado Ltd, French Provencale Fabrics;
Talisman; Caroline Thomas; Tiger, Tiger (King's Road)
Ltd; Paul Wu; Wallis; Laura Ashley; Lumiere; Dolcis; Sacha;
Visuals; Ally Capellino; Warehouse and Adrien Mann.